Heroes
of the Hour

Heroes
of the Hour

Brief Moments of Military Glory

Bryan Perrett

CASSELL&CO

Cassell & Co
Wellington House, 125 Strand, London WC2R 0BB

First published 2001

British Library Cataloguing-in-Publication data:
A catalogue record for this book is available from the
British Library

ISBN 0-304-35862-2

Distributed in the USA by Sterling Publishing Co. Inc.,
387 Park Avenue South, New York, NY 10016-8810

Edited, designed and typeset by Roger Chesneau

Printed and bound in Great Britain by MPG Books Ltd,
Bodmin, Cornwall

Contents

Preface

I T IS SOMETIMES SAID that decorations such as the Victoria Cross and Congressional Medal of Honor are frequently won but seldom awarded. This may well be true and, if so, it is simply a reflection of life itself. The same can be said of fame. Every nation has its well-remembered heroes, who are few in number simply because they are heroes. The names of George Washington, Napoleon Bonaparte, the Duke of Wellington, General Ulysses S. Grant and Kitchener of Khartoum are familiar to those with even a nodding acquaintance of the basic outline of history. Yet some of their most notable contemporaries, who assisted them to pre-eminence and themselves earned considerable fame in their day, have now become shadowy figures—if, indeed, they are remembered at all, notwithstanding their remarkable achievements. Often, these latter were momentous and repay study in their own right. As individuals, such men were as diverse as human nature itself. The lives of some were honourable throughout. Others saw no vice in treachery, or were flawed in other ways. The only characteristics they possessed in common were that they were soldiers of outstanding ability and, for good or ill, they exercised a decisive influence on the conflicts in which they fought.

One man's rebel is another man's patriot, goes the saying. Benedict Arnold joined the American colonists in rebelling against their King and Mother Country. Although he was not actually in command at the time, he was largely responsible for the colonists' critical victory at Saratoga, which brought France and Spain into the war on their side, and his contribution to the cause of American Independence was therefore of enormous value. Despite this, his avaricious nature soon led him to quarrel with his new masters and he deserted to the British, who rewarded him suitably and employed him for a time as a field commander. Treachery is neither easily forgotten nor forgiven, and Benedict Arnold, twice a traitor, found himself friendless when the war ended, a figure despised by both nations.

Serving in the same war was Banastre Tarleton, the son of a rich Liverpool slaver. Tarleton's exploits as a junior officer included the capture of General Charles Lee, who was regarded by Congress as being second only in importance to George Washington. The young officer's potential was recognised, and, as a result of the workings of the British commission-by-purchase system, he was appointed commander of a loyalist unit known as the British Legion. With the Legion, Tarleton showed himself to be a cavalry commander of rare distinction, winning one victory after another. His methods, including relentless pursuit, had much in common with Rommel's, but, like Rommel, he tended to repeat his tactics and did so once too often, with serious consequences. During its career, the Legion, whose members were engaged in what amounted to a savage civil war, behaved with counter-productive cruelty, generating hatred and fear wherever it went, earning its commander the name of 'Bloody'. Ironically, though Tarleton did possess pronounced sadistic tendencies, the title was awarded by the rebels for an engagement in which he had no control over events. His return home was celebrated with bonfires and the ringing of church bells. He never commanded troops in action again, preferring to become a hanger-on of the Prince of Wales's set, although he could have made a valuable contribution during the French Revolutionary and Napoleonic Wars.

General Louis Desaix was a man of very different stamp and background. Of aristocratic lineage, he nevertheless supported the principles of the French Revolution. He took part in Napoleon's Egyptian campaign, being responsible for the capture of Malta and the conquest of Upper Egypt. He then joined Napoleon for the 1800 campaign in northern Italy. Of the climactic Battle of Marengo, Napoleon was fond of remarking that within an hour he had turned his army's apparent defeat into a smashing victory. It was his first battle as head of state, consolidating both his position and, apparently, his reputation for brilliance, and he instructed his historians to record it in these terms. The truth was that he fought a bungled battle and was on the point of being routed when Desaix reached the field and delivered the decisive counter-attack, losing his life in the process. Subsequently, Napoleon went to considerable lengths to conceal his indebtedness to the dead hero.

Major George Baring was a Hanoverian officer who served with the King's German Legion in the Peninsular War and was then given the task of holding the vital outpost of La Haye Sainte with a small garrison during the Battle of Waterloo. Recognising that possession of the farm was the key to Wellington's position, Baring and his Germans beat off a series of ferocious French attacks throughout the afternoon and early evening. Only when their ammunition supply failed completely were Baring and a handful of survivors forced to abandon the position during hand-to-hand fighting in which they were hopelessly outnumbered, but by then it was too late for Napoleon to take advantage of the situation. After the war Baring joined the reconstituted Hanoverian Army and, as the King of England was also the King of Hanover, he received the equivalent of a knighthood and promotion as a reward for his exemplary services.

James Scarlett was one of the few generals to emerge from the Crimean War with his reputation enhanced. Initially, he commanded the Heavy Brigade within the British Army's troubled Cavalry Division, but chose to remain aloof from the asinine squabbles of Lords Cardigan and Lucan. Never having seen active service before, he possessed the wisdom to seek advice from those who had. To his troops he was something of a kindly, avuncular figure. The charge of his outnumbered brigade during the Battle of Balaclava trounced the Russians roundly, thwarting their plans to capture the British supply port, and was the most successful cavalry action of the war. After Lucan and Cardigan had left for home, Scarlett became commander of the Cavalry Division. He was not a man to seek fame or advancement, and, indeed, the outstanding performance of the Heavy Brigade was eclipsed almost immediately by the supreme courage and discipline displayed in the Charge of the Light Brigade, although in later years it, too, became the subject of a poem by Alfred Lord Tennyson. Scarlett was an unassuming sort of hero who, in his own eyes, simply performed the task he had been set with the minimum of fuss. It was, perhaps, understandable that the egregious behaviour of some of his contemporaries should have attracted the greater attention.

The Great or Indian Mutiny, arising from deep and mutual mis-
understandings, was probably the greatest tragedy in the history of the
British Empire. It was more than a mutiny, as several princely rulers
decided to throw in their lot with the rebels, but it was not a national war
of independence, for without the assistance of other princes and loyal
Indian troops it would have proved extremely difficult to restore order.
In such desperate time, the hour produced the men. One such was
Major William Hodson, the commander of an irregular cavalry regiment.
Hodson, a brilliant swordsman, loved fighting for its own sake. With icy
courage, he and a handful of his troopers faced down thousands of
mutineers to arrest the King of Delhi. He then returned to arrest the
King's decadent sons, who were guilty of some of the worst atrocities
committed against European women and children. Once again, Hodson
and his small escort were surrounded by a huge mob of mutineers who
seemed on the point of making a rescue attempt. To put an end to the
matter, Hodson shot the princes on the spot. To many he was a hero who
at a stroke deprived the mutineers of figureheads to whom they could
rally, and therefore saved many lives in the longer term, although to
others less immediately involved his action was high-handed and, lacking as it did the sanction of the judicial process, reprehensible. Hodson
was killed during the final capture of Lucknow but his name lived on his
regiment, which was absorbed into the Indian Army.

Major General Sir Hugh Rose commanded the Central India Field
Force during the Mutiny. Few expected him to do well, yet the achievements of his force were truly astonishing. Heavily outnumbered, it fought
its way across mountain ranges and arid plains in heat that literally
exploded thermometers, storming fortresses and winning battle after
battle. Among Rose's principal opponents were the notorious Tantia Topi
and the equally notorious Rani of Jhansi, who dressed and fought as one
of her own troopers and whose name was linked with a particularly vile
massacre. In any circumstances other than the desperate conditions
prevailing in India at the time, Rose would have been regarded as one of
the great commanders of the Victorian era. Outside the Army, however,
he was largely forgotten, and it is only recently that the full measure of
his worth has been recognised by historians.

In the equally tragic circumstances of the American Civil War, the huge armies raised by North and South were usually commanded by regular soldiers, whose names are still familiar to us. Below them the intermediate levels of command were held by officers who had been professional or business men until the outbreak of war, yet who were now required to make military decisions with a minimum of formal training. One such was Benjamin H. Grierson, who, as a colonel commanding a brigade of Union cavalry, was set the mission of raiding deep into enemy territory to destroy the Confederate rail communications with the fortress of Vicksburg. After completing this task successfully, he appreciated that his brigade would be cut to pieces by its pursuers if he attempted to return north, and he therefore decided to head for Federal-controlled territory on the southern reaches of the Mississippi. In so doing he performed the extraordinary feat of arms of having ridden right across the Confederacy from north to south, for which he received popular acclaim and promotion. After the war he chose to remain in the Army and was given command of the black 10th Cavalry. Although the regiment performed well during the Indian wars on the frontier, he never achieved the fame of such contemporaries as Custer, Miles and Crook and gradually dropped from view.

Lew Wallace had fought as a junior officer in the United States' war against Mexico but was by profession a lawyer and state politician. On the outbreak of the Civil War he was granted a commission as Major General of Volunteers, but he enjoyed mixed fortunes. He handled his division well during the campaign against Forts Henry and Donelson, but at the Battle of Shiloh he failed to make his presence felt and, having incurred Grant's enmity, was banished to administrative appointments. By 1864 Grant had deprived the Confederate Army of Northern Virginia, commanded by General Robert E. Lee, of the power to manoeuvre by locking it into a war of attrition. Anxious to break free, Lee sent one of his ablest subordinates, Jubal Early, to menace Washington from the Shenandoah Valley, hoping that this would panic the capital's politicians into withdrawing a large part of Grant's army to contain the threat. By now Wallace was commanding the Baltimore District, apparently far removed from the seat of war. However, he read the strategic implications correctly and, mustering such troops as he could, he marched to meet Early at Monocacy, imposing a day's delay on him despite losing

11

the battle. This provided Grant with just sufficient time to detach a single corps for Washington's defence. Early's advance came to naught and Lee did not recover the power to manoeuvre, making his defeat inevitable. For a brief period Wallace became the toast of the capital, and even Grant praised his prompt action. Today, although Wallace is widely known as the author of the book *Ben Hur,* few are even aware of his military service.

Having been awarded the Victoria Cross during the early months of the Second Afghan War, Lieutenant Walter Hamilton was already a hero when he was appointed to command Sir Louis Cavagnari's escort at the British Residency in Kabul, following the apparent termination of hostilities. The escort consisted of 75 men drawn from the Guides, a crack Indian Army unit and one that can be seen as a forerunner of the modern SAS, but the Residency, overlooked as it was from most directions, was vulnerable to attack. When thousands of regular Afghan soldiers, reinforced by the Kabul mob, launched a treacherous assault on the compound, Hamilton and his men conducted an aggressive defence, fighting to the death but taking 600 of their attackers with them. The subsequent official investigation records that 'the annals of no army and no regiment can show a brighter record of bravery than has been achieved by this small band of Guides'. As a direct result of the incident open hostilities were resumed, and the war, the collective memory of which has faded into the shadows with the passage of time, was fought through to a successful conclusion.

Hector Macdonald was the son of a Highland crofter. Having enlisted as a private soldier, he rose in due course to general's rank and was knighted for his services. While serving as a sergeant during the Second Afghan War he was offered the Victoria Cross or a battlefield commission, and he chose the latter. He went on to serve in the First Boer War, and during Kitchener's re-conquest of the Sudan he commanded an Egyptian infantry brigade. In the opinion of some, he was the real victor of the Battle of Omdurman, for when Kitchener, having beaten off the first dervish attack, prematurely ordered a general advance, he did so leaving large bodies of the enemy unsubdued on his flanks. When these, amounting to more than one-third of the dervish army, renewed the attack, Macdonald coolly redeployed his regiments to meet the threat, holding his own until assistance arrived and earning the popular nickname of

'Fighting Mac'. During the Second Boer War he commanded the prestigious Highland Brigade. He then became Commander-in-Chief Ceylon, where, because his marriage remained a secret, jealousy among the colonial hierarchy resulted in unfounded accusations of homosexuality being levelled against him. Wishing to spare his wife and family the humiliation of a public inquiry, he took his own life. For many years afterwards it was rumoured that the German General von Mackensen was actually Hector Macdonald, despite the career of the former being well documented. Though he remains largely unknown elsewhere, 'Fighting Mac' remains a hero in his native Scotland.

Major General Charles Townshend was a complex character, driven by a burning desire for advancement and a constant craving for popular adulation, but he was nonetheless a competent soldier. In 1895 he conducted the successful defence of the isolated fort of Chitral on the North-West Frontier, earning the nickname 'Chitral Charlie'. The siege caught the public imagination, although the relief force actually had a much harder time. He saw further active service in the Sudan and was present at Omdurman. During the First World War he commanded a division in Mesopotamia and, having broken the Turkish line, pursued the beaten enemy for many miles up the Tigris in river steamers, gunboats and local craft, the incident becoming known as 'Townshend's Regatta'. He was now at the height of his fame, but, encouraged by his immediate superior, he attempted to extend his advance and capture Baghdad, contrary to his better judgement. His division won a battle at Ctesiphon but incurred such heavy losses that he had to withdraw. Arriving at Kut al Amara, he announced that he would defend the town as he had defended Chitral twenty years earlier. This was neither necessary nor desirable. The siege kept him in the public eye, but relief attempts resulted in more casualties than there were men present in Kut and were finally abandoned. When Kut surrendered Townshend promised to share his men's hardships but instead enjoyed a luxurious captivity in an island villa while many of his troops starved to death in Turkish prison camps. The survivors never forgave him, nor did the public. He was never employed again, and he died in the very obscurity he so dreaded.

Townshend and the others described in these pages belonged to a time when it was possible for individuals to change the course of history, and their actions enable us to see events from an often neglected perspective. Comparatively few men achieved such status in the era of total war, and those that did have not yet been forgotten. The reader might agree that, the world being a stage, there are occasions when the supporting actors sometimes out-perform the principals.

Benedict Arnold

Once a hero, twice a traitor

I
N 1775 THIRTEEN of the fourteen British colonies in North America
rebelled against their Mother Country. The basic issue was that the
colonists, no longer needing the protection of the British Army and the
Royal Navy since the expulsion of the French from Canada, objected
strongly to being taxed without representation in Parliament. This was
hardly surprising since this had been one of the primary principles upon
which the English Civil War had been fought 130 years earlier. Nevertheless, the London administration of the day remained intransigent upon
the subject and King George III, badly advised, was adamant that there
should be no change in the colonies' status. Attitudes on both sides hard-
ened until the Westminster government, foolishly resorting to the tool of
repression, provoked the colonists into armed insurrection.

Within the thirteen colonies there was at first no clear majority in favour
of severing all political ties with the United Kingdom. Approximately one-
third of the population were in favour of complete independence, about
the same number, known as loyalists, were for retaining some form of connection, and the rest simply wanted to get on with their lives. These subdi-
visions were unevenly distributed. In the maritime New England colonies,
where trade was most affected by London's taxation policies, those favour-
ing complete separation were in the majority; in the central colonies, sepa-
ratists and loyalists were approximately equal in number; and in the southern colonies loyalist support was at its strongest. In the fourteenth colony,
Canada, formerly New France, there was minimal support for the rebellion. There, the language, customs and religion of the largely French
population were respected by the British, whose rule was infinitely pref-
erable to the corrupt form of government once imposed by Old France.

One of those who favoured separation on the outbreak of the rebellion was Benedict Arnold, the son of a long-established and highly respected New England family. Born in Norwich, Connecticut, on 14 January 1741, he was apprenticed to an apothecary in his youth but had served for a while in a local militia regiment during the 1754 war against the French and Indians. Returning to his mortar and pestle, he moved to New Haven in 1761. He possessed a shrewd business sense, expanding his activities into trade and shipping with Canada and the West Indies, the rewards enabling him to secure election to a captaincy in the local militia.

Having marched his men to Boston, where the New England militia besieged the British garrison, he recognised that only the rebels' lack of cannon prevented the town from becoming untenable. He persuaded the Massachusetts Committee of Safety that this could be remedied by capturing the guns of Fort Ticonderoga. The Committee accepted his plan, granting him the rank of colonel with which to lead their contingent, which would be joined by one from what is now the state of Vermont under the command of Ethan Allen. Ticonderoga, a strong fortification on a peninsula at the southern end of Lake Champlain, lay on the direct route between the Hudson valley and Canada. During the days of the French it had witnessed much fighting but had now become something of a military backwater, manned by a small care-and-maintenance detachment that ran a slack routine. The approach of Arnold and Allen went undetected, but when they reached the lake they found that they had only sufficient boats for 83 of their 270 men. Nevertheless, on the night of 10 May they rowed silently across and scaled the walls to find the garrison sound asleep. Without the loss of a man, the Americans captured the fort and with it 122 guns, arms, munitions and stores, as well as several small vessels. Two days later they captured another post, Crown Point, without encountering resistance. In due course some of the guns would be transported to Boston, with the result that Arnold predicted.

Arnold's superiors were delighted with the result of the expedition. They were, however, less than pleased not only by his inflated claim for personal expenses, amounting to approximately £45,000 in today's money, but also by his angry reaction to their auditors. At Ticonderoga he did not get on with Ethan Allen and asked for another appointment. He was assigned to the ill-considered invasion of Canada, during which he would lead a force of 1,100 men from Massachusetts across what is now Maine, up the Kennebec and Dead Rivers, then down the Chaudière River to the point where it met the St Lawrence near Quebec. Simultaneously, Major General Philip Schuyler, with 1,000 men, was to advance from Ticonderoga along the traditional invasion route, capture Montreal and join Arnold at Quebec, which was the expedition's ultimate objective.

Arnold began his march on 12 September. It was to be an epic of hardship, completed by canoe and bateau in increasingly harsh winter conditions. By the time the St Lawrence was reached on 8 November, desertion, disease and starvation had reduced his command to 600 men. On 13 November he crossed the river to join Major General Richard Montgomery, who had succeeded Schuyler when the latter fell ill. Montgomery had taken Montreal but now had just 300 men at his disposal. Despite this, he was determined to assault the formidable defences of Quebec and on New Year's Day decided to use darkness and a driving blizzard to conceal his lack of numbers. This was what Sir Guy Carleton, the Governor-General of Canada, had been expecting, and his 1,800 men were ready and waiting. Montgomery was killed in the first minutes of the attack. Arnold, hit in the left leg, was dragged to the rear by his men. Nevertheless, a party of Americans under Colonel Daniel Morgan— of whom more in the next chapter—did penetrate the defences, holding out in the town until forced to surrender at dawn. The attack had been a disaster. American losses amounted to 60 killed or wounded, plus 426 captured; British casualties came to five killed and thirteen wounded.

Surrounded by a hostile Canadian population, the newly promoted Brigadier General Arnold and the remnants of the force maintained a tenuous presence near the city until 6 May 1776, when British transports arrived with Major General John Burgoyne and substantial reinforcements for Carleton. Abandoning his guns, Arnold withdrew to Montreal, joining Brigadier General John Sullivan, the new commander of the American forces in Canada. Having himself received reinforcements, Sullivan mounted a counter-attack at Trois Rivières on 6 June. The affair was botched and resulted in his precipitate retreat. Despite this, he remained determined to hold on to Upper Canada to the bitter end. The more clear-sighted Arnold, seeing that there was nothing to be gained in either of the Canadas, Upper or Lower, wrote to him, commenting, 'Let us quiet them and secure our own country before it is too late.'

The army withdrew to Crown Point, followed by Carleton. Both sides understood that the next move would be dictated by whoever controlled Lake Champlain and began building gunboats and other small war vessels. Arnold was placed in command of the American flotilla, the presence of which inhibited a further British advance in the direction of the Hudson valley until the campaigning season was over. At length, on 11 October, the two flotillas clashed west of Valcour Island. Although Arnold managed to escape to Crown Point with five of his gunboats (one of which was discovered in 1997), the remaining eleven were sunk or set on fire to prevent their capture.

The strategy for the 1777 campaign in the north was dictated by Burgoyne, who returned to England on winter leave. Known as 'Gentleman Johnny', he was a largely absentee Member of the House of Commons, a poet, a playwright, a successful gambler and a sportsman. More importantly, he was well connected and, moving in that level of society where decisions were made, he wasted no time in putting forward a plan that he believed would end the rebellion in the American colonies. The epicentre of the rebellion, he judged correctly, lay in New England, which could be isolated by a triple thrust converging on Albany in the Hudson valley. The first thrust would be made by General William Howe's army marching up the river from New York; the second would involve a force under Colonel Barry St Leger advancing along the Mohawk to its confluence with the Hudson; and the third would be delivered by his own troops entering the Hudson valley by the traditional route from the north. The plan was approved by Lord George Germain, who, as Lord George Sackville, had so disgraced himself at the Battle of Minden in 1759 that he was declared unfit to serve the Crown in any military capacity whatsoever, yet was now, as Secretary of State for the Colonies, inexplicably responsible for the conduct of operations in America. On paper, the plan looked workable enough; in reality, it ignored the vast distances and the difficult terrain involved, as well as the fact that none of the three forces could either support or even communicate with each other. Having given Burgoyne his approval and sent him back to Canada with a commission as commander of the northern sector, Germain committed the greatest blunder of his career by informing Howe of the plan yet leaving it to his discretion whether he participated or not. Howe, senior to Burgoyne, could continue to do as he liked and there was nothing the latter could do about it. As we shall see in the next chapter, he chose to advance in an entirely different direction, against Philadelphia, thereby depriving Burgoyne's plan of one of its most vital elements.

In April 1777 a British force from New York raided Danbury, Connecticut, where it destroyed an American supply depot. Arnold, on leave from the northern front, quickly mobilised the local militia, harassing the raiders as they withdrew. At Ridgefield he attempted to intercept them and inflicted further loss, his horse being killed under him during the fighting. Congress was so pleased with the outcome that it not only promoted him to major general but also provided him with a new horse 'as a token of their admiration of his gallant conduct'. He then re-joined the Americans' northern army, once again commanded by Philip Schuyler, at Stillwater on the Hudson.

In July the second element of Burgoyne's plan was activated. Leaving Fort Oswego on Lake Ontario, St Leger commenced his advance towards the Mohawk valley. The size of his command—consisting of less than 900 men, the majority of whom were loyalists or Indians, plus a few light guns—was absurdly small for such an undertaking. He found his path barred by Fort Stanwix, located on the site of modern Rome, New York, and instituted a siege. On 6 August his Indians and loyalists ambushed an American relief column, mauling it so severely that it was forced to turn back. Simultaneously, however, the garrison of Fort Stanwix made an effective sortie, destroying the Indian encampment. Learning of these developments, Schuyler decided to send a second relief column, consisting of 1,000 volunteers, under Arnold's command. This was a courageous decision as Schuyler's army was only 4,500 strong and Burgoyne, advancing from the north, was now just 25 miles away; in fact, Arnold was the only one of Schuyler's officers who did not oppose the decision. American spies penetrated St Leger's camp, spreading word that Arnold was on the way and exaggerating his strength. This was too

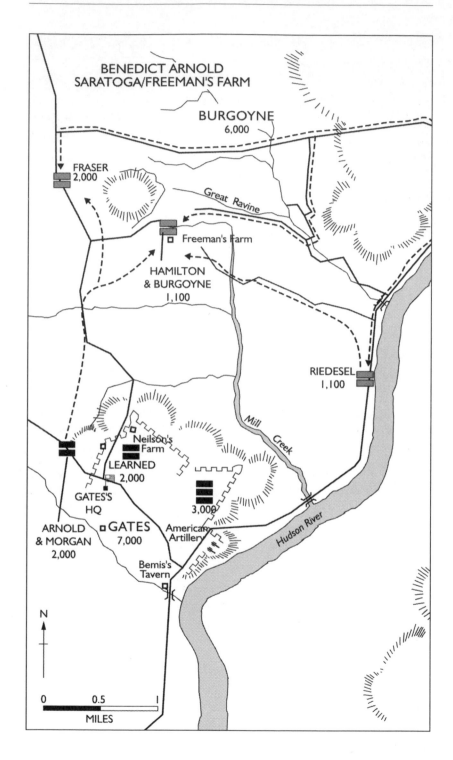

BENEDICT ARNOLD
SARATOGA/FREEMAN'S FARM

BURGOYNE
6,000

FRASER
2,000

Great Ravine

Freeman's Farm

HAMILTON
& BURGOYNE
1,100

RIEDESEL
1,100

Mill Creek

Neilson's
Farm

LEARNED
2,000

GATES'S
HQ

ARNOLD
& MORGAN
2,000

GATES
7,000

American
Artillery

3,000

Hudson River

Bemis's
Tavern

N

0   0.5   1
MILES

much for the Indians, who, having already lost all their possessions, simply decamped. St Leger had no alternative but abandon the siege and, leaving his guns and stores behind, retire hastily to Oswego. The second element of Burgoyne's plan had now come to naught.

The advance of Burgoyne's own army, 7,200 strong, had begun at the end of June. At first all had gone well. By heaving his artillery up Mount Defiance he rendered Fort Ticonderoga untenable. The garrison had abandoned the post on the night of 5/6 July, and on 7 July its rearguard was caught and mauled at Hubbardton. At this point Burgoyne lost his head. Instead of taking the easier route to the Hudson along Lake George, he decided to enter the valley by way of Wood Creek and Fort Ann. The Americans harassed the column constantly, blocking the road with felled trees, so that it took about three weeks to complete the journey. On 3 August he received confirmation that Howe would not be marching north from New York. A more prudent commander would have consolidated his position or retired, but Burgoyne, filled with groundless optimism, decided to press on in the vague hope that he would meet St Leger at Albany. This ignored the cardinal rule that the further an offensive proceeds the more its power declines, while for the enemy the reverse is true. Indeed, from that moment on, reinforcements began to reach Schuyler in growing numbers. To emphasise the point, a strong force of Burgoyne's German mercenary contingent, sent to forage near Bennington, was badly cut up on 16 August, sustaining 1,000 casualties. Undeterred, Burgoyne crossed to the right bank of the Hudson near Saratoga and advanced against the main American position, which he believed to be located on Bemis Heights. Congress had now appointed Major General Horatio Gates to command its army, which, its ranks further filled by tales of atrocities committed by Burgoyne's Indian allies, now numbered 7,000 men.

Having removed St Leger from the equation, Arnold had re-joined the army. He was not a popular figure among his peers, being regarded as opinionated and self-seeking. He certainly resented the promotion of others for deeds he regarded as inferior to his own, and he did not get on with Gates, who referred to him as 'a pompous little fellow'. The principal difference between them was that Gates did not believe that his militia and volunteers were equal to a stand-up fight with Burgoyne's regulars, and for that reason he had fortified the Heights, intending to fight a purely defensive battle; Arnold, on the other hand, believed that Burgoyne would attempt to work round the American position to the west, rendering it untenable, and he advocated offensive action against the British while they were engaged in their flank march.

Arnold had read the situation correctly and, fortunately for the Americans, he was commanding the left wing of Gates's army when Burgoyne advanced on 19 September. Thick woodland and broken terrain prevented the British from forming any impression of their opponents' position, whereas their own progress was reported regularly by the American scouts. Arnold repeatedly asked Gates for permission to attack with his own troops and eventually this was granted. He penetrated the space between Burgoyne's right and centre columns, forcing the latter back to an area of cleared land and a small house known as Freeman's Farm, which changed hands several times during heavy fighting. Arnold was everywhere, leading attacks and counter-attacks, bringing up troops and rallying those who had been repulsed. Believing that it was possible to inflict a sharp reverse on Burgoyne, he repeatedly asked Gates for reinforcements, but few were forthcoming. Meanwhile, Burgoyne summoned his left column, consisting of German troops under Major General von Riedesel. This fell on the flank of Arnold's men, forcing them to retreat at about the same time Gates ordered Arnold off the field. When dusk put an end to the fighting the British retained possession of the battlefield but had sustained 600 casualties, twice those of the Americans; they were, furthermore, shaken by the vehemence with which the American counter-stroke had been delivered.

It is just possible that, had Burgoyne chosen to withdraw at that moment, he might have saved much of his army, but that was not in his mind. Two days after the battle he received a communication from Sir Henry Clinton, commanding at New York while Howe was campaigning in Pennsylvania. Clinton told him that, having received reinforcements from England, he was prepared to mount a diversion up the Hudson to relieve the pressure on Burgoyne's army. Burgoyne therefore decided to delay renewing his attack on Bemis Heights to allow Clinton's measures to take effect. The decision proved fatal, for, when the moment arrived, his remaining 5,000 troops, subsisting on reduced rations, were confronted by an American army that was now 9,000 strong. Clinton kept his promise, but while his diversionary attack achieved some tactical successes, it was mounted too late to affect the issue.

Nor was all sweetness and light across the lines. In his despatch to Congress regarding what became known as the Battle of Freeman's Farm, Gates jealously omitted to mention Arnold's critical part in the action. Furious, Arnold stormed into his headquarters and a monumental row followed. According to the eyewitness accounts of staff officers, 'matters were altercated in a very high strain' and 'gross language ensued'.

During the next few days the quarrel was maintained by letter, to the point that Gates ordered Arnold to hand over his command to Major General Benjamin Lincoln and told him to seek employment elsewhere. Etiquette required that Arnold should leave at once but, like Achilles, he chose to remain sulking in his tent.

On 7 October Burgoyne again attempted to turn Gates's position on Bemis Heights, and again he was vigorously counter-attacked by the American left wing. Colonel Daniel Morgan's sharpshooting riflemen took a severe toll of the British officers, as they had in the earlier battle. Arnold, unable to remain passive, galloped on to the battlefield and assumed *de facto* command. Under his inspired leadership the Americans forced their opponents back on two redoubts that had been constructed to cover the western approaches to Freeman's Farm. The redoubts were then stormed, the effect being to render the rest of Burgoyne's position untenable. At the moment of victory, Arnold was shot in the left leg, the same which had been injured at Quebec, and his horse, killed by the same volley, broke it when it crashed on top of him. Although in agony, he exhibited a surprisingly chivalrous side to his nature, for as his soldiers ran past to bayonet the Hessian who had shot him, now himself lying wounded, he called out, 'Don't hurt him, he's a fine fellow! He only did his duty.'

The Battle of Bemis Heights spelled the end for Burgoyne, who had sustained a further 600 casualties in contrast to the 150 suffered by the Americans. Abandoning his sick and wounded, he began a ponderous retreat to Saratoga the following day but was pursued and surrounded by Gates, whose army now outnumbered his remaining troops by three to one. He asked Gates for terms and on 17 October the two concluded

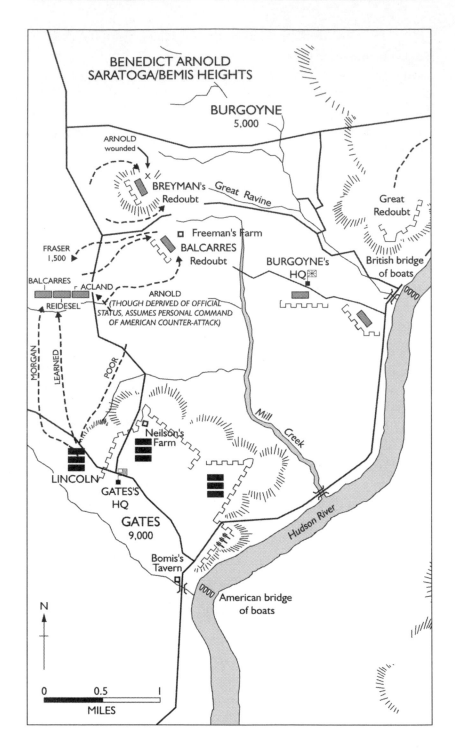

BENEDICT ARNOLD
SARATOGA/BEMIS HEIGHTS

BURGOYNE
5,000

ARNOLD
wounded

BREYMAN's _Great
Redoubt_   _Ravine_

Great
Redoubt

FRASER
1,500

☐ Freeman's Farm
BALCARRES
Redoubt

BURGOYNE's
HQ

British bridge
of boats

BALCARRES

ACLAND

ARNOLD
(THOUGH DEPRIVED OF OFFICIAL
STATUS, ASSUMES PERSONAL COMMAND
OF AMERICAN COUNTER-ATTACK)

REIDESEL

MORGAN

LEARNED

POOR

Neilson's
Farm

_Mill
Creek_

LINCOLN

GATES'S
HQ

GATES
9,000

Hudson River

Bomis's
Tavern

American bridge
of boats

N

0   0.5   1
MILES

a Convention under which his men were to be disarmed, marched to Boston and repatriated on condition that they took no further part in the war. To its shame, Congress repudiated the agreement and the men were held in Virginian prison camps; by the end of the war, many of them had managed to make good their escape.

Generously, Burgoyne conceded that Arnold had been largely responsible for his downfall. The surrender at Saratoga, however, did not merely end major operations in the northern sector of the war, for its strategic consequences were of immense importance. France, keen to avenge her ejection from Canada and taking due note that the colonists were quite capable of standing up to their Mother Country, not only recognised the United States of America but also declared war on the United Kingdom in 1778, to be followed by Spain in 1779 and Holland in 1780. In the long term, the colonists' victory was assured, and, thus far, no man had done more to achieve it than Benedict Arnold.

It took months for Arnold's leg to heal, and even then he walked with a limp. In July 1778 General George Washington appointed him military governor of Philadelphia after the British had evacuated the city. Philadelphia society, which still contained numerous open and covert loyalists, was much grander than that of provincial New England and he quickly succumbed to the round of balls, parties and other social events. A widower, he also became besotted with and duly married Miss Margaret Shippen who, at nineteen, was half his age. The Arnolds threw extravagant parties and generally lived beyond their means until they were deeply in debt. To remedy the situation, Arnold became involved in dubious financial dealings. However, his overbearing manner and arbitrary decisions had made him enemies. The Executive Council of Pennsylvania laid charges of fraud and peculation against him before Congress. At his court martial only two, relating to the illegal granting of a passport to a vessel and the use of public wagons for private purposes, were proved. By order of the court, he was subjected to a public reprimand from Washington. Simultaneously, the accounts for his period of command in Canada were being audited. They contained numerous irregularities, including the unauthorised deduction of large sums. Aggrieved by further criticism, he wrote bitterly to Washington: 'Having become a cripple in the service of my country, I little expected to meet such ungrateful returns.' There were, too, other causes for his growing bitterness. He was daily witnessing the dirty, self-seeking side of Congressional politics at close quarters and was beginning to wonder whether such a system had been worth fighting for. Again, having once fought against Catholic France, he disliked and distrusted the Franco-American alliance. Gradually, his disillusionment with the American cause became complete.

In 1780 he was appointed commandant of the strategically important post of West Point on the Hudson. He immediately opened a correspondence with Sir Henry Clinton, now the British commander-in-chief in North America, offering to surrender the fort and its 3,000-strong garrison in exchange for a suitable consideration. Naturally, Clinton found the suggestion acceptable and sent his adjutant general, Major John Andre, up the river in the sloop HMS *Vulture* to meet Arnold. The terms agreed included the payment of £10,000 to Arnold, who would also receive a brigadier-general's commission in the British Army. Arnold handed over a plan of the fort and other documents, which Andre concealed in his stockings. Unfortunately for him, the *Vulture* had been forced to move and, being unable to re-board her, he had to return to New York on foot, carrying a pass in the name of John Anderson, signed by Arnold. A few miles from safety he was arrested by suspicious militiamen and detained when the compromising documents were discovered. When, on 25 September 1780, Arnold was informed of his capture, he promptly had himself rowed out to the *Vulture* in his barge. Not until he knew that Arnold was safe did Andre disclose his true identity. He was, nevertheless, tried, convicted and hanged as a spy, being denied the soldier's privilege of a firing squad. Many American officers regretted his death, for they had grown to like and respect him during his captivity, and, in sharp contrast to Arnold's blatant treachery, he had striven to carry out his orders in as honourable a fashion as circumstances would permit.

Arnold's new career revealed all the savagery of the turncoat. In December 1780 Clinton sent him to Virginia with a force of 1,600 men, mainly loyalists and American deserters, to destroy depots used to supply the American armies in the south. His first objective was Richmond, much of which was thoroughly looted and burned to the ground on 5 January 1781. In May, having inflicted further devastation on Petersburg, Lord Cornwallis, whose army had just completed its long march from

North Carolina, sent him back to New York. In September Clinton despatched him to New London, the base for many American privateers, in his home state of Connecticut. There he burned ships, warehouses and most of the town. For good measure, he also stormed the nearby Fort Griswold, denying quarter to its 150-strong garrison, the majority of whom were slaughtered. In December he sailed for England with his wife and briefly advised the government on the conduct of the war.

With the conclusion of peace, Arnold's public life came to an end. Once hailed as one of the principal heroes of the American Revolution, his name had become and remains a synonym for treachery within the United States, despite his immense contribution to the cause of Independence. During the war other disenchanted American officers had changed sides or left the service, but they had done so out of conviction, and that was accepted. Arnold, however, had done so for personal gain, earning his countrymen's loathing and contempt. Whatever his qualities as a soldier may have been—and they were considerable—the inner demons that drove him were the need to be at the centre of events, the lust for rank, power and wealth, and the enjoyment of high living. In the end, they destroyed him.

His immediate usefulness ended, he found himself treated with cold indifference in London. As he had failed to deliver West Point he received only one-third of the £10,000 he had set as the price for his treachery. In British eyes, he was twice a traitor who had first fought against his King and then betrayed his own people. Such a man could not be trusted and was therefore unfit for further military employment. For the same reasons, he was denied the *entrée* into Society. There was a certain natural justice in his situation, for he found himself excluded from the very things he valued most. To support himself, Arnold returned to commerce, with only modest success. He died on 14 June 1801. His son William became a junior officer in the 19th Light Dragoons, with whom he served against his father's former countrymen on the Niagara front during the War of 1812.

Banastre Tarleton

The Redcoat Rommel

JOHN TARLETON was a successful Liverpool businessman with interests in shipping, in import and export, in plantations in Jamaica and other West Indian islands as well as Curaçao and, by no means least, in the infamous slave trade. For all that, he was a loving husband and father, and his attitude to the last of his interests mirrored that of many of his contemporaries, who strove to justify this revolting traffic in human beings by stating blandly that it was the duty of good men to rescue the African from the wretched condition into which the Almighty had inexplicably consigned him, and introduce him to the twin benefits of useful toil and imposed Christianity, so freely available in the plantations of the New World. There were many in Liverpool who abhorred the trade and would ultimately play a leading role in putting an end to it, but in the middle of the eighteenth century they remained a minority who, with some justice, claimed that every brick of their town had been cemented by an African's blood.

John's second son, Banastre, named after his maternal grandfather, was born in 1754 and received his early education at the Liverpool Free School. He wrote good, clear, incisive English, in sharp contrast to the verbose style then fashionable, and could turn his hand to poetry as well. He was a fine sportsman and rode well. When he went up to read law at University College, Oxford, in 1771 he was a rather wild, over-indulged young man, very much a product of the violent Liverpool environment in which slavery and privateering were frequently the roads to riches. Little is known of his career as an undergraduate, but he no doubt found the reading of law extremely dull and spent much of the summer terms playing cricket, at which he excelled. His new acquaintances, including the future Lord Rawdon, with whom he would later serve in America, would have seen a handsome, stocky, red-haired young man with an engaging style and great charm of manner. They would have noticed, too, that he had already developed a voracious appetite for the opposite sex, and that he was much given to the advertisement of his own virtues. In 1773 his father died, taking care that all his family were well provided for. Banastre's legacy amounted to £5,000, an enormous sum which translated into today's value would be approximately £100,000. It was enough to turn the heads of most nineteen-year-olds, and Banastre was no exception.

After he came down from Oxford he continued with his law studies at the Middle Temple, perhaps out of respect for his father's wishes. There is no doubt that he disliked the subject and found its practitioners pompously boring. As his enthusiasm for the profession waned, so his penchant grew for drinking, gambling, womanising and roistering. Like his father, he dearly loved a lord, and his inheritance enabled him to keep up with the younger members of the aristocracy at the gaming tables. In such circles, too, were to be found a better, more experienced class of hussy than he had been used to, and it was entirely characteristic of him that should a lady not succumb to his demands immediately he would pursue her remorselessly with expensive gifts until she did. His favourite haunt was the Cocoa Tree, where he and his cronies developed a taste for practical jokes, including the perennial favourite of overturning sedan chairs. One night at Covent Garden he stopped the performance by reading aloud a satirical poem he had composed, mercilessly ridiculing one of his rivals.

Of course, it could not last for ever. There was a general opinion that Master Tarleton would make but an indifferent lawyer, and opinion he doubtless shared, for he withdrew from the Middle Temple early in 1775. At about the same time the last of his legacy ran out and there was nothing for it but to return to Liverpool. His mother and his elder brother Thomas took him severely to task, as they would do many times in the future. Thomas certainly did not want him in the business, nor was he prepared to support him. It was suggested that a spell in the Army might do him good and enhance the family's standing, and to this suggestion he readily agreed. His mother therefore purchased a cornet's commis-

sion for him in the fashionable 1st Dragoon Guards at a probable cost of
£2,000.

Banastre reported for duty at Norwich in the spring of 1775. The
darker side of his nature was not yet apparent, and to the regiment he
simply seemed to be a somewhat extrovert junior officer with a fund of
amusing and risqué experiences to recount. He was put through his paces
as a troop leader and seems to have mastered the basic elements of his
new profession very well indeed. He did not, however, remain with the
regiment for long, for on the outbreak of rebellion in the American colonies he immediately volunteered for active service and in December his
request for transfer was favourably endorsed.

In London he held a farewell party for his old friends at the Cocoa
Tree. As the drink flowed the talk was of General Charles Lee, a renegade British officer who had thrown in his lot with the rebels and was
much reviled for doing so. Lee was a man of startling contradictions. He
was cultured, spoke several languages and read the classics for pleasure
in their original Greek and Latin, yet he was foul-mouthed, was given to
coarse humour, drank to excess and was something of a lecher. He believed in personal cleanliness but went about in the scruffiest clothes. He
could be the pleasantest company, although he was unsparing in his opinions, possessed a vile temper and was inclined to betray friends and enemies alike. He was tall and skinny, with a prominent nose that earned
him the nickname 'Naso'.

As a junior officer Lee had been present at Braddock's defeat on the
Monongahela and Abercromby's repulse at Fort Ticonderoga, the two
worst British reverses in what became known in America as the French
and Indian Wars. He had lived among the Mohawk Indians, who called
him Boiling Water because of his volatile temper. His restless spirit then
took him back to Europe, where he fought in various causes in Portugal,
Poland and Russia. He had been forced to leave Italy in a hurry after
shooting dead his opponent in an illegal duel that cost him two fingers.
Returning to England, he was sharply critical of the King and his minis-
ters and was said to be the author of the notorious *Letters of Junius*. Arriving back in America in 1773, he convinced a majority of Congressmen
that his knowledge of war was without equal throughout the Colonies.
Unfortunately, when it came to the point of rebellion, Congress had a

moral duty to appoint a native-born American, preferably a Virginian, as its commander-in-chief, and the logical choice was George Washington, another veteran of the French and Indian Wars. Initially, Lee ranked third in the American military hierarchy, just below Artemis Ward of Massachusetts. This he resented bitterly, and when Ward resigned after the rebels had captured Boston he began to plot the downfall of Washington.

Technically, Lee was not a traitor, having resigned from the British service before he entered the American. Just the same, his desertion angered his countrymen and many of the party at the Cocoa Tree would gladly have watched him hang. Flushed with drink and righteous indignation, Cornet Tarleton leapt upon a table brandishing his sabre, vowing that he would personally cut off Lee's head. Roaring with laughter, his friends heaved him back to his seat; no one was going to pay too much attention to the ravings of a drunken subaltern. Yet there were those present who would remember the words as being prophetic, for within a year Tarleton had ruined Lee, coming as close to fulfilling his boast as made no difference, and had embarked upon a meteoric career as one of the finest leaders of light cavalry in the history of the British Army.

For the moment, Tarleton would be serving as a troop officer with the 16th Light Dragoons. The light dragoon was a peculiarly British type of cavalryman whose origins lay in the Jacobite Rebellion of 1745. The Duke of Kingston, who had been impressed by the hussars of the Austrian Empire, raised a regiment of light dragoons for service in Scotland. The training given to the light dragoon was more exhaustive than that given to the average cavalry trooper. He was taught to fight mounted or dismounted, to fire from the saddle, to skirmish, to throw up defences and, above all, to use his initiative. He went about his business at top speed and neither hedge, ditch nor river delayed him. He carried a sabre, pistols, carbine and bayonet, a hedging bill and a spade. He wore a distinctive leather helmet and had a tremendous regimental *esprit de corps*. He was just about the most versatile soldier in the army, but he was, first and foremost, a cavalryman, and that meant reconnaissance, forming screens, raiding, pursuit and, if necessary, charging in close order. Kingston's regiment performed so well that several more light dragoon regiments were raised as part of the regular establishment. Given that uncleared virgin forest still covered much of the American colonies, they were better suited to such an environment than heavier cavalry, which relied on the massed shock action of a charge delivered across open terrain.

Arriving in the war zone, Tarleton took part in General Sir Henry Clinton's abortive expedition to Charleston, South Carolina, in June 1776, the defences of which had been previously strengthened by Lee. When the British ships sustained serious damage from a battery on Sullivan's Island, covering the seaward approaches to the harbour, Clinton decided to re-embark such troops as he had landed and re-join his superior, General Sir William Howe, who was about to attack New York. On 27 August Howe, a sound tactician, won a convincing victory on Long Island, forcing Washington to abandon both it and New York itself. He beat Washington at Harlem Heights on 16 September and again at White Plains on 28 October. The following month he took Forts Washington and Lee on the lower reaches of the Hudson. Washington was forced to commence a retreat across New Jersey with his rearguard commanded by Lee. Congress, shaken by the scale of the disaster, fled from Philadelphia to Baltimore, granting Washington what amounted to dictatorial powers. At this point Howe could have probably put an end to the matter, but he lacked the killer instinct of a great commander and simply dispersed his troops into winter quarters.

During these operations Tarleton simply performed the usual duties of a troop officer and, while he was noted for his dash, there had been few opportunities for him to distinguish himself. That would change dramatically on Thursday 12 December 1776, when Lieutenant Colonel William Harcourt, commanding the 16th Light Dragoons, personally led a troop-strong patrol with the object of discovering the whereabouts of Lee and his troops, who, since Washington had retired across the Delaware, were suspected of being somewhere to right and rear of the British advance. The patrol consisted of Captain Nash, Lieutenant Leigh and Cornet Tarleton, the troop's officers, Captain Eustace, who was an aide to General Cornwallis, and 25 troopers. The presence of Harcourt and Eustace indicate the importance which was attached to its mission.

Leaving the little town of Pennington, New Jersey, the patrol rode north through the deserted, wintry landscape throughout the day, reaching the hamlet of Hillsborough on Milestone Creek during the evening. Next morning Harcourt got the patrol moving again well before dawn, heading in the direction of Morristown with Tarleton and six troopers acting as point. A solitary armed rebel was captured, but he was almost certainly a deserter and had nothing of interest to say. Some way beyond, local people told Harcourt that Lee was no more than five miles away. They also warned him that rebel troops were closing in behind the patrol.

Three miles further on, Tarleton captured two armed men. He threatened to kill them unless they told him where Lee was, but, incoherent with fear, all they could say was that the general was about a mile away. Taking two troopers, he galloped to a hill overlooking the road. A mounted American could be seen approaching and, before he knew what was happening, the dragoons had captured him. He was a courier, *en route* to General Sullivan at Pluckemin, and he had just left Lee's headquarters. Harcourt had now closed up with the main body, but the prisoner seemed disinclined to talk further until Tarleton offered to sabre him. Sullenly, the man revealed that Lee's escort was about the same size as the patrol. He accompanied Harcourt and Tarleton back to the hill and pointed out the general's headquarters, which were located in a tavern.

Harcourt had accomplished the primary mission of locating Lee and his troops. The question now facing him was whether he should prejudice the patrol by attempting a *coup de main* to seize Lee, or carry out the less spectacular but useful job of shadowing the rebel troops. He decided on the former. Tarleton with one party would attack the house and secure Lee while Eustace and another held off the general's escort; simultaneously, Harcourt and the remainder of the troop would position themselves between the house and the American encampment, preventing any interference.

The plan worked perfectly. The first those in the tavern knew of the attack was the eruption of a swarm of yelling, red-coated dragoons from the nearby woods. Eustace chased Lee's escort into the outbuildings in which they were quartered and kept them pinned inside with gunfire. Tarleton set his horse at full gallop for the two sentries guarding the main entrance to the inn. They dropped their muskets and ran. At the cornet's order the snatch squad opened fire with their carbines and pistols, shooting through every door and window. Inside, Lee's staff and two French volunteer officers replied with their own weapons. The banging of small arms and smashing of glass lasted for about eight minutes, at the end of which the tavern's owner, a Mrs White, rushed into the open, begging Tarleton to spare her life and shouting that Lee was inside. Tarleton fired twice through the now closed front door, warning the occupants that he knew Lee was within and that if he and his staff surrendered immediately they would come to no harm; if they did not, the house would be burned down and everyone in it slaughtered. The back door was promptly flung open and several men tried to make their escape. The first was shot dead and the second, one of the French officers, was floored by a sabre stroke; the remainder retreated inside.

Lee decided to surrender. Renewed gunfire almost riddled his aide when he opened the front door, and almost immediately Lee emerged to give himself up. Tarleton must have asked himself whether this pathetic figure with a battered hat above the prominent nose, its skinny body clad in a blue coat faced in stained red and its legs enclosed in greasy leather breeches, was really the infamous General Charles Lee. At that moment Harcourt and his men came galloping up with the trumpeter blowing the Recall. There was just time to get the general mounted and snatch up some of his papers, and then the troop put as much distance as they could between themselves and Mrs White's tavern. Harcourt, mindful of the earlier warning that rebel troops might now be behind him, took a different route home, and for thirteen miles his men did not draw rein.

One of the great ironies of the affair was that Lee had been captured by men of the regiment he had once commanded. Greatly amused, they proceeded to get his horse drunk as soon as they reached safety. Lee was himself warmly received by a number of old friends, but he remained understandably depressed. His papers revealed that he was intriguing with all and sundry for the removal of Washington and for his own assumption of overall command. This was a not improbable outcome to his power struggle, for he was very popular with the American rank and file whereas the reputation of the repeatedly defeated Washington had sunk to its lowest ebb. In retrospect, the loss of Lee at this stage of the war can be seen as a long-term gain for the Colonists. As we shall see, he was not the great captain he believed himself to be, and if he had replaced Washington the conflict might have had a different ending. In

England, his capture was talked of as though it ended the problem in the Colonies and Harcourt received a personal note of thanks from the King.

On 18 December Tarleton wrote to his mother, giving his dateline as Prince's Town. He described the patrol in his clear style and his account is the best we have of the taking of Charles Lee. He concluded: 'This is the most miraculous event—it appears like a dream . . . Colonel Harcourt's own conduct was masterly—it deserves every applause. This coup de main has put an end to the whole campaign.'

Unfortunately, it had not. On 26 December Washington riposted, capturing the Hessian-held outpost of Trenton, and on 3 January 1777 he won a narrow victory at Princeton. These engagements, though small, were important in that they restored the flagging morale of the American army. Howe's cautious response was to abandon the scattered outposts in New Jersey and concentrate his troops in New York while he planned the coming year's campaign.

Washington, uncertain how to react to Burgoyne's advance in the north, stubbornly refused to be drawn into another pitched battle, so Howe decided to create the circumstances in which he would have to fight one. On 23 July 1777 much of the army was shipped from New York to the head of Chesapeake Bay, where it disembarked at Elkton, posing an obvious threat to Philadelphia. Washington barred the way at Brandywine Creek but was again outmanoeuvred, sustaining a serious defeat on 11 September. After further scrappy fighting Howe entered Philadelphia a fortnight later, beating off a botched raid against his main encampment at Germantown on 4 October. The result was that, while the British made themselves comfortable in the city, Washington's army spent a hard winter in miserable conditions at Valley Forge.

The war was now becoming global in character. The West Indies provided a vital element of the British economy, and since they had been denuded of troops to deal with the rebellion it was necessary to despatch fresh regiments to garrison them. Tarleton's home town raised an infantry regiment, the Liverpool Blues, for service in Jamaica. The workings of the purchase system enabled an officer serving with one regiment to purchase promotion in another, and, partly because of their influence in the town and partly because of his part in the capture of Lee, Tarleton's family were able to secure him a captaincy in the Blues. The colonel of the regiment wrote to Tarleton requesting him to report for duty, but the latter, not only knowing how thoroughly yellow fever and other tropical diseases decimated British regiments serving in the West Indies but also having little appetite for the transfer, refused. The colonel then promoted a junior captain to major over his head. Sir Henry Clinton, taking the view that this was high-handed and unfair, recommended that Tarleton should also be promoted. This was accepted and he became a major, nominally belonging to his parent regiment, the 1st Dragoon Guards. As he obviously he could not remain with the 16th Light Dragoons, he became brigade major of the army's cavalry brigade. This also included the 17th Light Dragoons, who had been active around New York and marched overland to join the army in Philadelphia during the winter. Shortly afterwards, Tarleton was promoted to the rank of acting lieutenant colonel to give him the status appropriate to his duties. Naturally, his meteoric rise resulted in considerable jealousy among others not so fortunate. For example, one of the leading diarists of the campaign, Captain John Peebles of the Black Watch's Grenadier Company, refers to him with heavy sarcasm at this period as 'Lieutenant Colonel Cornet Tarleton', although his attitude would change. Nevertheless, Tarleton's decision to remain in America had been a sound one, if for no other reason than that only a tiny handful of the Liverpool Blues ever saw their homes again: the dreaded Yellow Jack had done for the rest. Furthermore, Philadelphia provided him with a fine social life. At one stage, having been discovered in bed with another officer's mistress, he narrowly avoided a duel.

France had now entered the war on the Colonists' side. Howe, criticised because his failure to support Burgoyne had contributed to the Saratoga disaster as well as for his apparent inability to administer the *coup de grâce* to Washington, tendered his resignation in May 1778 and was replaced by Clinton. The latter was immediately required to detach troops for the defence of the United Kingdom and the West Indies and in the circumstances he could only abandon Philadelphia. While the army marched overland to New York, some 3,000 loyalists were evacuated by sea. During the retreat, the 17th Light Dragoons provided an escort for the twelve-mile-long baggage train, which had been sent ahead, while the 16th Light Dragoons were employed on flank and rearguard duties.

Washington followed, seeking a favourable opportunity to bring Clinton to battle. On 27 June that opportunity seemed to present itself as the routes of the two armies converged near Monmouth Court House. Commanding the American advance guard was Charles Lee, who had been exchanged after a comfortable captivity of eighteen months and who, despite their differences, still enjoyed Washington's confidence. During the evening Washington ordered Lee to attack the British rearguard the following day, and to call a conference of his officers to determine a co-ordinated plan of attack. Dismissive of Washington's wishes, Lee did call a conference at which he simply told his subordinates to be alert for orders which he would personally give on the battlefield itself. This was not the sort of liberty to take with Clinton, who, aware of probable American intentions, ordered Tarleton to bring up the 17th Light Dragoons from the baggage train.

When, next morning, Lee advanced with 5,000 men and twelve guns, he found himself denied information regarding the position of Clinton's rearguard by a screen formed by both light dragoon regiments. Uncertain how to proceed, Lee issued his units with orders followed by counter-orders, the result being complete chaos. They came into action piece-meal and, being sharply repulsed, took to their heels until rallied personally by Washington. Clinton then counter-attacked with his infantry, pushing the enemy back for three miles until the latter's main body arrived on the field. During an afternoon so hot that several men died from heat stroke, the Americans, drilled and disciplined to regular standards throughout the winter and spring by General Baron Augustus von Steuben, stood their ground impressively but failed to prevent Clinton from resuming his withdrawal to New York.

It is worth mentioning that in a war that involved an above-average number of useful villains, von Steuben was neither a general nor a baron, but simply a German volunteer who had arrived in Washington's camp with forged credentials. As for Lee, when Washington slated him publicly for his disobedience, he demanded a court martial. His request was granted and, being found guilty, he was dismissed from the service. Monmouth was to be the last major battle to be fought for the next two years.

In New York the 17th Light Dragoons absorbed the horses and some men from the 16th, who embarked for home. For the remainder of the war military activity around the city was restricted to raiding, with minor successes for both sides. With Britain's military resources stretched to the limit, Clinton knew that he would not receive sufficient reinforcements to return to the initiative in the northern and central states. On the other hand, his political masters in London were aware that loyalist support was strongest in the southern states, which could be pacified by arming the loyalists themselves and getting them to play a more active role in the war. New York itself contained thousands of loyalist refugees, and among the units raised from them was the British Legion, command of which was given to Lieutenant Colonel Banastre Tarleton.

The Legion consisted of both light dragoon and infantry elements and contained a large number of Pennsylvania men who had lost everything at the hands of those who had once been their friends and neighbours. Like other loyalist units, it was uniformed in green. In addition, Tarleton was given a 60-strong troop of 17th Light Dragoons as stiffening. This troop always kept itself a little apart from the rest of the Legion for reasons that reflected the nature of the war. Its members, for example, were used to regular army discipline, which was much stricter than that of the loyalists. Again, as professional soldiers, they accepted that the killing stopped when the battle was over, whereas the loyalists' minds seemed always set on bloody vengeance. Most of all, they were never fully convinced that they could rely on the loyalists if the going got rough. The relationship is best illustrated by the fact that when their scarlet coats became worn they preferred to patch them rather than accept an offer of new loyalist green. The one thing the two factions had in common was respect and liking for Tarleton himself. While still only 26 years old, to the regulars he was an experienced professional of proven ability, while to the loyalists his record had already made him a hero.

Clinton temporised about accepting London's remote-control instructions to commit his troops in the south. In October 1779, however, the British garrison at Savannah, Georgia, decisively repulsed a Franco-American assault. The French hastily re-embarked their contingent, while the Americans withdrew to Charleston. Everywhere throughout the south loyalist hopes soared while those of the rebels plummeted. It was beginning to seem as though not only Georgia but also the Carolinas might be recovered. Deciding to reinforce success, on 26 December Clinton sailed for Tybee, Georgia, with 8,500 men, including the Legion.

Within days of clearing the Hudson the convoy ran into the worst gale experienced for a generation. The ships scattered for their own protection, arriving in ones and twos at their destination, where it took some little time to reorganise the expedition. During the gale the Legion had lost all its horses and without them Tarleton could not serve as the eyes of the army. With characteristic drive he set about putting the matter to rights, borrowing suitable boats from the Quartermaster's Department to scour the area of Port Royal and the nearby islands 'in order to collect at that place, from friends and enemies, by money or by force, all horses belonging to the neighbourhood'. Thus, with his troopers mounted on a motley collection of nags and farm horses, he embarked upon a campaign which, in a few short months, would earn him fame or infamy, depending upon one's point of view.

His first task was to move the Legion to Beaufort and there await the arrival of General James Patterson, who was marching north from Savannah towards Charleston. At Beaufort Tarleton organised a sweep of the surrounding country, and at Salkehatchee Bridge he surprised a party of 80 American militiamen, killing and wounding several before the rest took to their heels.

On 21 March 1780 the Legion effected a junction with Patterson at Horse Shoe and then acted as advance guard while the combined force marched on Jacksonsboro. Two days later the Legion cavalry crossed the Edisto River and was engaged in a skirmish with rebel militia and dragoons at the plantation of Lieutenant Governor Thomas Bee. In this engagement ten Americans were killed and four captured, and the stock of horses slightly augmented. As the day wore on the American cavalry began to make its presence felt and there were one or two inconclusive brushes with Lieutenant Colonel William Washington's Light Horse and Count Casimir Pulaski's Hussars, the latter commanded by Major Paul Vernier since the death of Pulaski, a Polish volunteer, during the abortive assault on Savannah.

The following day Washington, a second cousin of the American commander-in-chief, mounted a successful counter-attack on the column, taking several prisoners, including a loyalist colonel. Tarleton des-

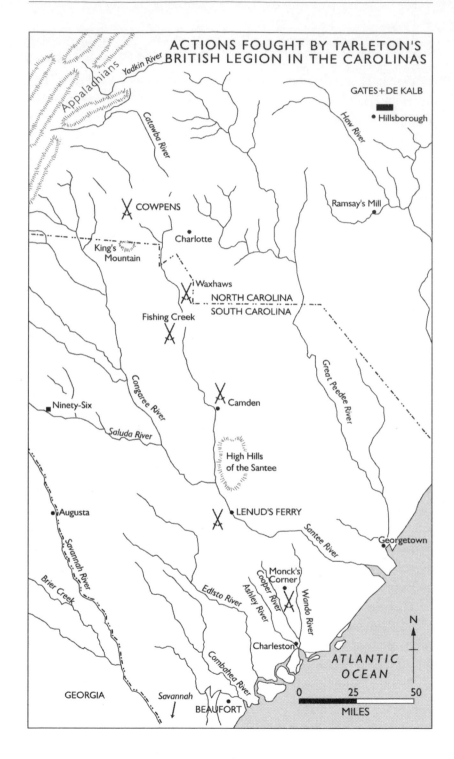

ACTIONS FOUGHT BY TARLETON'S
BRITISH LEGION IN THE CAROLINAS

Appalachians
Yadkin River
GATES + DE KALB
Hillsborough
Haw River
Catawba River
COWPENS
Ramsay's Mill
Charlotte
King's Mountain
Waxhaws
NORTH CAROLINA
SOUTH CAROLINA
Fishing Creek
Great Peedee River
Congaree River
Ninety-Six
Camden
Saluda River
High Hills of the Santee
Augusta
LENUD'S FERRY
Santee River
Georgetown
Savannah River
Monck's Corner
Cooper River
Ashley River
Wando River
Brier Creek
Edisto River
N
Charleston
ATLANTIC OCEAN
GEORGIA
Savannah
BEAUFORT
Combahea River
0   25   50
MILES

patched a rescue force at once but this got into difficulties through the 'error' of the officer commanding and he was forced to extricate it in person. In his own account of the campaign he says little beyond this, but it was clearly not one of his better days and he seems to have ended it in a black mood.

While this bickering on the flanks was taking place, Clinton was marching steadily on Charleston. The town lay at the end of a long narrow peninsula lying between the Ashley and Cooper Rivers and was a natural trap. George Washington had dreaded the possibility that the local American commander, Major General Benjamin Lincoln, would allow himself to be bottled up inside the town with most of his troops, and that is exactly what happened. By 30 March Clinton had established a solid front across the peninsula, opening his first siege parallel the following day. As the American cavalry remained at large in the open country behind, the primary mission for Tarleton and the Legion was to contain them and prevent any interference with the siege operations. On 5 April Tarleton failed in an attempt to surprise William Washington, but the latter withdrew to 23 Mile House.

The Legion went into camp at Quarter House, six miles from Charleston, where it was joined a week later by Major Patrick Ferguson and his famous unit of loyalist riflemen and by a weak brigade made up from companies of the 33rd and 64th Regiments under the command of Lieutenant Colonel Webster. Intelligence reports suggested that Washington had pulled back to Monck's Corner. He had been joined by Brigadier General Isaac Huger, who now had under his command not only Washington's Light Horse and Pulaski's Hussars but also Colonel Daniel Horry's Cavalry and other units recently arrived from Virginia. It looked very much as though some sort of attempt was to be made to break Clinton's siege.

A night attack on the Americans was planned, and during the evening of 12 April the Legion began its march on Monck's Corner, followed at some distance by Ferguson's and Webster's infantry. Some hours after starting, the dragoons riding point surprised a man carrying a despatch from Huger to the Charleston garrison. Rather than render the man incoherent with fear by threatening him, Tarleton offered him some money, and in return the grateful prisoner told all of Huger's dispositions. The cavalry were bivouacked on the near bank of the Cooper River, while the remainder of the force was encamped on the far bank, save for a small militia unit in a meeting house called Biggin Church, near a bridge of the same name. Tarleton made his plans accordingly. The Legion cavalry would ride straight into Huger's camp while Major Cochrane, with the Legion infantry, would deal with the militia in Biggin Church. Both would continue their march in total silence.

As the country on both sides of the road was largely swamp, Tarleton had little room for manoeuvre, but his approach went undetected and by 03:00 he was in a position to launch his attack. Huger had a vedette out, but the first the American advance guard heard of the Legion was a sudden thunder of hooves. In a second the sentries were either ridden or cut down and then the yelling dragoons swept on into the sleeping encampment, slashing at dazed figures as they rose in confusion from their blankets. Pistols banged and men screamed, and then suddenly the Americans broke, running for the safety of the swamp. Among the fugitives were Washington and Huger, forced into a watery hiding place to avoid detection. Some men did their best, like Major Paul Vernier of Pulaski's Hussars. Fearfully cut up, he was carried to a table in a nearby house where, before he died, his cursed his own troops for their cowardice and the loyalists for their barbarity in continuing to sabre him after he had surrendered.

At Biggin, Cochrane had gone in with the bayonet and the militia had fled at once, allowing him to capture the bridge intact. It had taken but a few minutes to destroy Huger's command. British casualties, amounting to one officer and two troopers wounded, were absurdly light. The Americans suffered fifteen killed and seventeen wounded, and 100 of them were now prisoners. Fifty wagons containing clothing, arms and ammunition were captured, but what pleased Tarleton most were the 83 troop horses he had taken, which would replace many of the nags he had rounded up near Port Royal. In his account of the campaign he commented that Huger had made two cardinal mistakes, the first by allowing his cavalry to camp on the 'enemy' bank of a river at night, and the second by not posting scouts ahead of the vedette, where they could have given advance warning of the Legion's approach.

In the aftermath of this easy victory, an ugly incident took place. Nearby was the plantation of Fair Lawn, the home of the loyalist Sir John Colleton.

Some of the Legion made their way there and found a number of women in residence. Selecting the three prettiest, they raped them, and when a doctor's wife tried to stop them she was slashed with a sabre. The remainder of the women ran from the house and placed themselves under the protection of the first British officer they could find. It then became apparent that they were actually loyalist refugees who had gone to Fair Lawn to escape from Huger's men.

Tarleton evidently ruled his own loyalists with a very light hand and, initially at least, he seems to have tried to defend the culprits, no doubt commenting that it was all very unfortunate and regrettable, and that he would deal with the matter personally. Furious, Webster would have none of it and demanded the immediate arrest of the guilty men; Ferguson, a man of high principles, wanted them shot on the spot. Faced with such opposition, Tarleton was forced to send them back to Charleston under close arrest, where they were court martialled and flogged.

While Clinton and Cornwallis, the latter responsible for the security of the army's rear, were more than happy with the outcome of the affray at Monck's Corner, they were less than pleased by its disgraceful aftermath. While issuing fresh orders to Tarleton, Cornwallis referred sharply to the subject:

> I commit the care of the country between the Cooper and the Wando to your charge. You will please report to me whenever you move so that I may know where to find you. I must recommend you in the strongest manner to use your utmost endeavours to prevent the troops under your command from committing irregularities, and I am convinced that my recommendation will have weight when I assure you that such conduct will be highly agreeable to the commander-in-chief.

Tarleton cleared the designated area without further incident, leaving the Charleston garrison even more isolated. By the beginning of May, however, the survivors of Monck's Corner had been reinforced and evidently felt strong enough to attempt a sweep of their own. On the 5th, Colonel Anthony White, with Horry's Cavalry and the remnants of Washington's regiment, crossed the Santee River at Dupin's Ferry and headed south-east, planning to re-cross the river further down at Lenud's Ferry, where Colonel Abraham Buford was posted with a regiment of Virginia militia. The following morning White's troopers surprised an officer and seventeen men of the Legion infantry foraging at Wambaw, taking them prisoner. Their capture was witnessed by a loyalist civilian, who also learned of White's intended route from careless talk and set out to bring help. During the afternoon he ran into Tarleton, who, by pure coincidence, was leading 150 of his dragoons towards Lenud's Ferry from the opposite direction. Tarleton decided on offensive action at once.

White reached the ferry first, but instead of withdrawing in an orderly fashion, by troops, he allowed his men to gather in a formless crowd around the crossing point, relying on the flimsy protection of a few vedettes. Taking in the situation at a glance, Tarleton decided to drive in the vedettes and pursue them into their main body without pause. The vedettes, all but engulfed in the galloping wave of green dragoons, wheeled at once and sped for the ferry. The scant warning they provided barely gave their comrades time to mount, let alone form, and seconds later the Legion cavalry smashed into the jostling mob like a thunderbolt, hacking and slashing. Within the first minute, five American officers and 36 troopers went down, dead or badly wounded. The remainder of White's men either threw down their arms or ran for the river. Among those who dragged themselves out on the far bank were White himself and William Washington, emerging from his second ducking at Tarleton's hands.

'This corps being totally surprised, resistance and slaughter soon ceased,' wrote Tarleton in his despatch. He had captured seven officers and 60 men, together with all the Americans' horses, so that his infantry, released from their brief captivity, were able to ride home. His standing among his men, and with the army's senior officers, could not have been higher. In England, the press reported his exploits in glowing terms, creating a national hero in what was a dismal and increasingly unpopular war.

The siege lines outside Charleston had now been developed as far as the third parallel. General Lincoln, recognising that an assault could be expected at any time, surrendered on 11 May. It was the worst American defeat of the war: 5,400 men marched into captivity or gave their parole, and Clinton took possession of large quantities of cannon, small arms and munitions as well as four frigates. In a somewhat mean-spirited manner, he permitted the garrison only conditional honours of war when they marched out, forbidding their bands to play a British

march and insisting that their colours remain cased. Leaving Cornwallis with 8,000 men to pacify the south, Clinton then returned to New
York.

Colonel Abraham Buford's regiment of Virginia militia were one of
the few formed bodies of American troops remaining in the area. They
had survived the disaster of Lenud's Ferry because they were encamped
on the far bank of the river, but following the fall of Charleston they were
reported to be marching north as fast as they could go. Cornwallis hurried after them, sending Tarleton and the Legion on ahead. Tarleton
now exhibited a tenacity comparable to Rommel's in that he allowed his
own troops no rest during the relentless pursuit of a retreating enemy. At
length the point was reached at which the Legion infantry began to collapse with exhaustion. Without hesitation, he mounted one of them behind each dragoon and the march continued. On 29 May, having covered 105 miles in 54 hours, he caught up with Buford near the little
settlement of Waxhaws. Permitting the weary horses to stand a while, he
sent forward a flag of truce to demand Buford's surrender. Buford declined, tried to continue his march, then rashly deployed his regiment
into line rather than square when he saw the Legion preparing to charge,
ordering the men to hold their fire until the horsemen were only thirty
yards distant. This would have been a severe test even for seasoned veterans, but for militia it was a disaster. As the dragoons came thundering
in, a ragged volley spluttered out. A few horses were killed, including
Tarleton's, which fell on top of its stunned rider, pinning him to the
ground. The Virginian line was simply ridden over and collapsed under
a rain of whirling sabre cuts. Then the Legion infantry arrived with the
bayonet. Furious at the imagined death of their leader, the loyalists showed
no mercy, hacking and stabbing repeatedly at those already on the ground.
It took all the efforts of the British officers of the 17th Light Dragoons to
get them to stop. Buford was among the few who survived the massacre,
having galloped out of harm's way before the issue was decided. Even
when Tarleton was found to be alive, the rebel wounded were treated
shamefully, the only assistance provided for them being handfuls of tow
to stuff into their gaping wounds.

Naturally, such actions were counter-productive. As word of the massacre spread, rebel attitudes in the south began to harden. Ever after,

men would speak of 'Tarleton's Quarter' when no mercy was shown, and the Legion's commander would go down in American history as 'Bloody Tarleton'. He probably deserved the epithet, for he was to boast that during the war he had killed more men and ravished more women than any man alive, while his method of schooling a horse consisted of endless thrashing with a cruel whip until the animal's spirit was broken. It was ironic that at Waxhaws, the episode for which the epithet was awarded, he was personally unable to influence events. Be that as it may, both he and his apparently invincible Legion were particularly hated in a climate where hatred had replaced reason. What amounted to a civil war had broken out across the southern states, where one atrocity begat another as loyalist and rebel guerrilla bands ravaged each other's territories, often killing such prisoners as they took. British officers, used to the conventions of formal warfare, expressed their horror at the savagery displayed by both sides.

After Waxhaws, the Legion re-joined Cornwallis. Congress, seriously alarmed by the turn of events in the south, despatched Major General Horatio Gates, the accredited victor of Saratoga, to restore the situation. Effecting a junction with Major General Baron de Kalb, Gates advanced on Camden, his army now numbering two regular regiments, contingents of North Carolina and Virginia militia and a small unit of dragoons, producing a total of approximately 4,000 men. Cornwallis hurried to meet him with 2,200 men, including the Legion. The two armies met six miles north of Camden on 16 August. On the American left the militia fled without firing a shot on the approach of Webster's brigade and the Legion infantry, carrying away their own dragoons with them. Webster immediately wheeled left, taking de Kalb's regulars in flank while they were engaged with Lord Rawdon's infantry to the front. Seeing his chance, Tarleton immediately led the Legion cavalry round the open American right flank and charged de Kalb from the rear. De Kalb was killed and his regiments were overwhelmed. The battle cost the British 312 casualties; American losses amounted to 800 killed and wounded, 1,000 prisoners and eight guns captured. In making his escape, Gates covered a remarkable 180 miles in three and a half days.

Two days after the battle Tarleton, with 350 men and one gun, was sent after an American guerrilla unit commanded by Colonel Thomas

Sumter, known as 'The Gamecock'. At dusk he detected the enemy's camp fires across the Wateree River. He bivouacked without lights or fires of his own, hoping to ambush Sumter if he attempted to ford the river at dawn. After breaking camp, however, the guerrillas marched off up the west bank of the river. Tarleton crossed and set off in pursuit, pushing his men so hard that by the time Fishing Creek was reached his infantry had begun to drop by the wayside. Mounting 60 of them double behind his 100 dragoons, he pressed on. Five miles beyond, the Legion's point cut down two sentries and reported to Tarleton that Sumter's new camp lay just beyond a rise and that his men, having piled their arms, were cooking, sleeping or swimming. As usual, Tarleton decided upon an immediate attack. The dragoons charged straight in, killing 150 of them, capturing 300 and taking 44 supply wagons, for the loss of only sixteen men killed or wounded. An added bonus was the rescue of 100 British prisoners, although Sumter himself, in his shirtsleeves and riding bareback, made good his escape.

Shortly afterwards, Tarleton went down with swamp fever. The Legion, required to operate against guerrilla bands in the hinterland behind Georgetown, performed less well under his subordinates. It is from this period that most of the atrocity stories come, as its members would go to extreme lengths to obtain intelligence from a reluctant and frightened population. Yet Tarleton himself was no better, for on his return to duty he threatened the widow of an American officer that if she did not give him the information he wanted he would exhume her husband so that he 'could look upon the face of valour'.

By now Sumter had returned to the field. The Legion, reinforced with infantry, was sent after him, and, following the usual pattern of pursuit, brought him to battle at Blackstocks on the Tyger River. A hard-fought action ensued in which Tarleton was forced to lead the dragoons in a desperate charge to extricate his infantry, who had got into difficulties. Sumter was seriously wounded, and when darkness put an end to the fighting both sides broke contact. The engagement was, perhaps, symptomatic of the fact that the tide was slowly beginning to turn against the British in the south. On 7 October Patrick Ferguson's unit of loyalist riflemen, 1,000 strong, was surrounded by an equal number of guerrillas on King's Mountain and surrendered when Ferguson was killed. The victors granted them 'Tarleton's Quarter', shooting some after they had surrendered, hanging others later and subjecting the wounded to the same abominable treatment the Legion had given its prisoners at Waxhaws.

With Washington's approval, Congress appointed Major General Nathanael Greene to command in the south. In December, while Cornwallis retired to winter quarters at Winnsborough, North Carolina, he took the offensive, detaching 1,000 men under Brigadier General Daniel Morgan to make a wide sweep to the west. Cornwallis reinforced the Legion with two weak infantry regiments, the 7th and the 71st, and sent it after Morgan while he followed with the main body of the army. Morgan, however, a veteran of the French and Indian Wars, was a canny opponent. He had studied Tarleton's methods and, knowing that he tended to repeat his tactics of hard pursuit followed by immediate attack, planned accordingly. On 17 January 1781 he allowed the Legion to catch up with him at a hill called the Cowpens, between the Pacelot and Broad Rivers on the North/South Carolina border, where he had prepared a position in depth. He deployed his inexperienced and very nervous militia behind a skirmish line, telling them that they would be permitted to retire and rally behind his regulars after they had fired three volleys. Once Tarleton's men were engaged with the latter, they would be counterattacked on one flank by Colonel William Washington's cavalry and on the other by the re-formed militia. The plan worked and the British infantry suddenly found itself encircled. Tarleton ordered his own cavalry to charge and retrieve the situation, but only the troop of 17th Light Dragoons, now reduced to some 40 men, followed him; the 200 loyalists of the Legion cavalry, used to easy victories and not liking what they saw, turned and rode off. For a moment, Tarleton, Washington and their men cut at each other, then Tarleton was hustled off the field by his scarlet-coated dragoons. Behind him the 7th and 71st, outnumbered and surrounded, fought on hopelessly but were eventually compelled to surrender; they never forgave him for abandoning them.

Morgan's well-deserved victory, sometimes described as an 'American Cannae', had been won at the cost of only twelve killed and 60 wounded; Tarleton's losses amounted to 100 killed, 229 wounded and 525 captured. Throughout the south those who favoured independence rejoiced at the news that at last the hated Legion had been roundly beaten.

There were, too, British officers who resented Tarleton's close relationship with Cornwallis and in consequence were troubled by guilty feelings of *Schadenfreude*. Cornwallis, infuriated by the reverse, set off after Morgan, but Morgan was retreating rapidly across North Carolina into Virginia, re-joining Greene on the way. Short of supplies and with his pursuit blocked by the swollen River Dan, Cornwallis decided to head for Wilmington on the North Carolina coast. Greene followed, forcing him to fight a successful holding action at Guilford Court House on 15 March. The Americans sustained 1,300 casualties and lost four guns, but Cornwallis's 500 casualties were more than he could afford.

During these operations, and indeed for the rest of the campaign, Tarleton and the Legion were kept on a much tighter rein. They did have their successes, but these were neither as spectacular nor as decisive as of yore. Cornwallis marched his army into Virginia, where, joined by a force under Benedict Arnold, he spent much of the summer trying to bring the Marquis de Lafayette's small army to battle. Tarleton and his dragoons were sent to raid Charlotteville, where the State Legislature was sitting, and succeeded in capturing seven of its members. At the end of July Cornwallis received orders from Clinton to occupy a deep-water harbour, possession of which would enable to the fleet to maintain communication between the two. He selected Yorktown on the York River, which he reached and began to fortify early in August, sending Tarleton to do likewise at the little settlement of Gloucester on the opposite bank.

Yorktown, located on a peninsula, proved to be a trap. Lafayette closed in while Washington and Lieutenant General Count Jean de Rochambeau marched south from New York. By the end of September Cornwallis, unable to receive either reinforcements or supplies from Clinton because the Royal Navy had temporarily lost command of the sea, was closely besieged by the American and French armies. Across the river, Tarleton continued to act vigorously, capturing twenty pilots destined for the blockading French fleet during one raid but losing two fingers from his right hand during a cavalry skirmish. For his part, Cornwallis conducted a lacklustre defence, abandoning critical ground voluntarily and losing two vital redoubts in consequence. On 19 October he surrendered, receiving the same terms as had been offered to General Lincoln at Charleston a year earlier. With wry humour, the British marched out with their bands playing a popular song entitled *The World Turned Upside Down*. Peace was not formally concluded until the following year, but to all intents and purposes the surrender of Yorktown ended the war for, further south, Greene, though defeated in every battle he fought, had so eroded his opponents' strength that only Charleston and Savannah remained to the British.

Although relations between captors and captives were professional and courteous, with senior officers from both armies hosting dinner parties for each other, many of the victorious Americans would gladly have killed Tarleton on the spot. He was placed under French protection but was left under no illusions as to his danger when, returning to his tent one night, he found his mattress ripped to shreds. Most officers were permitted to give their parole and return home via New York, although some were required to remain with the surrendered troops, who were to be dispersed in camps throughout Virginia, Maryland and Pennsylvania. The diarist John Peebles, serving with the New York garrison, recorded that Cornwallis, Benedict Arnold, Tarleton and others embarked aboard HMS *Robust*, escort to a homeward-bound convoy, on 15 December.

In England, Tarleton was still an extremely popular hero. When he reached Liverpool on 16 February 1782 the church bells were rung, bonfires blazed in his honour and men pulled his coach through the streets. In London he was lionised, quickly becoming a member of the Prince of Wales's high-living set. The actress Mary Robinson, once the Prince's mistress, now became Tarleton's, and for some years the two enjoyed a stormy relationship. All of this went to his head in much the same way his inheritance had. Once again, he quickly ran up debts which his family refused to discharge. In 1784 he fled to France for a while to escape his debtors. In 1787 he published his *History of the Campaigns of 1780 and 1781 in the Southern Provinces of North America*, which ran to two editions. He also opened a gambling club in partnership with a Guards officer, but the venture failed. He was elected Member of Parliament for Liverpool in 1790, fighting the lost cause of the pro-slavery lobby and retaining his seat until 1812. Eight years later he married Susan Priscilla Bertie, an adopted daughter of the rich and influential Cholmondely family, whose £30,000 dowry kept him in the manner to which he had become accustomed.

He remained in the Army but never commanded troops in action again. Nevertheless, his connections ensured his promotion to Colonel in 1790 and to Major General four years later. In 1801 came promotion to Lieutenant General and the profitable colonelcies of the 21st and 22nd Light Dragoons and the 8th Hussars. As Commander of the Southern District of Ireland he produced an excellent plan based on mobile defence in the event of a French invasion, but in other respects his talents went unused throughout the French Revolutionary and Napoleonic Wars. After leaving Ireland he became Commander of the Severn Military District, based on Bath, one of most popular venues of Regency society—an appointment which no doubt pleased him greatly. He was appointed Governor of Berwick-on-Tweed in 1808 and became a general three years later. In 1812 he retired to Leintwardine in Herefordshire, where he lived the life of a country gentleman.

By now he had slipped into obscurity, the deeds of his youth eclipsed by those of a younger generation of officers fighting Napoleon's marshals in Spain and Portugal. When honours were liberally bestowed following the decisive victory of Waterloo, he wrote petulantly to Lord Bathurst, the Secretary of War, recalling his own successes 35 years earlier. For old times' sake, the Prince Regent granted him a knighthood and in 1820 he was awarded the Knight Grand Cross of the Order of the Bath. He died in 1833, remembered by the children of Leintwardine as old man of ferocious aspect.

At the regimental level, Banastre Tarleton remains one of the most remarkable light cavalry commanders ever. Properly governed, he could have risen to greatness and he would undoubtedly have earned a place in the history of the Napoleonic Wars. Instead, he wasted his talents as a hanger-on of high society. In the United States he remains one of history's hate figures. In his own country, despite having once been a national hero, he has been all but completely forgotten. His one military legacy was the elegant Tarleton Helmet, a peaked, fur-crested, hard skullcap he had worn while commanding the Legion, later adopted by the Royal Horse Artillery and light dragoon regiments.

General Louis Desaix

Victor of Marengo

WHEN THE FRENCH TROOPS who had served in America during the War of Independence returned to France they brought with them concepts of freedom which until then were unimaginable to the average citizen. This infusion of ideas is sometimes regarded as being one of the principal causes of the French Revolution, but it can also be seen as an accelerant to a process of historical inevitability. The manner in which France was governed was reactionary, corrupt, unjust and controlled by those few who had a vested interest in maintaining the *status quo*. The burden of taxation rested most heavily upon those who could least afford it, yet there were sections of the wealthy nobility who were exempted from tax altogether. Reforms were desperately needed, but the cost of the recent war had left the national exchequer all but bankrupt, and even if funds had been available the will to implement them was absent. France was a powder magazine waiting to explode.

When the explosion came in 1789 there were a number of junior officers serving in the old Royal Army who agreed that the country required radical change. One such was Louis Charles Antoine Desaix, also known as the Chevalier de Veygoux, who had been born into a noble but impoverished family in 1768. He received his commission in the Old Army in 1783 but, having embraced the principals of the Revolution, quarrelled with his family in 1791. Unfortunately, the history of revolutions confirms that once a group of revolutionaries have seized power, they ruthlessly eliminate any fellow revolutionaries who might present a threat to their position. In this world of suspicion, denunciation and judicial murder, Desaix was especially vulnerable as an officer of the army with links to the former aristocracy, narrowly escaping the guillotine because of his irreproachable service to the cause.

As most of the senior officers of the Old Army had been dismissed or executed or had fled abroad, the promotion prospects of junior officers remaining in the New Army were considerably enhanced. Desaix, recognised as a man of ability, was promoted to *général de brigade* in September 1793 and to *général de division* the following year. Confronted by enemies in every direction yet unable to field much more than a semi-trained *levée-en-masse*, the commanders of the New Army were forced to develop new tactics to meet the changed conditions. These consisted of a cloud of skirmishers who would hug the enemy's battle line but disperse if attacked, then re-form when the threat had passed. Under cover of the skirmishers, columns of attack would be formed, relying on speed, mass and weight to smash their way through the enemy line. Where the French differed from their opponents was in motivation, for they were fighting not only to preserve such gains as the Revolution had made but also to prevent the cruelties of the *ancien régime* being reimposed. Faced with such motivation and an unconventional method of fighting, the conscript armies of the European powers, which still employed the stiff linear tactics of Frederick the Great, found themselves unable to cope. During 1795 and 1796 Desaix served on the Upper Rhine and in Germany, building up a considerable reputation for himself in a series of engagements. Early in 1797 he moved to northern Italy, where he decided to hitch himself to the rising star of General Napoleon Bonaparte.

There were those in the Directory, as the current governing body in France was called, who thought that Bonaparte's star was rising too rapidly for their own good. Therefore, when he put forward a plan to disrupt British trade with India and the Middle East by occupying Egypt, this was willingly accepted since it would remove him far from the seat of power. On 19 May 1798 the expedition sailed from Toulon, its first port of call being Malta, then ruled by the military-religious Order of the Knights of St John. The Knights, recruited from the younger sons of the Catholic nobility of western Europe, had once been a formidable force and, in 1565, had conducted an epic defence of the island against the assembled might of the Ottoman Empire. However, since the days of the

Great Siege they had become used to soft living and their once-strict internal discipline had deteriorated.

Bonaparte had decided to take Malta, which, being strategically placed in the central Mediterranean and possessing the finest naval harbour in the area, would be of immense value in protecting his long lines of communication. When Ferdinand von Hompesch, the Grand Master of the Order, declined to surrender the island on 9 June, Desaix was given the task of capturing it. He planned a three-pronged offensive in which he would personally neutralise the area round Marsaxlokk Bay on the east coast and then advance to the approaches of Grand Harbour, if possible taking one of the main gates. Simultaneously, Generals Vaubois and Baraquey d'Hilliers were to converge on Mdina, the island's ancient capital, from Qawra and St Paul's Bay, then join Desaix to close the circle around Grand Harbour. The neighbouring island of Gozo, defended by the incomplete Fort Chambray and a few hundred militia, was to be occupied by General Reynier.

Hompesch was hindered by internal dissent from the start. The Spanish Knights declined to fight at all and the Maltese were less than lukewarm in the cause of their noble masters. Rashly, instead of retiring within his magnificent fortifications, which could have held the French at bay for months, he tried to meet each of Desaix's thrusts in the open, with the result that the Maltese deserted. Roundly beaten, he made an abject surrender. When Bonaparte entered Valletta on 12 June the Knights, most of whom were drawn from the French aristocracy, were given hours to pack and leave the island that had been their home for over 250 years. In a thoughtless excess of revolutionary zeal, the French troops plundered the churches of their riches, then, leaving behind a garrison, resumed their voyage to Egypt. Most of this treasure was lost in the mud of Aboukir Bay when Nelson caught up with and destroyed the French fleet during the Battle of the Nile, but by then Bonaparte, Desaix and their troops were safely ashore.

Malta never served the purpose Bonaparte intended for it. The Maltese may have had little regard for their lordly masters of yore, but they were a devout people who bitterly resented the despoiling of their churches and other repressive measures imposed by the French. They rebelled and with British assistance drove the invaders inside their walls. Starving, the garrison finally surrendered in September 1800. At the request of its people, Malta was placed under British protection, remaining within the Empire until granted full independence in 1964. In 1999 the wheel of history apparently turned full circle when the Knights returned to the island, not as masters but as tenants, negotiating a lease on part of their first headquarters, Fort St Angelo.

The army with which Bonaparte landed in Egypt consisted of one cavalry and five infantry divisions, 131 guns and 40 mortars, engineers and a balloon detachment—a total of some 34,000 men. Egypt, though a province of the Ottoman Empire, was actually ruled by the Mameluke warrior caste, which would provide the backbone of the opposition to the French. The Mamelukes had originally been formed as a military élite with youths from the Caucasus, and they were still being recruited in that area. The true Mameluke was a fine horseman who indulged in wild charges, firing his carbine and numerous pistols as he did so, hurling javelins and finally closing with his scimitar, one of which he might hold in each hand. As an individual he was a very formidable opponent, but when faced with a disciplined force of approximately equal numbers he was less impressive. Each Mameluke had one or two armed servants who followed him into action, retrieving his discarded firearms and joining him in the fray if necessary. The Mameluke cavalry was approximately 10,000 strong, with about twice that number of armed servants. A second type of soldier whom the French would meet was the Janissary infantryman, another former élite, recruited from Christian boys in the Ottoman Empire's Balkan provinces. In earlier centuries the Janissaries had been the terror of Europe, but their special status had corrupted them to the point where they had become self-indulgent and undisciplined. In other respects, Bonaparte's opponents in Egypt were a typical oriental army raised on feudal lines, subsequently described by Sir John Moore as 'a wild, ungovernable mob' with little interest in the outcome of an engagement beyond personal survival.

The first major encounter between the two armies took place on 21 July, four miles from Cairo and within sight of the Pyramids, which gave their name to the battle. On the west bank the French advance was opposed by Murad Bey with 6,000 Mamelukes and 12,000 infantry, while in and around Cairo were a further 100,000 men, mainly feudal levies, under Ibrahim Bay. With his left flank resting on the river, Bonaparte formed his divisions into dense squares, echeloned to the south-west, where that commanded by Desaix formed the army's right wing. Against this flank the Mamelukes mounted one wild charge after another, only to be shot down in droves by concentrated musketry and artillery fire. On their less threatened left the French formed assault columns and secured a village on the enemy's line of retreat. Within an hour the Mamelukes were in full flight, leaving behind 2,000 of their number plus several thousand of their infantry. French losses amounted to 29 killed and some 200 wounded. Having watched Murad's defeat from across the river, Ibrahim's horde vanished in the direction of Sinai. Three days later the French entered Cairo unopposed.

Bonaparte now divided the army. While he chased Ibrahim across Sinai and ultimately into Syria with the main body, Desaix was sent up the Nile in pursuit of Murad with just 3,000 men. Although outnumbered by three to one, Desaix defeated him at El Lahun on 7 October. His nine-month campaign, which took him as far south as Aswan, was remarkable for its hard marching, expertly fought actions and logistic organisation, particularly as between January and May 1799 he was forced to detach General Belliard to capture the Red Sea port of Kosseir, through which Murad was receiving reinforcements from Arabia. Murad remained at liberty, but he was safely contained.

Notwithstanding his intellectual conversion to republicanism, it seems that Desaix had inherited the ideal of *noblesse oblige*. His cared for his men's welfare and in return earned their trust and affection. Simultaneously, his ability won him the respect of his enemies. The Upper Egyptians, unused to integrity among their masters, clearly preferred his period of rule to that of the Mamelukes, remembering him as 'the just Sultan'.

Meanwhile Bonaparte's campaign in Syria was not yielding the expected results. Although a Turkish army was defeated at Mount Tabor on 16 April, his every attempt to capture the city of Acre failed. In May he raised the siege and withdrew into Egypt. On 25 July he routed another Turkish army shortly after it had landed in Aboukir Bay. His mind, however, was in Paris, where the corrupt and useless Directory was in the midst of a crisis arising from defeats in Europe. Seeing an opportunity to advance his career, he sailed secretly for France on 23 August, leaving General Jean-Baptiste Kléber in command. By sheer luck he was able to evade the British blockade, reaching Paris on 16 October. The following month the Directory was deposed in a *coup* and replaced by a Consulate, the new system being ratified by a plebiscite. As none of his fellow consuls enjoyed as much popular support, Bonaparte became First Consul, which in practical terms meant that he had become *de facto* head of state and was just one step short of formally assuming the throne.

The campaign in Egypt was to continue for a further two years, ending in the ejection of the French following the intervention of a British army. Desaix, however, had sailed for France shortly after Bonaparte, although his ship was intercepted by the Royal Navy and he remained a prisoner for some months until exchange formalities could be concluded. He rejoined Bonaparte at Stradella in northern Italy on 10 June 1800. At this juncture the overall situation was that an Austrian army under General Baron Michael Melas had been besieging Genoa and presenting a threat to Provence. Bonaparte, commanding the French Army of the Reserve, had entered Italy through the Great St Bernard Pass, hoping that his sudden appearance would compel Melas to raise the siege and move to protect his lines of communication with Austria. Unfortunately, the starving French garrison had surrendered on 4 June. Furthermore, the Austrian Fort Bard, lying at the southern exit from the St Bernard Pass, had offered such tough resistance from 25 May until 2 June that while Bonaparte had about 27,000 men with him, his transport had been so delayed that only eighteen guns had arrived.

Melas reacted as Bonaparte hoped he would. Leaving a garrison in Genoa, he marched towards Alessandria with the rest of his army, numbering 26,000 infantry, 5,000 cavalry and 100 guns, intending to give battle. His movement was so slow that Bonaparte, approaching Alessandria from the north, had little idea of his real strength or intentions. Prisoners suggested that the Austrians might be marching north to the Po or trying to escape across the Apennines. During the evening of 13 June the French advance guard passed through the village of Marengo and became heavily engaged with Austrian troops holding an entrenchment on the near bank of the River Bormida, covering two bridges leading to Alessandria. Having taken two guns and several hundred prison-

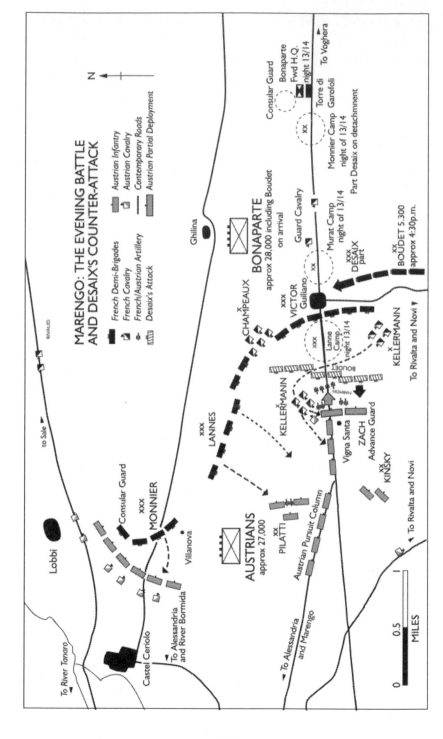

MARENGO: THE EVENING BATTLE
AND DESAIX'S COUNTER-ATTACK

French Demi-Brigades
French Cavalry
French/Austrian Artillery
Desaix's Attack

Austrian Infantry
Austrian Cavalry
Contemporary Roads
Austrian Partial Deployment

N

RIVALID

to Sale

Lobbi

Consular Guard
xxx
MONNIER

Villanova

Castel Ceriolo

To Alessandria
and River Bormida

To River Tanaro

Ghilina

BONAPARTE
approx 28,000 including Boudet
on arrival

xxx
CHAMPEAUX

xxx
LANNES

AUSTRIANS
approx 27,000

xx
PILATTI

Austrian Pursuit Column

To Alessandria
and Marengo

Guard Cavalry

Murat Camp
night of 13/14

xxx
VICTOR
Guiliano

xx

Lanne
Camp
night 13/14

x
KELLERMANN

MARENGO

BOUDET

Vigna Santa

ZACH
Advance Guard

xx
KINSKY

x
KELLERMANN

To Rivalta and Novi

To Rivalta and Novi

Consular Guard

Bonaparte
Fwd H.Q.
night 13/14

Torre di
Garofoli

To Voghera

xx

Monnier Camp
night of 13/14

Part Desaix on detachment

xxx
DESAIX
part

xx
BOUDET 5.300
approx 4:30 p.m.

0   0.5   1
MILES

ers, the advance guard fell back on Marengo, where it encamped. Bonaparte somehow received the impression that the bridges had been destroyed and, having reached the conclusion that the force defending them was possibly a flank guard screening the imagined Austrian retreat, he remained confident that he and not the enemy retained the initiative. His faulty appreciation led him to make the worst errors of his entire career. Unsure of the route Melas might be taking, he dispersed his divisions across a wide area in the hope of covering every eventuality, then settled down for the night. As part of this process, at 03:00 on 14 June he despatched Desaix with Major General Boudet's division to make a reconnaissance in force southwards towards Novi. After Boudet's had men tramped off, the Army of the Reserve slumbered on, oblivious to the deadly threat that was developing in the pre-dawn darkness to the west.

At 06:00 the Austrian army began crossing the bridges spanning the Bormida and, covered by a screen of skirmishers, broke out of its entrenchment to advance on the French. At this point Bonaparte refused to believe that the attack was anything more than a feint, and declined to recall either Desaix or Major General Lapoype, whose division was now far to the north and unlikely to arrive before evening. He had about 18,000 men and fifteen guns immediately available, but these were still scattered in their bivouac areas along the previous day's line of march. In fact, only six infantry regiments, deployed near Marengo, were in position to meet the Austrian assault. Nevertheless, although it was unknown to Bonaparte at the time, the situation could have been much worse, for in response to a rumour that French troops were active in his rear, Melas had detached almost half his cavalry to deal with the threat; the consequence of their absence would become apparent as the day wore on.

Although the Austrians were slow to develop their attack, they possessed the heavier firepower. In addition, as three of Bonaparte's four remaining divisions were committed piecemeal, they were generally present in superior numbers. Resisting doggedly, the French were slowly forced to give ground. At his headquarters, situated some miles behind the front at Torre di Garofoli, Bonaparte was informed at about 10:45 that the bridges across the Bormida had *not* been destroyed the previous night. Horrified, he galloped up to the firing line, which he reached at 11:00. It was immediately apparent that he had the entire Austrian army on his hands. His left was unstable, but the greater danger lay to his right, where the enemy had begun to outflank Marengo. He gave orders for his last reserve, Major General Monnier's division, supported by the 800 men of the Consular Guard, to mount a counter-attack on the extreme right, in the area of Castel Ceriolo. This would take time to prepare, but, luckily for Bonaparte, at noon the pressure eased while the Austrians replenished their ammunition pouches.

At 13:00 they came on again. Bonaparte, anxious to preserve the integrity of his line and worried by the danger to his flanks, gave his divisional commanders orders to withdraw from Marengo. Wounded and fugitives were now streaming away to the rear in such numbers that his staff set up rally points to halt the latter. At 14:00 Monnier's division went into action, foiling a move by an Austrian cavalry division to cut into the French rear. Here the fighting was so severe that at one stage the French 72nd Line found itself beating off simultaneous cavalry charges from front and rear. On Monnier's left the Consular Guard, later to form the core of the Imperial Guard, closed to within 50 yards of the Austrian infantry and engaged in a murderous fire fight, interrupted only by the need to form square and beat off three cavalry charges.

Yet, despite the heroic efforts of Monnier and the Guard, by 15:00 it was apparent that Bonaparte's army was on the brink of a decisive defeat. Melas certainly thought so. Exhausted and suffering from a minor wound, he retired to Alessandria to rest, leaving his chief of staff, General Zach, to deliver the *coup de grâce*. What Zach needed was cavalry with which to conduct the pursuit, but such cavalry as remained was already engaged with Monnier. In its place he formed a large column of grenadiers with which to smash through the battered French left-centre and pursue its remnants off the field. The issue, it seemed, had been decided, yet within a short space of time the entire complexion of the battle had changed.

Desaix's southward march towards Novi had been slowed by floods, so that he had not gone as far as he had anticipated when, at dawn, he heard the distant thumping of cannon from the direction of Marengo. This intensified until it became a steady rumble, indicating that a major engagement was in progress. By 10:00 he was sufficiently worried to halt Boudet's division, but to conform with his orders he despatched his aide, the future General Jean Savary, Duke of Rovigo, with a troop of hussars to verify whether the Austrians were present in Novi. By 13:00 Savary was able to confirm that they were not. That being the case, Desaix decided that the appropriate course of action would be to march towards the sound of the guns. Shortly afterwards, a messenger arrived from Bonaparte with orders to re-join the army.

Leaving Boudet to bring up his division as quickly as possible, Desaix spurred towards the battlefield, joining Bonaparte at about 15:00, by which time the French had been pushed back four miles and were barely holding together. The First Consul asked his opinion, to which he dryly replied that this particular battle was undeniably lost but that as it was only mid-afternoon there was still time to win another. His arrival on the field proved to be a steadying influence on the shaken French troops, who were aware of his exploits in Egypt and with whom he was popular. This, together with the lengthy period taken by Zach to form his grand assault column, gave Bonaparte and Desaix just sufficient breathing space to rally the army into some sort of order and prepare a counter-stroke.

When Boudet's panting division reached the field at about 16:00, Desaix deployed it in echelon to give it a combination of firepower to the front and protection against cavalry on the flanks. On the left was the 9th Légère with one battalion in line and two in column; to the right rear was the 30th Line with two battalions in line; and to the right rear of the 30th was the 69th Line with one battalion in line and two in column. The division lay directly in the path of Zach's assault column, now 6,000 strong and led by two brigades in line. As the column lumbered forward shortly after 17:00, Desaix instructed Savary to deliver an urgent message to Bonaparte:

'Tell him that I cannot wait any longer; that I am without any cavalry; and that he must direct a bold charge to be made upon the flank of that column while I charge it in front.'

Savary galloped across to Bonaparte, who listened attentively. 'Have you seen the column yourself?' asked the First Consul.

'Yes, General.'

'Is it very numerous?'

'Extremely so, General.'

'Is Desaix uneasy about it?'

'He only appeared uneasy as to the consequences that might result from hesitation. I must add his having particularly desired that I should tell you that it is useless to send any other order than that he should attack or retreat—one or the other; and the latter movement would be at least as hazardous as the first.'

'In that case, let him attack,' said Bonaparte. 'I shall go in person to give him the order. You will find General Kellermann and tell him what you have just communicated to me, and desire him to charge the enemy without hesitation as soon as Desaix shall commence his attack. You will point out the spot through which Desaix is to debouch, for Kellermann does not even know that he is with the army.'

Savary found Kellermann at the head of the rallied French cavalry, numbering about 600 men. He had just delivered his message when the renewed rattle of musketry confirmed that Desaix was in action. As the enemy column cleared a hamlet named Vigna Sacra, Desaix gave the order for Boudet's division to advance against it. Soon the 9th Légère was exchanging vicious volleys with the leading Austrian brigades. Desaix, riding ahead, was shot through the heart and reeled from the saddle. This, together with its own casualties, briefly unsettled the regiment. Events now followed hard one upon another. General Auguste Marmont, commanding the French artillery, had concentrated such guns as he was able to lay hands on and these had begun carving lanes through the flank of the column with case-shot, delivered at close range. One of the enemy ammunition wagons was hit, erupting in a tremendous explosion. Before the Austrians could collect their wits, Kellerman, leaving Boudet's embattled division on his left, had passed through the intervals between the guns. While half his troopers faced down a unit of Austrian cavalry, he wheeled the remainder left into line and charged into the flank of the disordered column, cutting his way through from left to right. Incredibly, large numbers of Austrians simply flung down their arms and the rest took to their heels. The French, never more formidable than when they sensed victory, reacted with their characteristic élan all along the line, chasing the now demoralised enemy back whence they had come.

The Battle of Marengo was over. The cost to the Army of the Reserve was about 6,000 men killed or wounded, but Austrian losses were much heavier, amounting to 9,400 killed or wounded, 8,000 men taken prisoner and 40 guns lost. Melas, his nerve broken and no longer able to feed his troops, signed the Convention of Alessandria the next day, agreeing to surrender all of Piedmont and Lombardy in return for permission to retire into Venetia.

The death of Desaix, who had snatched a notable victory from the very jaws of defeat, was regretted by the entire French Army. As was usual at the time, some suitable last words were attributed to him, although the truth was that he had died seconds after being hit. Bonaparte commented that his death was 'the greatest loss I could possibly have sustained'. This was no doubt meant sincerely enough at the time, although his perspective was to alter quickly. As Marengo was the first battle that Bonaparte fought as head of state, his intention was that it should hold an honoured place in history. He did not intend to have his shortcomings exposed, nor was he inclined to share glory with others. His official historians re-wrote the story of the battle until in its final form the French withdrawal from Marengo was all part of Bonaparte's master plan to draw the enemy forward and keep them occupied until, as the First Consul intended, Desaix arrived on their flank to strike the decisive blow. Likewise, on the very evening of the battle, he was sparing in his praise for Kellermann, who had just made one of the most decisive cavalry charges of the era.

Six years later this tendency would again become apparent. At Auerstadt on 14 October 1806, Marshal Louis Davout, who had served under Desaix in Egypt, trounced the main body of the Prussian Army despite being outnumbered by two to one; the same day, at Jena, Napoleon, with twice Davout's strength, defeated a Prussian force of approximately equal size. Davout's achievement was undoubtedly the greater, and for that reason he was granted the honour of being the first to enter Berlin. Nevertheless, Napoleon remained jealous of his success and he was never given a really independent command again.

Desaix was probably as good a general as Bonaparte, although he lacked the latter's burning ambition. What might have happened if he had not marched to the sound of the guns at Marengo opens up wide areas for debate. In the short term, Bonaparte would have sustained a severe defeat and been compelled to embark on a difficult retreat. Melas, once the threat to his line of communications had been removed, would have been able to consolidate his hold on northern Italy and perhaps launch an invasion of Provence. Closer to home, the First Consul's political enemies would have been quick to expose his fallibility. Once his public standing had been damaged, the Imperial crown may have lain beyond his reach and history would have followed a different path. Napoleon owed a great deal to Desaix but was never inclined to acknowledge the full extent of the debt.

Major George Baring

Defender of La Haye Sainte

HE NAME OF GEORGE BARING will be familiar to everyone with more than a passing interest in the Battle of Waterloo. For an afternoon and an evening, as commander of the 2nd Light Battalion King's German Legion and with the responsibility of defending the farm of La Haye Sainte, he was a prominent actor in one of history's most decisive dramas. We do not know a great deal about him, although he seems to have been well liked by his men and sometimes played the flute for the benefit of his brother officers. Some sources have suggested that he was British, and, indeed, because of a shortage of German officers in the King's German Legion, suitable British candidates were granted commissions without the need to purchase them. There was nothing remarkable in this, for, as the King of England was also the Elector of Hanover, regular social and commercial contacts between the two countries was the norm. However, as his name is absent from the British personnel records of the time, he has also been described as a somewhat shadowy figure. In fact, he was born in Hanover in 1773, almost certainly to a family of British descent, hence his English-sounding name. He was fluent in English, but thought and wrote in the German idiom.

Following the breakdown of the Peace of Amiens in 1803, a French army invaded Hanover. As the country had no defensible boundaries and its army was too small to offer resistance, the occupation was bloodless. It was also humiliating and bitterly resented, for the Hanoverian Army was forced to disband on parole after handing over its arms, ammunition and horses. Nevertheless, the Duke of Cambridge, son of George III, had been administering the Electorate and he devised a plan whereby officers and men of the disbanded regiments would form a contingent to serve with the British Army, despite the fact that this meant virtual exile. Many volunteered, joined by others who felt a sense of loyalty to the ruling house or resentment at the loss of their country's independence. Known at first as the King's Germans, they were embodied in England into what amounted to an army corps consisting of cavalry, infantry, artillery and engineer units. With slight differences, the King's German Legion wore the same uniforms as the British, as had been the case with the old army. Organisation, too, followed the British pattern, although orders were given in German.

In October 1805 the Legion, now 6,000 strong, formed part of the British expeditionary force that landed in the Elbe and temporarily liberated Hanover. About a quarter of the men, disliking their exile, deserted, but several times that number chose to enlist. Unfortunately, the crushing defeat inflicted by Napoleon on the Austrian and Russian armies at Austerlitz made French troops available for service in northern Germany and the expeditionary force, finding its position untenable, re-embarked in February 1806. Prussia, which had long cast greedy eyes on Hanover, then invaded on her own account and put a stop to overt recruiting. Prussia's triumph was short-lived, for in the same year the French came close to destroying her army at the battles of Jena and Auerstadt. Whatever pleasure the citizens of Hanover may have felt was temporary, for the southern part of the country was incorporated into the newly created Kingdom of Westphalia, ruled by Napoleon's brother Jerome, while in 1810 the northern part came under direct French rule. This did not stem the flow of men wishing to join the Legion, which also drew recruits from elsewhere in Germany and other parts of Europe.

It was during the Peninsular War in Portugal and Spain that the Legion established its reputation as a first-rate fighting force. It did not fight as an entity, its units being integrated with British formations. British and Hanoverian troops had fought together in various wars of the eighteenth century and had developed a liking and respect for each other. In the Peninsula the British looked upon the Legion as the only troops that were their equal and could be relied upon implicitly. Indeed, as Wellington commented in a letter to the Duke of York, 'It is impossible to have better soldiers than the real Hanoverians.' The Germans were acknowledged to be the better horse masters, and when it came to reconnaissance and scouting the Legion's 1st Hussars were said to be the best in the business. Again, all armies of the period sang on the march to make the miles pass by the more quickly. British regiments tended to bawl their songs, but the Germans orchestrated theirs carefully for the qualities of different voices so that they were a pleasure to listen to. Legion units fought in every major battle of the war, so distinguishing themselves that in August 1812 their officers were granted permanent commissions in the British Army. Some units were so reduced by casualties that they had to be broken up or sent back to England. Such losses bore down heavily on exiles to whom their regiment was now their only home, but they did not impair their fighting qualities.

Baring was an experienced officer who served in the Legion's light infantry, an élite branch of the service in which personal initiative was encouraged. The 1st and 2nd Light Battalions took part in Sir John Moore's invasion of Spain in 1808 and the subsequent harrowing retreat across snow-covered mountains to Vigo and Corunna. On 16 January 1809 Moore turned to give battle at Corunna, inflicting a sharp defeat on his pursuers, commanded by Marshal Nicolas Soult, at the cost of his own life. This enabled his exhausted army to be evacuated by sea to England. Between them, the two battalions had lost 425 men during the campaign, including 209 drowned as a result of shipwreck on the way home. They reached England with their uniforms in tatters and their boots, if they still possessed any, worn down to the uppers. Naturally, it took time for them to absorb and train sufficient recruits to restore them to operational strength, so that it was not until the spring of 1811 that they returned to the Peninsula. There they remained for the rest of the war, taking part in the bloody battle of Albuera the same year, winning further battle honours at Salamanca on 22 July 1812 and Vittoria on 21 June 1813, then fighting their way through the Pyrenees and into southern France during the winter of 1813/14. During these events Baring served with the 1st Light Battalion as a captain, winning a brevet to the rank of major, and then on the Staff. On 4 April 1814 he was posted to the 2nd Light Battalion.

Meanwhile far distant events had begun to have an influence on the Legion's subsequent career. In 1812 Napoleon's Grand Army had come to grief in the snows of the Russian winter. As its survivors straggled back into central Europe it became apparent that the Emperor was, after all, fallible. In February 1813 Prussia sided with Russia and large areas of northern Germany followed suit. Hanover formed volunteer battalions for service against the French during what became known as the War of German Liberation. These did not form part of the British Army, although a cadre of 40 gunners was sent by the King's German Legion to train the new army's artillerymen. Napoleon fought a vigorous campaign but was forced back into France. In April 1814, with all the powers of Europe in arms against him and Paris under attack, he bowed to demands for his abdication and retired into exile on the island of Elba.

Most post-war British governments are driven by an immediate need to cut military expenditure to the bone, but on this occasion common sense prevailed as far as the King's German Legion was concerned. On the conclusion of hostilities the Legion returned to England. Its non-Hanoverian volunteers were discharged and the intention was that the remainder should return to Hanover, forming the basis of the Electorate's new standing army. Its independent life, however, was prolonged by Napoleon's escape from Elba. Thus in June 1815 its units found themselves serving with Wellington's Allied army in Belgium. They were, in fact, some of the few Peninsular veterans to fight with the British contingent at Waterloo, many British regiments having been shipped straight across the Atlantic for the war with the United States.

On 15 June Napoleon crossed the Belgian frontier at the head of his 125,000-strong Army of the North. His opponents consisted of an Anglo-German-Dutch-Belgian force of 107,000 men under Wellington and a 128,000-strong Prussian army commanded by Field Marshal Prince Blücher. In the past, when confronted by converging hostile armies, Napoleon's strategy had been to separate them and defeat each in turn. This he intended to repeat, and on 16 June he attacked Blücher at Ligny, simultaneously detaching one-third of his army under Marshal Michel Ney to drive back Wellington's advance guard at Quatre Bras. The Prussians were defeated after a hard fight, but Napoleon made the critical error of believing that they would retire eastwards towards Germany through Namur and detached 33,000 men under Marshal Emmanuel de Grouchy to pursue them in that direction. The reality was that they were retiring northwards in order to maintain contact with Wellington, so that by the time Grouchy discovered the truth most of 17 June had been wasted. Meanwhile, although Ney had made little progress at Quatre Bras, the Prussians' departure made the position untenable and during the 17th Wellington withdrew some eight miles northwards to a gently sloping ridge named Mont St Jean, two miles south of the village of Waterloo.

This position had been previously selected by the Duke as it favoured the sort of battle he intended to fight. The army was drawn up on a four-mile frontage along the ridge, which overlooked a shallow valley to the south and was bisected by the Brussels–Charleroi road. Having no intention of making the enemy a present of No Man's Land, he established advance posts in two groups of buildings, the farm of La Haye Sainte beside the Brussels–Charleroi road, opposite his centre, and the château of Hougoumont, just east of the Brussels–Nivelles road, covering his right, with strict instructions that they were to be held regardless of the cost. He was satisfied with his dispositions but, as he watched the French establish themselves along a parallel ridge to the south, two doubts nagged at his mind. The first concerned the mixed quality of his own army. He had no reservations about those troops who had served under him in Spain, but a high proportion of the British and German contingents lacked experience and the loyalty of some Dutch-Belgian units, who only the previous year had fought for Napoleon, was dubious. His second cause for concern was whether Blücher's Prussians were close enough to take part in the battle that he knew would come on the morrow. During the evening a thunderstorm broke and, with two intervals, rain cascaded down throughout the night, turning the ground into a quagmire and making life a misery for those troops who were unable to find shelter.

Major Baring's 2nd Light Battalion KGL belonged to Major General Sir Charles Alten's 3rd (Anglo-Hanoverian) Division, which was positioned to the west of the Brussels–Charleroi road, close to a point where it was crossed by a sunken lane running along the crest of the ridge, with La Haye Sainte some 300 yards to its front. The battalion, together with the 1st Light Battalion and the 5th and 8th Line Battalions KGL, formed part of the division's 2nd (King's German Legion) Brigade, commanded by Colonel Christian von Ompteda. As dawn broke and the rain ceased, Baring and his battalion were ordered to form the garrison of La Haye

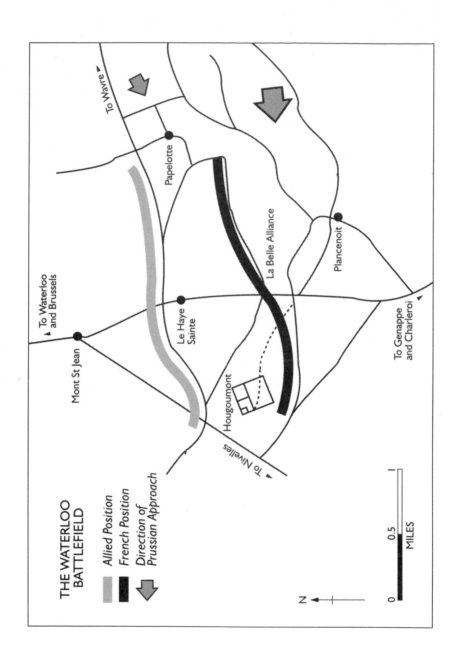

THE WATERLOO
BATTLEFIELD

Allied Position

French Position

Direction of
Prussian Approach

To Waterloo
and Brussels

Mont St Jean

Le Haye
Sainte

Hougoumont

To Nivelles

Papelotte

La Belle Alliance

Plancenoit

To Genappe
and Charleroi

To Wavre

N

0   0.5   1

MILES

Sainte, where they had spent the night The battalion consisted of six companies, but because its non-Hanoverian personnel had been discharged, its strength amounted to only 360 green-uniformed riflemen. It was armed with the Baker rifle, which was more accurate and possessed a longer range than the Brown Bess smooth-bore muskets of the line infantry, and to which a sword-bayonet could be attached for close-quarter fighting.

The farm's name meant The Holy Hedge, but few had the time to reflect upon its origins. The farm itself consisted of buildings and a high wall forming a rectangle surrounding a central courtyard. The house and stables occupied the north wall, this range of buildings being continued along the west wall by a cow shed. A barn occupied most of the south wall, with a pond at its eastern end. The east wall of the enclosure incorporated several pig sties, the roofs of which would serve in place of fire-steps, and bordered directly on to the road. Two doors and three large gates provided access to the farmyard from the outside. Unfortunately, the gates in the west wall of the barn, giving direct entry to the building from the fields, had been taken off their hinges during the night and broken up for campfires, rendering this area the most vulnerable to enemy attack. To the north of the buildings and closest to the ridge was a kitchen garden, bounded by a low wall towards the road but on the other sides by a hedge. Adjoining the south wall of the farm was a long orchard, running beside the road.

Most areas of human activity are subject to internal friction, and military operations are particularly so. No sooner had Baring received his orders than he was told to send off the battalion's pioneers to Hougoumont. This was most unfortunate, as the mule carrying the entrenching tools had been lost the previous day, leaving him with no resources with which to strengthen the defences. Nevertheless, old hand that he was, he recognised that it would be several hours before the ground dried out sufficiently to permit the passage of artillery and, that being the case, he had a little time in hand before the battle began. His men began knocking loopholes in the walls and constructing a barricade in the yawning gap left by the destruction of the barn gates. There was also time to cook some veal that had been discovered. Appreciating that, sooner or later, the farm would become isolated when the French attacked, Baring allowed for all-round defence, placing three companies in the orchard, two in the farm buildings and one in the garden. Looking southwards from the orchard, his view of the enemy was obscured by a low swelling in the ground.

It is one of the stranger aspects of the battle that both Wellington and Napoleon had something of a blind spot regarding La Haye Sainte, although many junior officers saw its potential and dangers at once. In Allied hands, it would be a painful thorn in the side of the French, provided it was held in strength. In French hands, it provided the key to Wellington's position and therefore the entire battle, since it could serve as a springboard for an assault that would smash through the Allied centre. Yet Wellington, though at the peak of his abilities, was apparently content that the post should be held by Baring's weak battalion alone. For his part, Napoleon, his genius in decline and his health poor, attached no special importance to the farm, although it would have been an easy matter for the grand battery of 74 guns he had concentrated opposite the Allied centre to batter it into rubble, rendering it untenable, rather than expend its energies on targets in the open.

Napoleon's plan was to make a strong feint against Hougoumont with Reille's II Corps, the intention being that Wellington would reinforce his right at the expense of his centre to meet the threat. Once the Allied left-centre had been weakened by this and protracted bombardment, d'Erlon's I Corps would punch a hole straight through it. At 11:30 the French grand battery opened fire and the Allied artillery replied. Shortly afterwards, Reille's corps began its attack on Hougoumont. Unfortunately for Napoleon, the garrison of the château repulsed one assault after another and Wellington did not denude his centre. Indeed, thanks to the urgings of Jerome Bonaparte, who was commanding one of his divisions, Reille allowed his entire corps to be sucked into the struggle for the château, involving the whole of the French left wing in a battle within a battle that lasted for the rest of the day. At about 13:30 d'Erlon's I Corps, 17,000-strong, began its assault in four dense columns, that on the left being directed at La Haye Sainte with cuirassiers covering its open flank.

Baring's account says that the farm had come under fire from skirmishers shortly after noon, but the probability is that it was later than

this.* He was in the orchard when the skirmishers appeared and he ordered his men to lie down, forbidding them to open fire until the enemy
attack developed. One round cut his bridle close to his hand and another
killed one of his officers standing nearby. Then, quite suddenly, the mass
of d'Erlon's left-hand column appeared over the low crest to his front
and, behind its drummers beating the *pas de charge,* advanced on a two-
regiment frontage with shouts of 'Vive l'Empereur!' The orchard was
attacked frontally while on both sides the French surged past to attack
the farm buildings and the kitchen garden. The riflemen took their toll,
which the French seemed to disregard, but, faced with overwhelming
numbers and already outflanked, they were pushed steadily back through
the trees towards the barn. At one point Baring's horse fell, its leg broken
by a musket ball, and he was obliged to take that of his adjutant.

Many things now seemed to happen at once. One of Baring's officers,
a Captain Meyer, reported that the enemy had surrounded the kitchen
garden, which, since he could fire into it from three sides, had become
untenable. Baring gave him permission to retire into the farm buildings.
Meanwhile, up on the ridge, Major General Count von Kielmansegge,
commanding the 1st (Hanoverian) Brigade of Alten's division, had been
watching the progress of the attack with the Prince of Orange, who commanded the corps. Both agreed that, unless something was done quickly,
La Haye Sainte would be lost before the battle had really begun. Keilman-
segge ordered the 600-strong Lüneburg Battalion to counter-attack immediately. It advanced steadily in line, pushing the French infantry back
down the slope. In the orchard, Baring's men joined in and recovered
some of the lost ground. The movement worried Baring as he was aware
of the presence of the cuirassiers covering d'Erlon's left flank and was
conscious that the flimsy hedge surrounding the orchard offered no defence against them. He was about to order a general withdrawal on the
farm when, as he feared, the cuirassiers deployed and charged. The sight
was too much for the young Lüneburg soldiers. They broke and ran,
carrying with them the companies in the orchard. Baring strove to rally
them, but he says that they were either unfamiliar with his voice or that it

---

* He was writing sixteen years after the event and his memory may not have been exact.
Standard time did not exist until the coming of the railway and tactical synchronisation
of watches did not take place until late in the Crimean War.

was not sufficiently strong to penetrate the din. Some regained the safety of the ridge, but many others fell either to the cuirassiers' long swords or to the fire of the French infantry who had just taken the kitchen garden. Fortunately, those in the farm buildings, commanded by three attached English officers, Lieutenants Graeme and Carey and Ensign Frank, kept their heads and remained where they were, taking a toll of the cuirassiers as they thundered by.

This marked the high-water mark of d'Erlon's attack. Those columns beyond the road had put a Dutch-Belgian brigade to flight but now their heads were being shot away by the steady, disciplined musketry of British infantry. Seeing that the enemy attack had been brought to a standstill, Wellington launched his counter-stroke. It consisted of the Household and Union heavy cavalry brigades, which struck the French at the full gallop. The assault columns burst apart and fled back down the slope, leaving a thick carpet of dead and dying behind them and losing two Eagles in the process. Some of the troopers even reached the grand battery to cut down a number of its gunners, but now their mounts were blown and they suffered severely when counter-charged by the French cavalry.

At La Haye Sainte the cuirassiers had simply been ridden over or bundled back whence they had come, while the French infantry who had followed up their charge, and those who tried to escape from the kitchen garden, were cut to pieces. The whole area round the farm was now covered with dead and wounded Frenchmen. Baring, nevertheless, knew that he had by no means seen the last of the enemy. The attack had cost him three officers killed and six wounded besides far more men than he could afford. In response to his urgent request for reinforcements, Ompteda sent down two companies from the 1st Light Battalion, which he deployed in the garden. He decided to leave the three English officers and their men in the farm building, but not to re-occupy the orchard, which was more trouble than it was worth.

The failure of d'Erlon's attack left Napoleon temporarily without an alternative plan. However, whatever course of action he decided upon, it was clear that the obstacle posed by La Haye Sainte would have to be removed. Ney, in tactical control of the battle, was ordered to take the farm, passing on these instructions to d'Erlon, who was busy rallying his

troops. Approximately half an hour after their first repulse, the French
came on again, in two columns as before. These advanced through the
orchard and almost encircled the farm, to be met by steady, accurate fire
from windows, loopholes and the walls. Baring, despite his long experience, commented that the enemy came on 'with the greatest rapidity,
despising danger, and fought with a degree of courage which I have never
before witnessed in Frenchmen'. He also noticed that, because of the
enemy's dense attack formation, many of his riflemen's bullets were finding more than one billet.

The French swarmed against the walls, tried to batter their way through
gates and doors and grabbed the defenders' rifle muzzles where they
protruded from the loopholes, an action which, even it did not obtain
physical possession of the weapons, at least prevented them from being
re-loaded. Very quickly they spotted the weak point offered by the missing barn gates. Here the most severe fighting took place at close quarters,
until the entrance was blocked by the bodies of seventeen Frenchmen,
piled one upon the other. These were used by their comrades as cover
for sniping into the interior of the farmyard. Baring's horse was shot
dead under him. His orderly, believing he had been killed, left with his
spare mount and it was some time before he could catch one of the loose
horses that were running about.

While the struggle raged on, the entire complexion of the battle suddenly changed. Both Wellington and Napoleon were aware that, although
Grouchy had caught up with the Prussian rearguard, the rest of Blücher's
army was approaching the battlefield from the east and would make its
presence increasingly felt as the afternoon continued. This placed Napoleon in a very difficult situation. He wished to preserve the infantry of the
Imperial Guard for its usual decisive role and, apart from his cavalry, he
was short of troops with which to meet the new threat. Reille's corps was
still locked in its private battle at Hougoumont; d'Erlon's corps had already been mauled and it was inevitable that its right wing would come
under pressure from the east, leaving only Lobau's VI Corps to hold off
the mass of the Prussians in the area of Plancenoit. It was while considering these options that the Emperor noticed not only that Wellington had
begun pulling back his units behind the crest of the ridge, but also that
there was a steady stream of men and vehicles heading for the Forest of

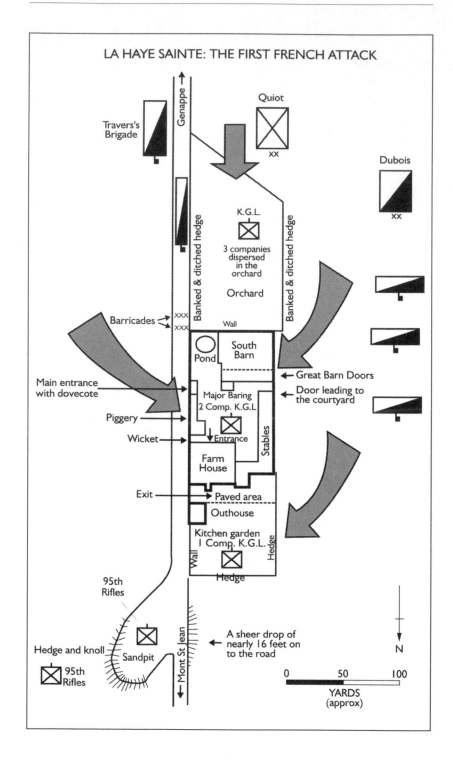

LA HAYE SAINTE: THE FIRST FRENCH ATTACK

Genappe

Travers's Brigade

Quiot
xx

Dubois
xx

Banked & ditched hedge

K.G.L.

3 companies
dispersed
in the
orchard

Orchard

Banked & ditched hedge

Barricades → xxx
xxx

Wall

Pond

South Barn

Great Barn Doors

Main entrance
with dovecote

Major Baring
2 Comp. K.G.L

Door leading to
the courtyard

Piggery →

Wicket →

Entrance

Stables

Farm House

Exit →

Paved area

Outhouse

Kitchen garden
1 Comp. K.G.L

Hedge

Hedge

95th Rifles

Wall

Mont St Jean

A sheer drop of
nearly 16 feet on
to the road

N

Hedge and knoll

Sandpit

95th Rifles

0   50   100

YARDS
(approx)

Soignies behind the Allied front. It looked very much as though the Allies were starting to withdraw, but the truth was that Wellington was simply using the crest to shelter his men from the worst effects of the French artillery fire, while those heading rearwards were wounded heading for the dressing stations, prisoners under escort and empty ammunition wagons leaving the line. Napoleon, choosing to take the more optimistic view, decided to employ his vast superiority in cavalry to turn the imagined retreat into a rout, just as a massed cavalry attack had finally broken the determined Russian resistance at Borodino three years earlier. Such a course would also leave the French infantry to deal with the Prussians when they arrived. Having taken these decisions, the Emperor, feeling unwell, decided to rest, leaving the conduct of the battle in Ney's hands. The latter selected the area between Hougoumont and La Haye Sainte for the great cavalry charge, as this provided a frontage 1,000-men wide. At a little before 16:00 Baring, still fighting off his attackers, observed the French deployment:

> Four lines of French cavalry had formed on the right-front of the farm: the first cuirassiers, the second lancers, the third dragoons and the fourth hussars. It was clear to me that their intention was to break the squares of our division in position, and by destroying them break the whole line. This was a critical moment, for what would be our fate if they succeeded? As they marched by the farm, I brought all the fire possible to bear on them. Many men and horses were overthrown, but they were not discouraged. Without in the least troubling themselves about our fire, they advanced with the greatest intrepidity to attack the infantry. All this I could see, and confess freely that now and then I felt some apprehension.

As the great tidal wave of horsemen flowed up the slope, the Allied artillery shot lanes through its ranks with ball and case shot. Undeterred, the French breasted the rise at a canter to see not the broken army on the verge of retreat they had been promised but serried ranks of squares bristling with bayonets. In vain did they circle the impenetrable hedges, struggling to hack or stab their way through the bayonets, receiving in return close-quarter volleys that sent riders and horses sprawling by the score. Suddenly, the now disorganised French were counter-charged by the less numerous Allied cavalry and driven back down the slope.

> Meanwhile [wrote Baring] the contest in the farm had continued with undiminished violence, but nothing could shake the courage of our men, who, following

the example of their officers, defied danger, laughing. Nothing could inspire more courage or confidence than such conduct. These are the moments when we learn how to feel what one soldier is to another, what the word 'comrade' really means. Such feelings penetrate the coarsest mind, but only he can fully understand who has been witness to such moments! When the cavalry retired, the infantry also gave up their fruitless attack. They fell back, accompanied by our shouts and derision. Our loss, on this occasion, was not so great as during the first attack. Our first care was for the wounded, but my greatest anxiety concerned our ammunition supply which, I found, because of the constant firing, had been reduced by more than half. I immediately sent back an officer with a request for ammunition, which was promised.

Between 16:00 and 17:30 Ney mounted a dozen cavalry charges, each more difficult to execute than the last because the whole area was strewn with dead and wounded men and horses. Baring was unable to maintain the galling fire into the flank of the enemy attacks to the extent he wished because of his anxiety over the ammunition. La Haye Sainte itself was given about an hour's respite, but when the French infantry attacked again he sent another officer back to the ridge to stress the urgency of the situation. Once again, however, the internal friction of armies was at work, for while the Baker rifle had a bore of 0.615in, that of the Brown Bess musket was 0.75in. There was no ammunition available for the former as, unknown to everyone, the cart carrying the two light battalions' supply was lying overturned somewhere on the road from Brussels. There was plenty of musket ammunition, but it was obviously of no use to Baring's men. Wellington was to comment later that he should have personally ensured that the garrison of La Haye Sainte was adequately supplied, but in the circumstances he could not think of everything. As it was, Ompteda did what he could to help by sending down the skirmishers of the 5th Line Battalion, whom Baring stationed in the courtyard.

After the fighting had raged for a further half-hour, Baring sent a third officer to request rifle ammunition. Ompteda had clearly discussed the situation with the Prince of Orange, for 200 men from a Nassau battalion arrived to supplement the defence. Savage fighting took place again at the open entrance to the barn. The French, unable to break into the building, tossed burning brands into the interior. Much of the contents had been dispersed as bedding the previous night, but enough remained to start a conflagration.

Our alarm was now extreme [commented Baring], for although there was water in the courtyard, all means of drawing it and carrying it were wanting, every vessel having been broken up. Luckily, the Nassau troops carried large field cooking kettles. I tore a kettle from the back of one of the men. Several officers followed my example and, filling the kettles, they carried them, facing almost certain death, to the fire. The men did the same and soon not one of the Nassauers was left with his kettle. The fire was thus luckily extinguished with the blood of many a brave man! Many of the men, although covered with wounds, could not be brought to retire. 'So long as our officers fight and we can stand,' was their constant reply, 'we will not stir from this spot.'

The attack lasted about 90 minutes, after which the French withdrew again. Someone had woken up to the fact that La Haye Sainte was vulnerable to artillery fire, which began to knock chunks out of the southeastern angle of the boundary wall. Baring was now beginning to suffer from reaction as the weight of responsibility for holding the post bore down on him. His depression deepened when it was discovered that, even after stripping the pouches of the dead, his men now possessed no more than three or four rounds apiece:

They made nothing of the diminished physical strength which their excessive exertions had caused, and immediately filled up the holes that had been made in the walls by the enemy's guns, but they could not remain insensible to the position in which they were placed by the want of ammunition and made the most reasonable remonstrances to me on the subject.

Yet another officer was despatched to the ridge, this time with a warning that unless supplies were forthcoming the farm could not be held against another attack.

At about 18:30 the French came on again, as before in two columns, one consisting of the 13th Light Infantry and the other of d'Erlon's corps engineers. About 1,000 men took part in the attack, which was therefore much weaker than those that had gone in before, but by now the casualties in the farm far outnumbered those still able the bear arms.

The enemy gave me no time for thought [wrote Baring]. They were already close by our weak walls and now, irritated by the opposition they had experienced, attacked with renewed fury. The contest commenced at the barn, which they again succeeded in setting on fire. It was extinguished, luckily in the same manner as before. Every shot that was now fired increased my uneasiness and anxiety. I sent again to the rear with the positive statement that I must and would leave the place if no ammunition was sent me. This was also without effect.

Our fire gradually diminished. I heard many voices calling out for ammunition, adding, 'We will readily stand by you, but we must have the means of defending ourselves!' Even the officers who, during the whole day, had shown the greatest courage, represented to me the impossibility of retaining the post under such circumstances. The enemy, who soon observed our wants, now boldly broke in one of the doors. However, as only a few could come in at a time, these were instantly bayonetted, and those behind hesitated to follow. They now mounted the roof and walls, from which my unfortunate men were easy targets. At the same time, they pressed in through the open barn, which could no longer be defended. Inexpressibly painful as the decision was to me of giving up the place, I gave the order to retire through the house into the garden.

The three British officers covered the withdrawal via the narrow passage leading through the house. Ensign Frank, already wounded, ran through his first assailant but at the same moment his arm was broken by a ball. He darted into a room and concealed himself behind a bed, where he remained for the rest of the battle. Two wounded riflemen who followed were pursued by the French with yells of 'No mercy for the green bastards!' and shot dead. In the passage the French tended to get in each other's way. With a shout of 'That's the scoundrel!' an officer grabbed Lieutenant Graeme by the collar. Graeme threw him off, parried several bayonet thrusts and escaped through the rear door into the garden with musket balls cracking past his ears. Carey also escaped, although he was wounded in the process, but in the retreat from the farm Captain Holtzermann and Lieutenant Tobin were captured.

Baring quickly reached the conclusion that the garden was untenable while the enemy held the farmhouse. He ordered the men back to the ridge as individuals, permitting those who had been sent down as reinforcements during the afternoon to re-join their regiments. Curiously, the French did not fire upon them as they pulled back. Baring continues his narrative:

With the weak remnant of my own battalion I attached myself to two companies of the 1st Light Battalion which, under Lieutenant Colonel Lewis von dem Busch, occupied the sunken road. Although we could not fire a shot, we helped increase the numbers. Here the combat recommenced with increased fury, the enemy pressing forth from the farm, and I had the pain of seeing Captain Henry von Marschalk fall—a friend whose distinguished coolness and bravery on this day I can never forget. Captain von Gilsa had his right arm broken, Lieutenant Albert was shot and Lieutenant Graeme, as he swung his cap in the air to cheer on the men, had his right hand shattered. None of them would take cover in the sunken road, notwithstanding my attempts to persuade them, but remained on the edge above. I was riding a dragoon's horse, in front of whose saddle were large pistol holsters and a cloak, and the firing was so sharp that four balls entered here, and another the saddle, just as I had alighted to replace my hat which had been knocked off by a sixth ball.

While the French skirmishers pressed ever closer to the Allied line, Ney brought up a horse artillery battery that went into action at only 300 yards' range. At this juncture the Prince of Orange gave way to panic. Stubbornly rejecting advice that a unit of enemy cuirassiers had arrived in the lee of the farm, he ordered Ompteda to deploy a battalion in line and counter-attack. The 1st and 2nd Light Battalions were in no condition for this, nor was the 8th Line Battalion, which had suffered severe casualties during the cavalry attacks of the afternoon and lost its King's Colour. The choice therefore fell upon the 5th Line Battalion. Led by Ompteda personally, its advance swept away the skirmishers and reached the garden of the farm, in which the brigade commander's sword could be seen rising and falling until he was shot down at close quarters. Then the cuirassiers charged and within a minute the battalion had been ridden over. Elated by their easy success, the cuirassiers headed for the main line, believing that they had the power to break it but apparently unaware of the troops concealed in the sunken road. Baring comments that at twenty paces they received such a volley that they wheeled about in the greatest disorder, and were then counter-charged by the Legion's 3rd Hussars.

All of this proved too much for neighbouring Allied units. A Hanoverian brigade pulled back out of range, a Nassau brigade took to its heels and a newly formed Hanoverian cavalry regiment, the Cumberland Hussars, bolted as far as Brussels. At about 19:00 a yawning gap appeared in Wellington's line around the vital crossroads. At last Ney possessed the key to the Allied position, but Baring had denied it to him for so long that it was now useless. The simple truth was that he lacked the troops with which to exploit his success. Reille's corps was still locked into its own battle around Hougoumont; Lobau's corps, though reinforced with the Young Guard, was barely holding its own against the Prussians at Plancenoit; d'Erlon's decimated troops, similarly menaced from the east, seemed incapable of further effort; and the magnificent

French cavalry had been almost destroyed during the afternoon. Urgent representations were made to Napoleon, but it was not until 19:30 that the Emperor began leading forward six battalions of the Middle Guard and three of the Old Guard. The problem was that the Guard was too far to the French rear and it would take time to bring it into action—time during which, minute by minute, Wellington was steadily closing the window of opportunity by moving formations into the gap from less threatened parts of his line.

From the ridge, Baring observed the approach of the Guard's columns. The thought had just crossed his mind that nothing seemed likely to terminate the slaughter but the entire destruction of one army or the other when his horse was struck fatally by a ball in the head:

> He reared up, and, in coming down again, fell on my right leg, pressing me so hard into the deep loamy ground that, despite all my exertion, I could not extricate myself. The men in the road considered me dead and it was not for some little time that one of them came out to set me free. Although my leg was not broken I had lost the use of it for the moment. I crept to the nearest house behind the front. An Englishman was charitable enough to catch a stray horse, place a saddle upon him and help me up. I then rode forward again and learned that General Alten had been severely wounded. I saw that the part of the position which our division had held was only weakly and irregularly occupied. Scarcely conscious from pain, I rode to the sunken road where I had left the rest of the men, but they had been obliged to retire to the village because of the total lack of ammunition, hoping to find some cartridges there. A French dragoon drove me from the spot but, shortly after, there arose along the whole line cries of 'Victory! Victory! Forward! Forward!' What an unexpected change! As I no longer had any men to command, I joined the 1st Hussars and followed the enemy with them until dark, when I returned to the battlefield.

During his period of incapacity Baring had been unaware that the climactic events of the battle had been taking place further along the ridge. The Guard had marched up the Brussels road until it was just short of La Haye Sainte. Then, instead of assaulting through the crossroads ahead, it had inexplicably struck off diagonally to the left, picking its way towards the Allied line over the debris of the failed cavalry attacks. No sooner had it reached the summit of the ridge than its reputation for invincibility was blown apart in a blaze of musketry.* As its bat-

* An account of this, one of the most famous episodes in the Napoleonic Wars, is contained in the author's *Last Stand!*

talions fled back down the slope the effect on the rest of the French was immediate. The cry went up that the Guard was beaten, so what hope was there for anyone else? Within minutes the army had disintegrated and was in panic-stricken flight. Only the Old Guard preserved its discipline, escorting the Emperor off the field, all but sacrificing itself as it did so.

Returning to the field, Baring re-joined what remained of his battalion. Of the 360 men who had been present at the beginning of the defence of La Haye Sainte, only 42 remained effective:

> Whoever I asked after, the answer was 'killed' or 'wounded'. I freely confess that tears came involuntarily into my eyes because of this sad news and the feelings of bitterness that possessed me. I was aroused from these gloomy thoughts by my friend Major Shaw, Assistant Quartermaster General to our division.* I was utterly exhausted and my leg was very painful. I lay down to sleep, with my friend, on some straw the men had collected together for us. On waking, we found ourselves between a dead man and a dead horse! I shall pass over, in silence, the scene which the field of battle, with all its misery and grief, now presented. We buried our dead friends and comrades. After some food was cooked and the men had, in some measure, refreshed themselves, we broke camp and set off after the enemy.

In fact, the 2nd Light Battalion had fought its last major action, for the Prussians led the Allied advance on Paris. With the powers of Europe again massed against him, Napoleon bowed to the inevitable and abdicated for the second time. At the subsequent Congress of Vienna, Hanover became a kingdom rather than an electorate, albeit sharing the same monarch as Great Britain. In 1816 a new Hanoverian Army was formed by merging the units established during the War of Liberation with those of the King's German Legion.

Understandably, the amalgamation between those who had fought in exile for long years and those who had only taken up arms when victory seemed assured was not without its frictions. For his remarkable achievements at Waterloo, Baring was created *Freiherr*, the approximate equivalent of a knighthood, was permitted to add the nobility's *'von'* to his name and received the rank of lieutenant colonel, retrospective to July 1813, which meant that he also received a financial reward in the form of back

---

* Later General Sir James Shaw-Kennedy.

pay. In the new army he reverted to the rank of major but was given command of the prestigious Guard Rifle battalion. As the Army was not actively employed again for another fifty years, promotion was slow. His last regimental appointment was as colonel commanding the Guard Grenadier Regiment, which indicates the esteem in which he was held. In 1831, now a major general, he contributed an article on the defence of La Haye Sainte to the *Hannoversches Militärisches Journal*.

When Queen Victoria ascended the British throne in 1837 the political link with Hanover ended as the constitution of the latter did not permit female succession. Contacts were, however, maintained at the personal level. When, having risen to the rank of lieutenant general and become a baron, Baring died at Wiesbaden on 27 February 1848, the British government contributed to the pensions of his widow and daughter. In other respects Whitehall was less prompt. It had produced a medal for the victory of Waterloo shortly after the event, but it was not until 1847 that it authorised the Military General Service Medal 1793–1814, with clasps commemorating the battles at which the recipients had been present. By then many of those eligible, including former members of the King's German Legion, were dead. Baring's medal and clasps were presented to his widow at a formal parade at Osnabrück on 17 August 1849.

In 1866 Hanover backed the losing side during Prussia's War with Austria. The Hanoverian Army defeated one corps of a 50,000-strong Prussian invasion army, but the odds were too great and it was forced to surrender. Thereafter it ceased to exist and Hanover was ultimately absorbed into the new German Empire. Nevertheless, German interest in Baring's achievements continued to the extent that a biography was published in Berlin in 1898, running to two editions.

Brigadier General
The Hon. James Scarlett

Commander of the Heavy Brigade

THE OUTSTANDING CHARACTERISTIC of the British Army has always been its regimental spirit, which, while essentially tribal, provides a source of immense strength when it is most needed. Unfortunately, when the Army embarked for what has become known as the Crimean War, it can be said to have amounted to little more than the aggregate of its regiments. Its senior generals were political appointees, most of whom were elderly men who had not seen active service since the Napoleonic Wars and had become set in their ways. There was an acute shortage of trained staff officers, service on the staff being regarded as unfashionable. The ordnance, procurement, supply, medical and transport departments were a bureaucratic tangle with overlapping or grey areas of responsibility, producing voluminous and time-consuming paperwork with little consideration for the pressing needs of the moment. At the intermediate levels of command there was a serious lack of experience in handling formations larger than a regiment. There was, too, a prejudice against what were called 'Indian' officers, which meant not only those who had commanded the native troops of the Honourable East India Company but also Regular Army officers who had chosen to serve in India, where their pay purchased a higher standard of living than could be obtained at home and who willingly transferred to incoming regiments when their own had completed its tour of duty.

Somehow, alongside the French, the Army had landed in the Crimea, won a muddled victory at the Battle of the Alma on 20 September 1854—largely because of the troops' dogged bravery and Russian incompetence—and then gone on to besiege the Russian naval base of Sevastopol. It was here that its deficiencies became steadily more apparent, nowhere more so than in the Cavalry Division, consisting of a Light and a Heavy Brigade.

The reader will probably agree that no one is more tiresome or dangerous than a stupid man who believes his behaviour to be the norm. By and large, illogical as it was, the system of purchasing commissions and promotion within regiments had served the Army surprisingly well, although it was fallible and in this case had produced two such men in the persons of Lieutenant General the Earl of Lucan, commanding the Cavalry Division, and Major General the Earl of Cardigan, commander of the Light Brigade. Much has been written about the two, and for those unfamiliar with the story the following few lines will suffice. The pair actually had much in common. They had both purchased command of their respective regiments, spending huge sums on horses and uniforms to present the perfect appearance on parade. Both were harsh commanding officers, being martinets of the worst type, prying into every detail during incessant inspections, parades and drills and inflicting severe reprimands on their officers and brutal floggings on their men for aught that seemed amiss. Both, naturally, were cordially hated in return. They were brothers-in-law who detested each other so intensely that the Army Commander, Lord Raglan, did his best to keep them apart and even allowed Cardigan to sleep on his own private yacht in Balaklava harbour. Lucan had seen some active service, fighting with the Russians against the Turks in 1828, but Cardigan had seen none, although his name was the better known as a result of a series of well-publicised scandals arising not only from his outrageous style of command but also from his private life. Lucan's stupidity can be defined as a simple lack of common sense; Cardigan's arose from a sincere belief that his birth, wealth and position entitled him to do just what he wanted, regardless of the rules or consequences.

Fortunately, the commander of the Heavy Brigade, Brigadier General The Hon. James Yorke Scarlett, was a man of a very different stamp. The second son of Lord Abinger, he was born in 1799 and educated at Eton and Trinity College, Cambridge. He entered the Army as a cornet in the 18th Hussars, demonstrating a serious interest in his profession when, placed on half pay for a period, he chose to spend his time studying in the Senior Department of the Royal Military Academy, Sandhurst. Later he sat as the Tory Member of Parliament for Guildford for five years, and he commanded the 5th Dragoon Guards from 1841 until 1853. Modest, kindly, unassuming and gifted with plentiful common sense, he was popular with his officers and men alike. Now in his middle-fifties, Scarlett was a somewhat stout, red-faced avuncular figure with a large white moustache and white eyebrows. Having little in common with Lucan or Cardigan, he pointedly stood aside from their vicious squabbling. A subaltern in the Light Brigade, contrasting him favourably with his own commander, commented, 'Good kind old fellow that he is, they [the Heavy Brigade] are all very fond of him and will follow him anywhere.'

Scarlett had been on the point of retiring from the Army when he was appointed commander of the Heavy Brigade. He had no experience of active service but was prepared to learn from those who had, and to his staff he appointed two of the 'Indian' officers his contemporaries regarded so askance. The first was Colonel William Beatson, who had fought in Spain during the First Carlist War and in India, where at one time he had commanded the Nizam of Hyderabad's cavalry. Beatson's appointment was strongly opposed by Raglan, Lucan and Cardigan, but he came along anyway, although he lacked official status. The second was Lieutenant Alexander Elliott, who had enjoyed a brilliant career as a cavalryman in India, where latterly he had been given command of the Commander-in-Chief's bodyguard and appointed *aide-de-camp*. Elliott was also a very able administrator, but ill health had forced him to leave India and start working his way up from the bottom in the British Army.

Lord Raglan, commanding the British contingent of the Allied army besieging Sebastopol, had chosen Balaklava as his supply port. The constricted harbour, which was little more than a long, narrow inlet, was quite unsuited for this purpose and soon became overcrowded with ships either seeking a berth or struggling to leave one. It quays, such as they were, had never been intended for the volume of supplies passing over them. Consequently, rations, fodder, ammunition, clothing, tents, blankets, medical supplies and countless other items soon became piled into mountainous dumps from which it was difficult to retrieve anything. The commissary officers, burdened by a system that involved requisitions, dockets, ledgers, sanctions and signatures, followed by physical checks if the items could be located in the vast jumble, did their best but were unable to cope. Even when all the necessary procedures had been completed, the transport system barely existed, so regiments had to detach carrying parties daily to fetch their requirements. Thus burdened, the troops had a seven-mile trek to make along the single track that wound from the Balaklava gorge to the British siege lines, involving a climb of some 700 feet.

Once clear of the gorge, the track passed through the village of Kadikoi, then swung away to the north-west over the Sapoune Heights. To the north-east of the village was a plain that extended as far as the Fedioukine Hills, subdivided into the North and South Valleys by a shallow ridge named Causeway Heights because along its crest ran the Woronzoff Road—so named because it connected Sevastopol with the estates of Count Woronzoff to the east. A series of six redoubts had been hastily thrown up along the length of the Heights, No 1 being on a detached feature known as Canrobert's Hill at the eastern end of the ridge and the remainder being sited approximately half a mile apart along the crest. No 1 contained three naval 9pdr guns and was held in battalion strength; Nos 2, 3 and 4 contained two naval 9pdrs each and were held by half a battalion; and Nos 5 and 6 were unarmed and unoccupied. The garrisons were Tunisian troops drawn from the Turkish contingent, supplemented by one British artillery NCO in each of the manned redoubts. At the western end of the ridge were the camps of the Cavalry Division, providing a link between the siege lines and Balaklava as well as patrols that were in daily contact with the Russians at the River Tchernaya beyond the North and South Valleys.

This constituted Balaklava's first line of defence. It was intended to do no more than buy time in which reinforcements could be brought up from the siege lines. As a precaution, however, Raglan created a second and final line of defence closer to the port. This consisted of an infantry brigade and an artillery battery stationed at Kadikoi under Major General Sir Colin Campbell and a second battery manned by Royal Marines on the hills above Balaklava to the east of the track. By the last week of October, however, the demands of the siege had reduced the brigade to a single regiment, the 93rd (later The Argyll & Sutherland) Highlanders.

Russian officers were, by and large, said to be the worst in Europe, although there were notable exceptions. One such was General P. P. Liprandi, commanding the Russian field army charged with breaking the siege. He was aware of every detail of the British defences, and it was obvious to him that, as it would take about three hours for reinforcements to arrive from the siege lines, Balaklava was there for the taking. Once the port was in Russian hands, not only would the British element of the siege operations would be reduced to impotence, the entire Allied army would in effect be penned inside an awkward triangular coastal enclave with his own troops on one side and the Sevastopol garrison on the other, dependent entirely on whatever supplies could be brought through the small French-held harbours of Kamiesch and Kazatch. For the task he had assembled no fewer than 22,000 infantry, 3,400 cavalry and 78 guns—a force which dwarfed the few troops immediately opposed to him.

The commander of the Turkish contingent, Rustum Pasha, had an excellent spy network in the Russian camp. He was accurately informed as to Liprandi's intentions, the size of his army and the date of his attack, which had been set for 25 October. All this intelligence was passed to Lord Raglan the previous day, but as there had already been several false alarms he simply asked to be kept informed. To his credit, it was Lucan's habit to stand-to the Cavalry Division an hour before dawn, and he took the warning very seriously. At first light on the 25th he and Lord George Paget, left in temporary command of the Light Brigade while Cardigan was aboard his yacht, were trotting along the South Valley to inspect the picquets. In the pre-dawn gloom two flags could be seen flying above No 1 Redoubt. A staff officer informed him that this signalled a general advance by the enemy. Seconds later came the boom of the redoubt's guns, confirming that the Russians were already within range. A picquet, spurring back along the valley, drew rein to report to Lucan. Three enemy infantry divisions had crossed the Tchernaya, they told him. The first was climbing the Fedioukine Heights, the second was heading for Causeway Heights and the third had already begun to attack No 1 Redoubt.

The alarm had now become general. Raglan ordered his 1st and 4th Divisions, commanded by, respectively, the Duke of Cambridge and Major General Sir George Cathcart, to march immediately from their camps to the Balaklava Plain. The former got his men moving within thirty minutes but the latter, grown awkward and cantankerous in his old age, argued with the aide bringing the order and did not comply for an hour. The French sent two infantry brigades and two cavalry regiments, which, because they had less distance to travel, reached the Sapoune Heights first.

Meanwhile the 500 Turks holding No 1 Redoubt were engaged in a desperate fight to buy time for their allies' counter-measures to take effect. They were being assailed by five infantry battalions, with six more in reserve, and were under fire from 30 guns. Even so, it was not until 07:30 that they were driven out, leaving 170 of their number behind them. By now No 2 Redoubt was coming under fire from the guns of the Russians' centre division, which had reached the eastern end of Causeway Heights. The garrison, observing the abandonment of No 1, fled, many of them to be speared by pursuing Cossacks as they ran. Lucan and Campbell promptly sent up their artillery batteries to support the defenders of No 3 Redoubt. However, as the Russian guns threw the heavier weight of metal, they began to sustain serious loss and were pulled back. The Turks, believing themselves abandoned, bolted, followed by the garrison of No 4 Redoubt, leaving the British NCOs barely enough time to spike the guns. Some of the fugitives paused briefly to loot the camps of the Cavalry Division, the tents of which had been struck, then headed for Balaklava; others, under firmer control, fell in on the flanks of the 93rd. It was now shortly after 08:00 and Balaklava's outer defences had been overrun.

The fight for the redoubts had been witnessed by Lord Raglan and his staff from the edge of Sapoune Heights, where the French were emplacing their guns. The entire battlefield lay spread out before them like a panorama, several hundred feet below. Lucan had sensibly drawn up the Cavalry Division to the east of its camps, ready to fall on the flank of any Russian advance on Balaklava. Raglan, however, believed that the division was too exposed and issued an order that was hastily drafted by his Quartermaster-General, Brigadier General Richard Airey. By the time the aide chosen to deliver the order had reached Lucan, the whole situation had changed.

Opening the pencilled note, Lucan read: 'Cavalry to take ground to left of second line of redoubts occupied by the Turks.' In the light of recent events, this was gibberish. Annoyed, Lucan asked the aide to define Lord Raglan's intentions. The aide, a Captain Weatherall, had heard enough of the army commander's conversation to be able to explain that the division was to withdraw to the western end of Causeway Heights, where it would be covered by the French guns firing from the Sapoune escarpment above. Lucan, aware that the small part played by the cavalry at the Alma had earned him the nickname of 'Lord Look-on', was very reluctant to incur further odium by withdrawing, but angrily complied. No sooner had the brigades retired to their new position than Cossack skirmishers began a further looting of the abandoned camps, killing the sick and spare horses in the process. At this point Lord Cardigan, well rested and fed and resplendent in his 11th Hussar uniform, arrived from his yacht to assume command of the Light Brigade.

A large body of Russian cavalry, deployed in six blocks, had now entered the North Valley, followed by some twenty guns and a mass of infantry. The enemy horsemen were lancers and hussars, wearing dark grey overcoats and old-fashioned shakos with back oilskin covers. The overall impression they created was one of black, lowering menace. Raglan deduced that they would be used to protect the right flank of an infantry advance against Balaklava. In the meantime he had decided that he had been wrong to interfere with Lucan's original deployment and sent a second order to the Cavalry Division. It took the aide about thirty minutes to descend the 600 feet and deliver the order, which read: 'Eight squadrons of heavy dragoons to be detached towards Balaklava to support the Turks, who are wavering.' By then, it was hopelessly out of date and also seemed like gibberish to Lucan, as the Turks had long since gone, although the 93rd seemed perfectly steady over at Kadikoi. At this stage it is important to remember that what was visible to Raglan was not visible to Lucan, Scarlett and Cardigan, whose view of the North Valley was interrupted by Causeway Heights, and who consequently remained in ignorance of the approaching Russian cavalry. Nevertheless, the order seemed to vindicate his judgement, and after giving Scarlett his instructions he decided to seek a better viewpoint. Aware that his ungovernable brother-in-law regarded the Light Brigade as a semi-independent command, he gave Cardigan a sharp reminder of their respective responsibilities. 'I'm going to leave you now,' he said. 'You'll remember that you

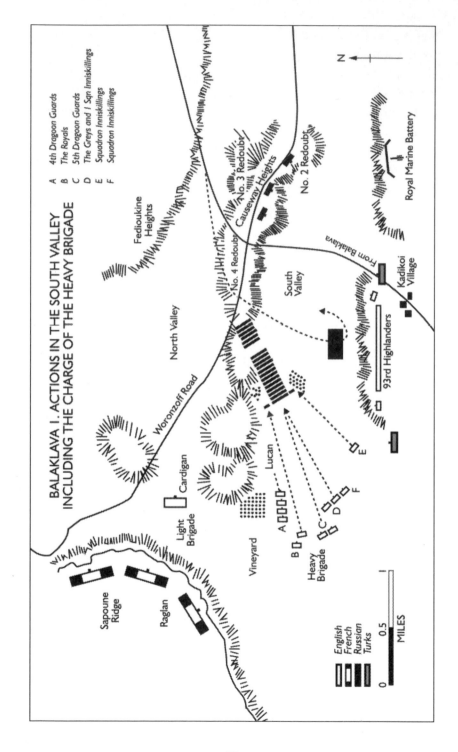

BALAKLAVA I. ACTIONS IN THE SOUTH VALLEY
INCLUDING THE CHARGE OF THE HEAVY BRIGADE

A   4th Dragoon Guards
B   The Royals
C   5th Dragoon Guards
D   The Greys and 1 Sqn Inniskillings
E   Squadron Inniskillings
F   Squadron Inniskillings

N

Fedioukine Heights

No. 3 Redoubt
Causeway Heights
No. 2 Redoubt

Royal Marine Battery

From Balaklava

No. 4 Redoubt

North Valley

South Valley

Kadikoi Village

Woronzoff Road

93rd Highlanders

Lucan

Cardigan

Light Brigade

Vineyard

A

B

C

D

E

F

Heavy Brigade

Sapoune Ridge

Raglan

English
French
Russian
Turks

0   0.5   1
MILES

are placed here by Lord Raglan for the defence of this position. My instructions to you are to attack anything and everything that shall come within reach of you, but you will be careful of columns or squares of infantry.' Scarlett was already briefing his regimental commanders, but, before he could move off, the scene changed dramatically yet again.

Four squadrons detached themselves from the main body of the Russian cavalry and, trotting over the crest of Causeway Heights, headed straight for Kadikoi. Their task was evidently to probe across the South Valley and test the strength of Balaklava's inner defences. At first it must have seemed easy, for only Campbell's field guns were visible, the 93rd having been told to lie down in a fold of the ground to protect themselves from the fire of the Russian guns on Causeway Heights. Campbell's battery went into action, as did the big guns of the Royal Marine battery on the hill behind, punching rounds through the close ranks of the approaching horsemen. Campbell, though aged 61, was a fiery, fire-eating general who had served his apprenticeship during the Peninsular War. So low was his opinion of Russian cavalry that he had already decided not to form a square to meet the attack, nor even pay the enemy the compliment of forming fours. Instead, he intended employing the maximum firepower possible by deploying the 93rd, who had been joined by 100 *invalides* and an unknown number of rallied Turks on the flanks, in two ranks.

When the Russians were within 900 yards and closing at a canter, he ordered the 93rd to stand and dress their line. It was a breathtaking moment. On the Sapoune Heights the *Times* correspondent, William Howard Russell, wondered how 'that thin red streak tipped with steel' (a phrase immortalised as 'the thin red line') could possibly withstand the charging squadrons. At 800 yards the Turks fired a ragged volley and fled. At 600 yards the 93rd fired their first volley. It did little damage, but it gave them time to reload. At 350 yards they fired their second volley. Several men and horses went down, but many more were hit and, to the Highlanders' astonishment, the Russians wheeled away to their left and rode back the way they had come. Their commander probably informed General Liprandi that the Highlanders would hardly have stood as they did unless they were supported by a much larger force that might also be lying concealed in ambush and, that being the case, it must be assumed that the approaches to Balaklava were held in greater strength than had previously been imagined.

The Russians had barely disappeared from view when Scarlett set his brigade in motion. It moved eastwards in open column of troops, with the 5th Dragoon Guards leading, followed by the Royal Scots Greys, the Inniskilling Dragoon Guards and 4th Dragoon Guards, leaving behind the two squadrons of the Royal Dragoons. The move was carried out at a walk as the horses had to pick their way through the looted camps, where fallen tents, guy ropes, picket lines, posts and holes were all hazards, as well as the tangled vines of an abandoned vineyard. Scarlett may have been the most amiable of commanders but, like many general officers, he had his personal fads and fancies. Instead of wearing his general's cocked hat, he wore the brass helmet of his old regiment, but when his aide, Lieutenant Elliott, reported for duty that morning he reprimanded him for wearing a peaked forage cap, insisting that he should replace it with his staff officer's cocked hat. Elliott did not like the hat because it was too large for him, but he solved the problem by folding a large silk handkerchief inside it.

The mass of Russian cavalry, some 3,000 strong, had now come under fire from the French guns on Sapoune Heights. At about the same time its commander, General Ryjoff, ordered it to wheel left across Causeway Heights in accordance with Liprandi's plan. Unknown to either, the Russians and the Heavy Brigade were now on a collision course. Glancing to his left, Elliott suddenly saw lines of lance points and serried ranks of horsemen breaking the skyline about 500 yards distant. Scarlett immediately decided to charge and wheeled his regiments left into line, taking ground to the right so that his left would not have to cross the encumbered ground. Ryjoff, halting, took ground to his left for the same reason, so that the centres of the two lines were approximately opposite each other. The Heavy Brigade, however, was outnumbered by five or six to one, so that the Russian line was much the longer. Scarlett, unperturbed, ordered the ranks to be dressed so that they would strike the enemy in as compact a formation as possible.

Lucan, who had observed the Russian advance as soon as he reached higher ground, came galloping up. He had a tendency to become flustered in a crisis and ordered Scarlett to charge, which he was about to do anyway. Across the valley, the enthusiastic Royal Marine gunners began sending long bowls into the Russian mass, every shot knocking down men and horses, until their commander forced them to desist when it became clear that a mêlée was about to take place.

Liprandi's sound plan was now compromised by a blunder on Ryjoff's part. Trumpets sounded in the Russian ranks and the mass moved forward as far as a dry ditch and halted, simultaneously pushing forward its outer wings to envelop the centre of the Heavy Brigade. This was obviously a manoeuvre from the Russian tactical manual, and it may have looked very fine on the St Petersburg review ground, but here it proved fatal. It was a curious decision, as Ryjoff could have chosen to engage the Heavy Brigade with his own centre while his wings simply bypassed the combat. Drawing their carbines, some of the Russians opened a popping fire, hitting a man here and there.

Scarlett, satisfied at last with the dressing of his lines, placed himself several horse-lengths ahead of them with Elliott, Trumpet-Major Thomas Monks and his orderly, Sergeant James Shegog. He ordered Monks to sound the Charge and the brigade began to move forward, gathering pace as it covered the 400-yard uphill slope separating it from the enemy. Once launched, there could be no turning aside from the moving ranks, but none sought to, as participants later spoke of being possessed of a wild demonic fury, knowing that during the next few minutes they would either kill or be killed. Although they had the advantage of the higher ground, the Russians made the further mistake of meeting the charge at the halt or, at best, a slow walk.

Short-sighted and possessing no aptitude for the sword, Scarlett vanished into the mass, laying about him to left and right. At his side was Shegog, a giant of a man and noted swordsman, taking strokes intended for the general on his own blade and dealing smashing, skull-cleaving blows in return. Most of the enemy's attention, however, was directed at Elliott, whom they believed to be the general because of his cocked hat. An officer, ignoring Scarlett, rode straight at him. Elliott parried his thrust and ran him through to the hilt, dragging him out of his saddle. Then the aide found himself deep in the Russian ranks, slashed at from every quarter. He was cut across the face, on the forehead and behind the ear. His cocked hat was cut through, but the silk handkerchief saved his life and although he lost consciousness for several seconds the press around him kept him in the saddle.

Seconds after Scarlett had been swallowed up, the leading squadrons of the Greys and the Inniskillings smashed into the enemy line, followed by the 5th Dragoon Guards. The horses instinctively headed between their opposite numbers, their impetus carrying them five ranks deep into the mass. Cutting and stabbing furiously at those around them in the dense press, the men also used their bridle hands to seize the throat of the enemy on the left and pitch them over their cruppers into the trampling hooves below. Very quickly it became apparent that the Russian greatcoats were too thick to be penetrated by the British sabre, so resort was made to vertical and horizontal cuts to the head. In this the dragoons, big men on big horses, had a height advantage over the smaller Russian light cavalrymen; in addition, the British sabres had been sharpened whereas those of the Russians were notably blunt, and their lances, while useful in a pursuit or against broken troops, were simply an encumbrance in a close mêlée like this.

The full extent of Ryjoff's mistake now became apparent, for while the foregoing was taking place the Russian flanks had continued to swing inwards. Scarlett had already despatched his brigade major, Captain Connolly, to bring up an Inniskilling squadron which had been moving in the direction of Kadikoi. This smashed into the Russian left wing during its wheel, taking its troopers on the vulnerable bridle hand and bowling some of them over, and attacking others from behind. Simultaneously, Lucan had sent an aide to order the 4th Dragoon Guards to attack on the opposite flank while he galloped on to bring up the Royals. The former charged straight through the Russian files from right to left and, seconds later, the Royals, who had already been heading for the action on their own initiative and had formed into line from column at the gallop, smashed into the Russian right.

Under pressure from three sides, the Russians became a jostled mob whose officers had completely lost control of the situation. They were, too, getting the worst of the mêlée. Beginning at the left rear, they began shredding away and suddenly the whole mass turned and bolted across the crest of Causeway Heights into the North Valley. The Heavy Brigade pursued for a short distance but then Scarlett ordered Monks to sound

Right: Benendict Arnold, a first-rate field commander whose reputation was forever stained by treachery. (Anne S. K. Brown Military Collection, Brown University Library)

Below: Arnold was seriously wounded while leading an attack on a redoubt during the Battle of Bemis Heights. He exhibited a surprisingly chivalrous side to his nature, ordering his men not to bayonet the Hessian who had shot him because the man had only done his duty. (Anne S. K. Military Collection, Brown University Library)

Above: Burgoyne surrenders to Major General Horatio Gates at Saratoga. In fact, the American successes at Freeman's Farm and Bemis Heights were largely the result of Arnold's drive and energy. Arnold had already quarrelled with Gates, and his resentment at the latter's receiving the credit for the defeat of Burgoyne's army began the sour process that would ultimately lead to his turning against his fellow countrymen. The figure in homespun beside the cannon's muzzle is Daniel Morgan, who was to defeat Tarleton's British Legion at Cowpens. (US Army Military History Institute)

Left: A print of Sir Joshua Reynolds' famous portrait of Banastre Tarleton, the original of which hangs in the National Gallery, London. The unnatural pose was chosen to conceal the fact that Tarleton had lost two fingers in one of his later engagements. One of the captured Colours shows the French royal cypher. (Anne S. K. Brown Military Collection, Brown University Library)

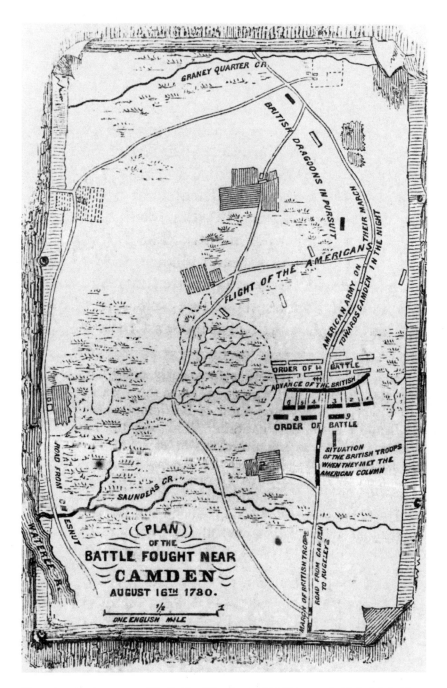

Above: A contemporary map of the Battle of Camden in which Gates was decisively defeated by Cornwallis and Tarleton. The map illustrates the nature of the partially cleared terrain in which the war was fought. (US Army Military History Institute)

Left: Although he was born into a noble family, General Louis Desaix embraced the principles of the French Revolution. A commander of great ability and integrity, he distinguished himself during the capture of Malta and Napoleon's campaign in Egypt. (Anne S. K. Brown Military Collection, Brown University Library)

Below: The Battle of Marengo—a drawing by Martinet. Desaix's counter-attack is in progress and in the centre Desaix's body can be seen being carried off the field. Napoleon, a beaten general until Desaix's arrival, was reluctant to acknowledge the debt and, as contemporary hagiography demanded, is shown controlling events, centre right. (Anne S. K. Brown Military Collection, Brown University Library)

Opposite page, bottom: Waterloo—Adolf Northen's spirited painting of the final moments at La Haye Sainte. Major Baring (mounted) is shown leading the last desperate counter-attack across the farmyard. The farmhouse is on the left; on the right the French have finally broken through the defences of the barn, which has been set ablaze for the second time; in the background are the pig sties and the main gate, which is on the point of being forced. The garrison's ammunition is all but exhausted and some of its men have resorted to hurling roof tiles at the enemy. (Niedersachsisches Landesmuseum, Landesgalerie, Hannover)

Above: Brigadier General The Hon. James Scarlett on the point of launching the Heavy Brigade on its dramatic charge. He is correctly shown wearing a dragoon's helmet rather than his general officer's cocked hat. Balaklava harbour is visible to the left of the picture. (Anne S. K. Military Collection, Brown University Library)

Below: Orlando Norrie's watercolour of the Charge of the Heavy Brigade at Balaklava, showing the 4th Dragoon Guards in the foreground with the Scots Greys to their left and a little in advance. Though largely eclipsed in public memory by the subsequent Charge of the Light Brigade, this was the most decisive cavalry action of the Crimean War. (Courtesy of the Director, National Army Museum, London)

Above: An artist's imaginative representation of Major William Hodson receiving the surrender of the aged King of Delhi. In reality, Hodson's *coup* was an astounding piece of cheek in which his formidable personality alone overawed thousands of armed mutineers. (Anne S. K. Brown Military Collection, Brown University Library)

Left: Hodson's summary execution of the Moghul princes attracted controversy since it lacked the sanction of the judicial process. This Victorian sketch suggests that he might be showing mercy to two captured mutineers; equally, while indicating the atrocities they have committed, he might be on the point of blowing their brains out. (Anne S. K. Brown Military Collection, Brown University Library)

Right: Many believed that the constitution of Major General Sir Hugh Rose was too delicate to withstand the rigours of campaigning in the furnace heat of the Indian summer. He was to prove them wrong.

Below: The 14th Light Dragoons were one of the most formidable elements of Rose's Central India Field Force. Here the regiment is seen executing one of its many successful charges against the mutineers. (Courtesy of the Regimental Association, 14th/20th King's Hussars)

Above: Benjamin H. Grierson in the uniform of a brigadier general of volunteers. (US Army Military History Institute)

Right: A remarkable photograph, taken by a Confederate official, showing Grierson's brigade nearing the end of its long ride across the Confederacy. The men can be seen standing at the heads of their horses, some at least of which have been temporarily unsaddled. The scene is probably the brigade's final halt before it re-entered Federal lines at Baton Rouge, Louisiana. (US Army Military History Institute)

Below: After the Civil War, Grierson commanded the 10th Cavalry, a regiment of black soldiers with white officers, for 23 years. The regiment saw much active service on the frontier with Mexico. Black units were highly regarded and known to the Indians as Buffalo Soldiers. (US Army Military History Institute)

Above: Major General Lewis Wallace enjoyed mixed fortunes during his military career but was finally hailed as the Saviour of Washington. Today he is better remembered as the author of the novel Ben Hur. (Anne S. K. Brown Military Collection, Brown University Library)

Above: Heavily outnumbered, advance units of Wallace's scratch force pull back across the railroad bridge at Monocacy Junction. Wallace's decision to fight a delaying action here resulted in defeat but prevented Jubal Early's Confederates reaching Washington at a time when the capital was almost defenceless. (US Army Military History Institute)

Above: C. B .Birch's statue of Lieutenant Walter Hamilton, Queen's Own Corps of Guides, leading a sortie by the doomed garrison of the British Residency at Kabul. Slightly over life-size, the figure is a good likeness of Hamilton, who had already been awarded the Victoria Cross for an earlier action in the campaign. (Courtesy of the Director, National Army Museum, London)

Right: General Sir Hector Macdonald enlisted as a private soldier and, entirely on his own merits, achieved the rank of general and a knighthood. (Anne S .K. Brown Military Collection, Brown University Library)

Above: At Omdurman, Macdonald's Brigade was simultaneously attacked by dervishes from two directions. He met the threat by forming the brigade into an L shape, feeding his regiments from left to right across the inner angle. He is said to have remained so cool that he reprimanded one unit for its sloppy drill. (Anne S. K. Brown Military Collection, Brown University Library)

Below: Evidently taken from the lower slopes of Djebel Surgham, this photograph shows Macdonald's Brigade in action. The brigade has completed its redeployment and the Camel Corps has come up on its right, joined by the Lincolnshire Regiment; on the right of the picture the artillery and leading elements of the 1st British Brigade are arriving. By now, Macdonald's men were down to their last few rounds of ammunition, but they had defeated both dervish attacks. (Anne S. K. Brown Military Collection, Brown University Library)

Above: The newly promoted Major Charles Townshend, photographed in the uniform of the Central India Horse, shortly after his successful defence of Chitral Fort. By the time he was given command of a division during the First World War, he had proved himself to be a capable, courageous and experienced officer. Unfortunately, his all-consuming self-interest was a fatal flaw that resulted in death and wounds for thousands of men. (Anne S. K. Brown Military Collection, Brown University Library)

Above: Chitral Fort seen from across the river. The fort was constructed before the days of breech-loading rifles and, overlooked as it was from many directions, its interior was vulnerable to sniper fire. (Courtesy of the Director, National Army Museum, London)

Below: Townshend's decision to allow himself to be besieged in Kut-al-Amarah was to have disastrous consequences. Fortunately for his cavalry, he sent them out before the Turks had completed their investment of this grubby, unimportant little town. Perhaps it is coincidence, but this contemporary entry in the sketchbook kept by Private Baggot of the 14th King's Hussars contains a real sense of foreboding. (Courtesy Regimental Association 14th/20th King's Hussars)

the Recall and its scattered regiments re-formed on their officers. It had taken just eight minutes' furious fighting from the time Scarlett had charged into the enemy ranks until the Russian formation disintegrated. Russian casualties were estimated at 200, most of them wounded; the Heavy Brigade's were a fraction of this. Raglan sent Scarlett a personal note of congratulation, commenting that 'The issue was never for a moment doubtful.' Lucan, chagrined that the engagement had been brought on and fought through without his playing more than a minor role, was a great deal less forthcoming.

The engagement had taken place within sight of the Light Brigade, standing idle some 500 yards distant. Time and again, Cardigan was urged to attack by some of his officers, especially when the Russians gave way, but he kept stubbornly repeating that he had been ordered to remain where he was. This was selective memory with a vengeance, for Lucan had also ordered him 'to attack anything and everything that shall come within reach'. Certainly, if the Light Brigade had pursued the beaten Russians, a role for which it was trained, it would have cut them up even more savagely. As Cardigan was no coward, it is open to question whether he was so stupid as not to recognise an obvious tactical opportunity or whether he was simply being bloody-minded and seeking to make trouble for Lucan. His subsequent excuse was that the Russians had never approached his position, but the fact was that he had been grossly negligent and should have been deprived of his command.

It was now about 10·30 and the main issue of the day had actually been decided. Without his cavalry screen Liprandi was not inclined to proceed with his attack on Balaklava. From his viewpoint on the Sapoune Heights, Raglan could see that the battered Russian cavalry had rallied at the far end of the North Valley, behind a line of guns. More guns could be seen at the far end of Causeway Heights and across the valley on the Fedioukine Heights. The Russians could also be seen to be abandoning Nos 3 and 4 Redoubts, blowing up the magazines as they did so. As the British 1st and 4th Divisions were now entering the battlefield he decided to take the offensive and recover the rest of the ridge. Airey dashed off another order for Lucan: 'Cavalry to advance and take advantage of any opportunity to recover the heights. They will be supported by infantry, which have been ordered. Advance on two fronts.' Once again, the

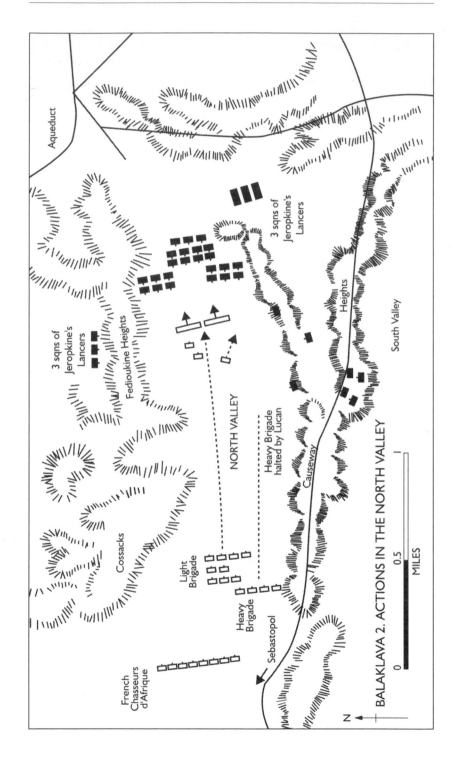

Aqueduct

3 sqns of
Jeropkine's
Lancers

3 sqns of
Jeropkine's
Lancers

Fedioukine Heights

NORTH VALLEY

Heights

South Valley

Heavy Brigade
halted by Lucan

Causeway

Cossacks

Light
Brigade

Heavy
Brigade

Sebastopol

French
Chasseurs
d'Afrique

N

BALAKLAVA 2. ACTIONS IN THE NORTH VALLEY

MILES

0   0.5   1

message was incomprehensible, but as the South Valley was now clear of the enemy Lucan decided to move his division round into the North Valley, where the Heavy Brigade was positioned to the right rear of the Light Brigade, and await the arrival of the infantry.

Observing Russian horse-teams at the far end of Causeway Heights, Raglan deduced that they were there to remove the guns from the captured redoubts. He had spent most of his professional life with the Duke of Wellington, who was said never to have lost a gun, and he had no intention of providing the enemy with trophies that would enable him to claim a victory, especially as the Cavalry Division lay within striking distance. What he seems to have forgotten is that, when viewed from far above, terrain features flatten and merge, and that the Russians on Causeway Heights were not only on higher ground than the Cavalry Division but also hidden by several rolling crests. He told Airey what Lucan was to do and the latter scrawled one of the most famous orders in history:

> Lord Raglan wishes the cavalry to advance rapidly to the front—follow the enemy and try to prevent the enemy carrying away the guns. Troop Horse Artillery may accompany. French cavalry is on your left. Immediate.

The aide selected to carry the order was Captain Lewis Edward Nolan, undeniably the best horseman in the Army and the author of books on cavalry tactics and horse management. He was also volatile, short-tempered and disinclined to suffer fools, especially Lucan and Cardigan. Plunging over the edge of the escarpment, he tore down its face along what amounted to little more than a goat track and found Lucan near the Light Brigade. Naturally, Lucan found the order no more intelligible than its predecessor and requested clarification.

'Lord Raglan's orders were that the cavalry should attack immedi ately!' was Nolan's sneering response.

'Attack, sir? Attack what? What guns, sir?' asked Lucan.

At this point Nolan should have offered a full explanation. Instead, flinging out his arm in the general direction of the Russian guns at the far end of the North Valley, he remarked with studied insolence, 'There my lord, is your enemy! There are your guns!'

If that was what had been intended, the Cavalry Division was to attack a battery one and a half miles distant and in the process cross a natural killing ground covered by artillery from both sides of the valley and in front, to say nothing of the fire of the enemy's infantry and the mass of rallied cavalry beyond the guns. What was being asked was nothing less than suicidal, but Raglan demanded immediate action. Yet, as has been already mentioned, in a crisis Lucan tended to become over-excited and lose his grip on reality, for if he had read the order a little more closely he would have found that it actually contained the key to his problem. The Russians were not 'carrying off' their own guns. In the very nature of the phrase, 'carrying off' implied captured guns, and the only guns the Russians had captured were in the redoubts at the far end of the ridge. Unfortunately, his mind could not grasp the equation. Reluctantly, he accepted Nolan's unintentional designation of the wrong objective. Pausing only to spit a mortal insult at Cardigan, Nolan trotted off to ride with the 17th Lancers in the coming charge.

Cardigan and Scarlett accepted their orders philosophically in the full knowledge that they were being required to perform a death ride. The division formed up with the Heavy Brigade echeloned to the right-rear of the Light Brigade, with Lucan and his staff between the two. At 11:10 a silence fell over the battlefield as it began to move forward. It trotted ever deeper into the North Valley, the dressing of its jingling ranks immaculate. Suddenly Nolan spurred diagonally across the front of the Light Brigade towards Cardigan, shouting something like 'Threes Right!' This would have been the correct order if, attempting to correct the terrible error resulting from his cavalier arrogance, he had wanted to bring the brigade back on to the intended axis of advance along Causeway Heights, a divergence of some 20 degrees from that being taken. We shall never know the truth, for at that moment a shell burst nearby. A splinter entered his chest and, screaming horribly, he careered back through the ranks before falling dead. Cardigan, imagining that Nolan had been intent on committing another breach of military etiquette, was seized by a rage so violent that he thought of little else throughout the charge.

The Light Brigade had now entered the killing ground and was being torn to pieces by the torrent of shot and shell from both flanks and ahead. Lucan was horrified by its dreadful wake of dead, dying and maimed men and horses strewing the ground. His own staff began to take casualties and he sustained a minor wound in the leg. Glancing round, he saw that the Heavy Brigade, slower and tired from its earlier exertions, had fallen behind but was also beginning to sustain losses. He now made the best decision of his entire period of command, commenting to his adjutant, Lord Paulet, 'They have sacrificed the Light Brigade—they shall not have the Heavy if I can help it!' The divisional trumpet-major sounded the Halt followed by the Retire. The calls went unheard in the Light Brigade, but the regiments of the Heavy Brigade reined in and retired out of range—all save one man. Brigadier General James Scarlett, still wearing his sabre-battered 'brass pot', had not heard the calls either and, spoiling for another fight, continued to canter down the valley. His senior aide, Colonel Beatson, put spurs to his horse and eventually drew up alongside the startled brigade commander, shouting that he was charging the Russians alone. Annoyed, Scarlett trotted back to meet Lucan, who repeated the comment he had made to Lord Paulet.

Meanwhile the Light Brigade continued to provide the supreme example of disciplined courage and self-sacrifice. Gripped by a berserk fury in their desire to avenge the deaths of so many of their comrades, the survivors swept through the battery, spearing or cutting down the gunners, attacking the already demoralised Russian cavalry beyond and driving them back to within sight of the Tchernaya. Then, recognising that there was no more to be done, they began making their way back along the strewn valley, although now they faced the additional hazard of Cossacks sent by Liprandi to intercept their retreat. They were, however, assisted by the French, who had watched the spectacle with a mixture of awe and pity and who now launched the 4th Chasseurs d'Afrique in a gallant charge that cleared the Fedioukine Heights.

First to arrive back was Cardigan, who had faultlessly led his men into the enemy battery but, having done so, thought it no part of his duty to engage in hand-to-hand combat like a private soldier. He was still livid about Nolan's apparent interference, commenting callously to Scarlett, 'Imagine the fellow screaming like a woman when he was hit!' He would have continued had not Scarlett interrupted him: 'Say no more my lord; you have just ridden over his body.' By degrees, the bloodied survivors of the Light Brigade came in, some riding wounded and exhausted horses, some staggering, some limping, some supported by their comrades, some crawling. The brigade had started its charge 678 strong, but now, just twenty minutes later, only 195 mounted men remained. Although more men would arrive, the loss of 500 horses meant that the Light Brigade was, for the moment, finished. In sharp contrast, the Heavy Brigade's personnel casualties *for the entire day* amounted to ten killed and 98 wounded, over half the losses having been incurred in the North Valley.

Cardigan was absolved from any responsibility for the disaster as he had merely obeyed the direct order of his divisional commander. Lucan, too, protested that he had acted under orders, to which Raglan tartly retorted, 'Lord Lucan, you were a lieutenant general and should therefore have exercised your discretion, and, not approving of the charge, should not have caused it to be made!' This was the nub of the matter, although, in mitigation, Airey's badly drafted order and Nolan's peremptory delivery of the same should also be taken into account. Lucan was summoned home and demanded a court martial, which was refused. Cardigan also left for home, on medical grounds, to receive a hero's welcome and an audience with Queen Victoria, and to be appointed Inspector General of Cavalry. This provides a perfect example of the Anglo-Saxon trait of celebrating a gallant failure rather than a victory gained at modest cost. It was, after all, the charge of Scarlett's Heavy Brigade that put paid to Liprandi's hopes of taking Balaklava, but to the public Cardigan was the hero of the battle. That very December, Alfred Lord Tennyson wrote his famous poem *The Charge of the Light Brigade*, lines from which remain in common use in the same manner as phrases from the Authorised Version of the Bible, the Book of Common Prayer and some of Shakespeare's plays. It was not until 1882 that Tennyson penned *The Charge of the Heavy Brigade*, of which few have even heard.

Following the departure of Lucan and Cardigan, Scarlett assumed command of the Cavalry Division amid a general sigh of relief. Recalling the events of 25 October in the North Valley, he commented that if his brigade had not been halted by Lucan he could have taken advantage of the alarm generated by the Light Brigade's charge and broken through to the Tractir Bridge over the Tchernaya, trapping large numbers of Russians on the wrong side of the river. This was by no means impossible, but it was not a probable result. Now Scarlett was forced to grapple with problems of a different kind. As the weather deteriorated, the ramshackle transport system collapsed and the division's horses were used to convey the steadily increasing numbers of sick down to Balaklava and return laden with food and ammunition. There was plenty of forage in Balaklava, but no means of bringing it forward. Those horses forced to remain on the Plain starved in hock-deep winter mud, gnawing on each other's manes and tails and even gun wheels until they collapsed and died. Of the 2,216 horses the division possessed at the end of October 1854, 932 died from starvation or disease during the next six months. Russell's reports in *The Times*, describing how men and animals alike were forced to endure terrible hardships over the winter months, thanks to administrative mismanagement, created a national scandal that led to the fall of the government. Thereafter, conditions underwent a steady improvement.

Scarlett was promoted to major general with the local rank of lieutenant general and was honoured with a knighthood in 1855. He worked hard to rebuild the division. Fresh horses arrived, as did recruits to fill the gaps in the ranks caused by casualties or disease. He subjected them to unremitting drill, often in the presence of the enemy, but did not think that they would reach the required standard for another year. The Russians did not know this, for after the events of 25 October they had kept their own cavalry out of harm's way. More regiments arrived, at full strength, so that the Cavalry Division now consisted of three brigades. It was, too, an efficiently run formation and one that held its commander in affectionate regard. 'He does his work like a gentleman and gives no unnecessary trouble,' wrote one officer. 'He is a real old brick,' said another.

The fall of Sevastopol all but ended active hostilities. Scarlett was well received on his return home but was not a man to seek popular adulation. He did not go to war again. His first peacetime appointment was as commander of the cavalry in the Aldershot District. This brought him into contact with Cardigan, who attempted, unsuccessfully, to drag him into his perennial quarrels with Lucan. After a period commanding the Portsmouth District he became Adjutant-General in 1860. In 1865 he received what was regarded as the prize home service appointment, namely command of the Aldershot District. He carried out these tasks with the same good-humoured, fatherly common sense that had characterised his command of the Cavalry Division. While by no means a reactionary, he was a little old-fashioned in some of his ways and responded to proposals regarding the abolition of the purchase system with a degree of reservation. On the other hand, he knew that the world was changing fast and accepted the fact. The American Civil War, the Austro-Prussian War and the Franco-Prussian War all clearly indicated that the future role of horse cavalry would be very different. When asked about this he chuckled and replied, 'I am too old to go to school again and unlearn the lessons of my life.' He retired from the Army in 1870 and died suddenly the following year.

Major William Hodson

Beau sabreur, *killer of princes*

B ORN IN 1821, William Stephen Raikes Hodson, the son of an archdeacon, was educated at Rugby, where he was a contemporary of Thomas Hughes, the author of *Tom Brown's Schooldays,* and may have served as the model for Brown's inseparable friend Harry East. He seems to have been a popular figure as, for some long-lost reason, he was given the nickname of 'Larky Pritchard'. Despite this, he was not one to tolerate nonsense, and, when discipline in one of the school's houses broke down, the Headmaster, Dr Arnold, appointed Hodson as its praepostor, with satisfactory results.

On leaving Rugby, Hodson took a law degree at Cambridge but decided that his future lay with the army of the Honourable East India Company. Aged 23, he was now too old to pass through the latter's military academy at Addiscombe, near Croydon in Surrey, but with the assistance of an old family friend, Sir William Napier, who was serving as Lieutenant-Governor of Guernsey, the difficulty was bypassed by granting him a commission in the Guernsey Militia, from which a transfer was arranged several months later. Arriving in India in 1845, Hodson joined the 2nd Bengal Grenadiers, with whom he fought throughout the First Sikh War, taking part in the battles of Mudki, Ferozeshah and Sobraon. During these engagements he revealed not only a love of fighting for its own sake, but also so formidable a talent as a swordsman that few of his opponents lived to speak of the encounter afterwards. He was subsequently posted to the 1st Bengal European Fusiliers, one of several European regiments maintained permanently in India by the Company. These regiments came as close to being a foreign legion as made no difference, although most of the men were British. They received better pay and conditions than soldiers of the Queen's (British regular) regiments 'rented' by the Company, in exchange for a lifetime in virtual exile. This probably encouraged some to enlist, as did the opportunity to acquire wealth by devious means in India, but there were undoubtedly a higher proportion of men in their ranks who had excellent private reasons to absent themselves from home than could be found in the Queen's regiments. They were routinely described as a rough lot who needed firm handling but invariably performed well in action.

Hodson evidently impressed his superiors, for in 1847 he was appointed second-in-command and adjutant of the Guides, a newly raised irregular unit of which more will be said in a later chapter. Initially, the unit also contained its share of desperate characters, but Hodson was equal to the task and, during the Second Sikh War, impressed them with his own feats of daring and tactical skill. In 1852 he assumed temporary command of the Guides while the corps' founder, Harry Lumsden, went home on leave. He now gave full rein to his personality, attracting friends and making enemies in equal numbers. As a man devoted to action, he had little interest in administration or even the proper channels of command. No respecter of persons, or rank for that matter, he was overbearing, blunt to the point of rudeness, high-handed and disinclined to compromise. Naturally, his superiors took exception and used the fact that the unit's accounts were in a muddle to convene a Court of Enquiry. After months spent unravelling the mess, the Court cleared Hodson of any imputations of irregularity. Simultaneously, however, he was in trouble for the arrest and detention of a tribal chief suspected of implication in the murder of the local British Resident, although such evidence as existed was circumstantial. Hodson was sharply criticised for his lack of judgement and sent back to the 1st Bengal European Fusiliers as a subaltern. There he applied himself conscientiously to his duties and got on so well with his commanding officer that in January 1857 the latter wrote to the Adjutant-General, commenting that in view of Hodson's experience and qualifications his talents were being wasted as one of the regiment's junior officers and that he should be considered for an appointment on the staff. The upshot was that Hodson was interviewed by Major General The Hon. George Anson, the Commander-in-Chief, who formed a very favourable impression of him.

The thunderclouds of what became known as the Great Mutiny had already begun to gather. Indian society still thought in feudal terms and in matters of religion and caste was instinctively conservative. Although apparently humane, the Company's reforms, including the abolition of *sati* (the live burning of widows on their husbands' funeral pyres) and the outlawing of *thagi* (ritual strangulation in honour of the goddess Kali) provoked hostility from those with vested interests in the preservation of these customs. Measures permitting widows to remarry and the imposition of a land title system where none had existed before provoked widespread anger. Some of the princely rulers benefited from their association with the Company, but others bitterly resented the loss of their powers. Many Hindus, especially Brahmins, saw in Christian missionary activity a British plot to destroy the caste system and imperil their souls. The year 1857 was also significant, since it was prophesied that the British would be driven from India forever during the centenary of the Battle of Plassey. To many, as tales of British incompetence in the Crimea began to spread, the moment seemed ripe. Much of India was further unsettled by the mysterious passage of *chapattis* between villages during the night. No one knew whence they came or what they signified, but the runner always brought instructions that fresh *chapattis* should be baked and passed on to other villages. To simple, superstitious minds the implications were that soon decisive and probably terrible events were about to take place.

Of the Company's Madras, Bombay and Bengal armies, the last was the largest and most experienced. It was also the most seriously affected by the present troubles because its ranks contained a high proportion of Brahmins, high-caste Hindus and Rajputs. The Hindus objected strongly to a new regulation compelling them to serve abroad, since this would probably entail a sea passage that, according to their faith, would lose them their caste. Furthermore, the close relationship which had existed between British officers and their sepoys during the Sikh Wars had become more distant following the arrival of a new and sometimes unsuitable generation of officers. Despite this, the generals, grown old in the Company's service, refused to believe that the troops were on the brink of mutiny. The detonator that initiated the explosion of fear, hatred and resentment was the ammunition for the new Enfield rifle. An agitator

107

claimed that it was greased with a mixture of cow and pig fat, and as the cow was sacred to the Hindus and the pig was abominated by Muslims the entire native element of the Bengal army was unwilling to accept it. The authorities promised to rectify the grievance but by now the troops had lost faith in them.

From January 1857 onwards the situation deteriorated rapidly. Some regiments refused to accept the new cartridges and were disbanded. At Meerut on 9 May 85 troopers of the 3rd Light Cavalry were court martialled, publicly stripped of their uniforms and sentenced to a period of hard labour for refusing them. One can understand the sepoys' dilemma, for none of the choices facing them was welcome. They could refuse the cartridges and face severe punishment; or they could accept them and risk losing their souls; or they could mutiny and destroy the system which apparently threatened them. On 10 May, a Sunday, the Meerut garrison mutinied while its British element was at church parade, destroying their own tenable case with a horrific display of savagery. British officers were murdered, their wives horribly violated, their children slaughtered and their homes burned.

The mutiny, accompanied by similar atrocities, spread like wildfire throughout the Bengal army. The mutineers then converged on Delhi, where they proclaimed Bahadur Shah II as Emperor of Hindustan. Bahadur was indeed a descendant of the once-mighty Moghul emperors, but he was now a confused old man in receipt of a pension from the Company and, although British officials paid him the respect due to his age and ancestry, he was known simply as the King of Delhi. He lived in the city's crumbling Red Fort, where faded grandeur merged with filth and squalor, surrounded by a crowd of decadent self-seekers who were constantly at odds with each other. Quite possibly he did not understand the full implications of what was happening, but he was undoubtedly gratified that Hindus and Muslims alike were suddenly anxious that he should become their ruler and appointed his son Mirza Moghul as commander of his newly acquired army.

In fact Mirza commanded nothing, nor did anyone else, for once the bonds of regimental discipline had been loosed the mutineers became a huge armed mob whose delegates were little better than a parliament of fowls. Some, indeed, believed that they had achieved what they set out to do and that no further effort was necessary. Consequently no concerted action was taken to destroy the remnant of British power in northern India when it was at its most vulnerable. On 1 July the mutineers were joined by a large contingent from the former Bareilly garrison under Bakht Khan, an Indian artillery officer with some forty years' service to his credit. Bakht soon persuaded the King to appoint him commander-in-chief in place of the ineffective Mirza Moghul, the principal result being that from this point onwards relationships between the senior rebel commanders were marked by mutual suspicion and recrimination.

What followed has been described as more than a mutiny yet not quite a civil war, for although the rulers of some states threw in their lot with the mutineers, others joined the British, and without loyal Indian troops it would have proved extremely difficult to bring the situation back under control. One of the most important sources of immediate reinforcement for the British lay with the Sikh population of the Punjab. The Sikhs pride themselves on being a martial race, and the battles of the Sikh Wars had been fought with a ferocity the British had not encountered since the Napoleonic Wars, engendering a mutual respect between the two sides. This respect was not extended by the Sikhs to the Company's Bengal Native Infantry regiments, some of which would have given way had it not been for the British presence. The Sikhs therefore tended to despise the Bengalis as soldiers and were not averse to restoring their own reputation by fighting against them.

General Anson quickly mobilised a field force, including the 1st Bengal European Fusiliers, to march against the mutineers in Delhi. On 18 May he ordered Hodson to raise a regiment of irregular cavalry. Hodson's duties prevented him from leaving the field force, but he had made close friends with many of the leading families in the Punjab and with Robert Montgomery, the province's Judicial Commissioner, and wrote to them requesting their help. Altogether, they raised no fewer than seven troops, the majority of the men being former members of the Khalsa, the original Sikh army. One troop, at Hodson's request, was formed from Afghans, to avoid an overbearing Sikh influence. The regiment, which would become known as Hodson's Horse, was uniformed likes the Guides in khaki but distinguished by red turbans, cummerbunds and sashes worn over the shoulder. The men were armed with whatever they felt most capable with, including swords, lances and firearms.

At first the Delhi Field Force was in an impossible situation. It numbered just 600 cavalry, 2,300 infantry and 22 field guns and occupied a slight elevation known as The Ridge to the north-west of the city. Here, nominally, it was besieging some 40,000 mutineers armed with several hundred artillery weapons, secure behind formidable walls. In reality, it was just able to beat off repeated rebel attacks. Reinforcements, including the first three troops of Hodson's Horse, began reaching the Delhi Field Force early in July, although battle casualties and disease continually thinned the ranks. The British, too, suffered from command problems. The strain on General Anson, a 70-year-old veteran of Waterloo, proved too much and on 27 May he died from cholera. On 5 July the disease also claimed the life of his successor, Major General Sir Henry Barnard. Command passed to Major General Thomas Reed, who was already so ill that a fortnight later he handed over to Colonel Archdale Wilson. Granted the temporary rank of major general, Wilson was conscious of the fearful responsibility he had inherited and was accused by his critics of being indecisive. Nevertheless, he reorganised the Delhi Field Force efficiently and, wisely, decided to delay an assault on the city until a train of siege guns had arrived with further reinforcements from the Punjab. In command of these was the dour, uncompromising Brevet Lieutenant Colonel John Nicholson, an officer in the Cromwellian mould who, like Hodson, had made a startling reputation for himself in the Punjab and on the Frontier. Although only a substantive captain, Nicholson was appointed temporary brigadier general and became the driving force of the siege, compelling Wilson to mount the critical assault when he judged the moment to be right.

During this period Hodson, now an acting major, had two jobs, for as well as commanding his own regiment in its role of protecting the rear of the Delhi Field Force he also acted as Wilson's intelligence officer. In the middle of August the rebels at last made an attempt to cut the flow of reinforcements from the Punjab by assembling a 2,000-strong force of infantry, cavalry and guns at the town of Rohtak, approximately 45 miles north of Delhi. Hodson's Horse, 233 strong but reinforced by 103 troopers from the Guides Cavalry and 25 men of the Jhind Horse, were sent out to deal with them. Hodson found the enemy holding a strong defensive position and decided to lure them out with a feigned retreat. Cheering wildly and waving their swords, the rebels swarmed out in pursuit of the trotting lines. Once he was satisfied that they were thoroughly disordered, Hodson ordered 'Threes about and at 'em!' He wrote to his wife:

> Never was there such a scatter! I launched five parties at them, each under an officer, and in they went, cutting and firing into the very thick of them. We cut down upwards of fifty in as many seconds. The remainder flew back into the town, as if not the Guides and Hodson's Horse, but death and the devil, were at their heels!

It seems that some at least of the rebels rallied and sallied forth again, but were dispersed and scattered by a second charge, after which Hodson made the citizens of the town feed and supply his men and horses.

The details of the siege and storming of Delhi do not directly form part of this narrative. Suffice it to say that, in spite of every effort made by the rebels, effective siege batteries were emplaced before the city walls and by the evening of 13 September had created suitable breaches for an assault. This was delivered the following morning and led by Nicholson, who was to lose his life in the fighting. All such assaults were desperate affairs, but when the mere 5,000 attackers faced 30,000 defenders who had nothing to lose it was bound to be especially so. The difference was that the British regiments fought in a spirit of vindictive fury that was usually alien to their nature. The massacre and mutilation of their women and children left no room in their hearts for mercy, so they sought only to kill and kill again, caring not whether they died themselves. Days of savage street fighting followed, sometimes inflamed when stocks of drink were discovered, until the streets, gardens and houses of the city were strewn with bodies, the whole nightmare scene being clouded with the acrid smoke of burning buildings. By the 20th all organised resistance had ended and the remnant of Bakht Khan's troops had either fled to the south or across the Jumna River. By then, the 3,000 men of the assault force remaining on their feet were engaged in systematic looting; the official Prize Agents managed to amass property valued at £750,000 for ultimate distribution, but the probability is that even greater sums remained in the troops' possession.

On 14 September the cavalry, including Hodson's Horse and a battery of horse artillery, had covered the right flank of the attack to counter a sortie by the rebels through the Kabul and Lahore Gates, aimed at the British position on The Ridge. The battery fired until the barrels of its guns glowed, but the cavalry, unable to charge because of walled gardens to its front and unwilling to retire because that would expose the guns to capture, could only sit and endure a hail of gunfire and musketry, not only from the rebels facing them but also from the western city walls. It was a stern test of discipline that was costly in men and horses alike. The situation eased slightly when the Moree Bastion and the Kabul Gate were stormed by the assault columns from within, but it was not finally resolved until the Guides Infantry and a Baluchi battalion arrived to push the enemy back through the Lahore Gate.

There was little part cavalry could play in street fighting, but on 19 September Hodson, accompanied by his second-in-command, Lieutenant Charles MacDowell, led a troop in a sweep through the suburbs of Kishengunge and Telewara. They cut down some 50 rebels on the way, but of far greater importance was the discovery that the enemy's main encampment had been abandoned, providing proof that at last the mutineers' will had been broken. Hodson noticed that the nearest of the city gates was lying open and apparently unguarded. Suspecting a trap, the troop cautiously made their way through with firearms cocked. It was not a trap, and shortly afterwards they came across a heap of looted treasure from which two bottles of beer poked provocatively. 'We uncorked and drank the Queen's health at once,' wrote Hodson to his wife.

His network of agents was already active, enabling him to recover the colours, mess plate and drums of the mutinied regiments, abandoned by the rebels in their flight. On 21 September he was informed that the King of Delhi and his family, having refused to withdraw with Bakht Khan's army, had taken refuge in the tomb of the Emperor Hamayun, some six miles outside the city. Such a fugitive could not be allowed to remain at liberty, for, as Hodson commented, 'His name would have been a tocsin which would have raised the whole of Hindustan.' Wilson agreed, but pointed out that after a week's remorseless fighting the troops were utterly exhausted. However, after some discussion he permitted Hodson to take 50 of his own troopers and guarantee the King and Queen their lives and personal safety, provided they surrendered at once, this being considered the only way by which their persons could be secured.

Hamayun's Tomb was a huge building crowned by several white domes, located in a large walled garden that was entered through a fine arched gateway. The structure had been built among the ruins of a much older city that had been abandoned when the Moghuls built their splendid new capital on its northern edge. The surrounding terrain therefore consisted of numerous overgrown, fragmented ruins in which lurked thousands of armed rebels who, while they not prepared to accompany Bakht Khan's retreating army, were still desperate and dangerous men. It was across this landscape, where an ambush could be expected every step of the way, that Hodson and MacDowell led their men.

Arriving at the great entrance arch, Hodson sent some of his agents into the tomb with Wilson's offer. The troop was surrounded by a vast and growing crowd of armed men, filling the hot air with the hum of their hostile muttering. Stony-eyed, the big, bearded, scarlet-turbaned Sikh troopers stared impassively ahead, their bored horses occasionally snorting or pawing the ground. For fully two hours nothing happened. Hodson later admitted that he had never known such nerve-wracking suspense, although he gave no hint of it.

At length the agents reappeared to report that the King would surrender only to Hodson personally. Hodson drew his sword and, alone, pushed his mount through the crowd to the archway, where a group of armed retainers stood. He shouted that the Government had promised that the prisoners' safety would be guaranteed. The attitude of the retainers seemed to relax. Queen Zeenat Mahal emerged in a closed *palki*, followed by the frail figure of the King and one of his sons, Jumma Bukht. Hodson, coldly respectful, received the surrender of their swords, and the party began its journey back to the city. It was followed for much of the way by the huge crowd, now largely silent, although the atmosphere remained potentially explosive. As the city walls came into view, however, the crowd began to disperse. At the Lahore Gate the Duty Officer asked who the prisoner was. Hodson's relief was evident in his airy answer: 'Only the King of Delhi!' The gate guard wanted to cheer him but Hodson cut them short, commenting that the King would take it as a compliment to himself.

Having handed over his prisoners to the civil authority at the Red Fort, Hodson made his report to Wilson, who expressed his delight. Remarking that he had not expected to see him or MacDowell again, he permitted the two officers to retain the magnificent swords that had been surrendered to them. Hodson then told him that two of the King's sons, Mirza Moghul and Mirza Kishere Sultanet, were also said to be hiding in Hamayun's Tomb, together with a grandson, Mirza Abu Bukht. Apart from having exercised ineffective command of the rebel army for a time, Mirza Moghul had connived at and actually witnessed the atrocities committed when the mutiny spread to Delhi, as had his brother. The young Mirza Abu Bukht was an even nastier specimen, who, even when emotions were running high, had disgusted his own people; one contemporary Indian source accuses him of lopping the limbs of European children in front of their mothers and much else besides. Hodson argued that these men could still provide a focus for the mutineers and asked permission to bring them in. Wilson, recognising that Hodson had already got away with one colossal piece of bluff and might not escape a second time, was reluctant to let him go. After a prolonged argument he gave way, passing the decidedly Delphic comment on the Princes, 'But don't let *me* be bothered with them!' That, of course, left the matter open for Hodson to interpret in a number of ways.

Once more, Hodson and MacDowell set off, accompanied by 100 of their men, including some of the Afghan troop and by a captured nephew of the King who was to act as a go-between. Halting some way short of the tomb, around which a huge armed mob began to gather immediately, Hodson despatched the nephew to tell the Princes that he had been sent to take them back to Delhi, dead or alive. Thirty minutes later the man returned to ask whether their lives would be spared if they gave themselves up. Hodson replied that he was only prepared to accept their unconditional surrender. The messenger disappeared again, but clearly informed the mob what was afoot as the Muslims among the rebels began to shout for the Princes to lead them in an attack on Hodson and his men. Once again, tension began to mount, for, faced as he was by thousands of armed men, Hodson was hardly in a position to take them by force. The two officers began debating the few dubious options remaining to them. At this point the King's nephew emerged again to say that the Princes were coming out; effete as they were, they were unprepared to take the risks involved in personal combat, as their followers wished.

Hodson sent ten men forward to bring out the prisoners and ordered MacDowell to deploy the remainder in line across the road, with clear instructions to shoot the Princes immediately at the first sign of trouble. The Princes, dressed in their finery, appeared in a small bullock cart, escorted by five troopers on either side. Hodson went forward to meet them. Formal bows were exchanged, but the crowd was now turning ugly and began to surge towards the cart. Hodson signalled MacDowell to bring the troop forward until it was between the mob and the cart, then accompanied the Princes some way along the Delhi road. Meanwhile the line of troopers had begun edging their mounts forward, slowly pushing the rebels back in the manner of police horses marshalling a football crowd. The situation remained unbearably tense. Hodson returned, having told the Princes' escort to make the best possible speed towards the city. Appreciating that there were limits to the speed that could be expected from a bullock cart, he decided to buy as much time as possible by keeping the mob fully occupied.

> They retired on Hamayun's Tomb, and step by step we followed them [wrote MacDowell later]. Inside they went up the steps, and formed up in the immense *harden* [open space] inside. The entrance to this was through an arch, up steps. Leaving the men outside, Hodson and myself (I stuck to him throughout), with four men, rode up the steps into the arch, when he called upon them to lay down their arms. There was a murmur. He reiterated the command, and, God knows why, they commenced doing it.

It was an absurd situation, but Hodson possessed immense personal charisma and knew exactly how to handle a crowd. Slowly but steadily swords and firearms clattered on to growing piles. MacDowell fully expected to be attacked by fanatics, but nothing happened and at length he emulated his commander's icy calm by pulling out his pipe and puffing at it in apparent contentment. After two hours over 1,000 men had been disarmed and Hodson judged that the prisoners' cart was well on its way. Leaving the piled weapons under guard, the rest of the troop set off on the road to Delhi.

'Well, Mac,' said Hodson, 'we've got them at last!'

The two began to chuckle, but their relief was short-lived. They had been followed closely by the mob from Hamayun's Tomb, many of whom had not been disarmed. Furthermore, by the time they caught up with the cart even more armed rebels had emerged from the ancient city ruins. As yet no one had struck a blow or fired a shot, but the escort was being jostled and it seemed that a determined rescue attempt was about to be made. MacDowell estimated that they were surrounded by some 6,000 rebels and recalled that he had never been so frightened in his life.

'What shall we do with them?' asked Hodson, indicating the prisoners as the troop closed up. 'I think we had better shoot them here. We shall never get them in.'

His Sikh troopers shouted their approval, as did the Afghans, who, while they were of the same religion as the prisoners, had nothing but contempt for cowards. Hodson ordered the Princes to get out of the cart and strip to their loincloths, then told them to get back aboard. The mob, no longer controlling events, fell back in awed silence. Taking a carbine from one of his men, Hodson shot each of the prisoners dead in turn. The spell was broken when a prominent member of the crowd suddenly began running away. Instinctively, MacDowell and one of the troopers went after him. After he had been ridden down he was recognised as the King's favourite eunuch, who had been guilty of many atrocities on his own account, and who had probably orchestrated the botched rescue attempt. The trooper ran him through with his sword.

The cart continued on its way. Once it had reached Delhi the bodies were taken from it and displayed for three days on the spot where the rebels had committed most of their atrocities. Many approved whole-heartedly of Hodson's action, but others, while glad that the mutineers had been deprived of a natural focus, thought that he had been high-handed and should have waited for the sanction of the judicial process. The King himself was tried and found guilty of the murder of 49 Christians in Delhi but was accorded clemency by Lord Canning, the Governor-General, and spent his few remaining days in exile in Rangoon. It is safe to say that no such mercy would have been granted to the Princes had they lived to stand trial. Even so, the merits or otherwise of their summary execution by Hodson would be keenly debated throughout the Victorian era. Shortly after the event Hodson expressed his own thoughts in a letter to his wife:

In twenty-four hours I disposed of the principal members of the house of Timur the Tarter [Tamerlane]. I am not cruel, but I confess I did rejoice at the opportunity of ridding the earth of these wretches. I intended to have had them hung, but when it came to the question of 'they' or 'us' I had no time for deliberation.

It is left to the reader to decide how he would have acted in Hodson's position.

Although some garrisons mutinied even after the capture of Delhi, the fall of the city and the end of the Moghul dynasty were mortal blows from which the Great Mutiny never really recovered. Furthermore, substantial reinforcements were already on their way from England, including a high proportion of Crimean War veterans, tilting the scales further against the rebels although much hard fighting remained and nothing could be taken for granted.

Much of the Delhi Field Force, including Hodson's Horse, was subsequently employed in putting down the rising in the state of Oudh, which was the homeland of many of the mutineers. In the capital, Lucknow, a small garrison had held out in the British Residency against incredible odds until, in November, a relief force had ensured its safe evacuation after heavy fighting. In the spring of 1858 an army under General Sir Colin Campbell, the Commander-in-Chief, was formed to finally wrest the city from the rebels.

Hodson's adjutant was Lieutenant Hugh Gough, originally from the Company's 1st Bengal European Light Cavalry. During the November relief operations Gough had distinguished himself by leading a charge across a swamp and capturing two guns from a large force of the enemy, despite the fact that his horse was wounded twice and he received a number of sword cuts through his turban. He describes Hodson's Horse at the time as 'a full-blown regiment, [its] men better equipped, clothed and drilled, and horses of a better stamp, with decent saddlery and accoutrements'. In his memoirs he recounts an action fought by the regiment on 25 February 1858 at a place called Jellalabad, when it was opposed by a mass of infantry and two guns:

We advanced and charged. We got well into them, and the whole affair seemed over. The rearmost gun was in our possession but somehow, owing to the ardour of the charge and pursuit, our regiment got quite out of hand, lost all formation and scattered; and they [the enemy], seeing our condition, regained their formation as we lost ours. It looked sadly probable that Hodson's Horse would in their turn retreat. Hodson at this crisis managed to get a few brave spirits together, but not more than a dozen. Fortunately, I too was able to rally our men to a certain extent, who seeing our supports [the 7th Hussars] coming up, now came on with a will and, charging the remaining gun, scattered the enemy in all directions.

What Gough does not say is that for his part in this action, and the action the previous November, he was awarded the Victoria Cross. That part of the citation relating to the fight at Jellalabad comments that 'He set a magnificent example to the regiment when ordered to charge the enemy's guns. He engaged himself in a series of single combats until at length he was disabled by a musket ball through the leg while charging two sepoys with fixed bayonets.' Like Hodson, Gough, who would become a general and a knight, was one of those rare individuals who become possessed by the joy of battle.

Campbell began the siege of Lucknow on 2 March, and much hard, bitter, close-quarter fighting was needed before the last pockets of resistance were eliminated three weeks later. On 11 March the 93rd Highlanders were fighting their way through a large palace complex known as the Begum Kothi. In one of the buildings a party under Sergeant William Forbes-Mitchell cornered a group of well-armed rebels in a room. Forbes-Mitchell, unwilling to risk the lives of his men needlessly, placed some of them to cover the door and sent others to fetch fused gunpowder bags that could be flung into the room. At this point Hodson appeared. There was no need for him to be there and this was a purely infantry matter, but he was itching to get into a fight. Forbes-Mitchell explained the steps he had taken, but Hodson paid no attention. Although the sergeant tried to restrain him, he rushed to the doorway and was promptly shot through the chest. He fell back and was able to mutter 'Oh my wife!' before he began choking on his own blood. Forbes-Mitchell had him carried away on a stretcher, but there was no hope. Shortly afterwards the powder bags arrived. After two or three has exploded in the room the stunned enemy came staggering out, being bayoneted in turn without loss.

So died William Hodson, an undoubted hero but one whose reputation would be dogged by controversy for two generations. His name, however, was to live on in his regiment, for when the Indian Army was reorganised after the Mutiny it was decided that recruits would be drawn only from the sub-continent's martial races and Hodson's Horse became part of the regular establishment. By the end of 1858 the regiment was large enough to be split in two, becoming the 9th and 10th Bengal Cavalry in 1861. Three years later the latter became the 10th Bengal Lancers and in 1878 was granted the title of 10th (The Duke of Cambridge's Own) Regiment of Bengal Lancers. In 1886 the 9th became the 9th Regiment of Bengal Lancers. Both regiments again changed their name in 1903, becoming respectively the 9th Hodson's Horse and the 10th Duke of Cambridge's Own Lancers (Hodson's Horse). When the cavalry arm contracted in 1922 they merged to become the 4th Duke of Cambridge's Own Lancers (Hodson's Horse). Following Independence and the division of the old Indian Army between India and Pakistan, regiments shed the royal honorifics from their titles but, being proud of their traditions, tended to retain such names as Hodson's to maintain a link with their founders.

Major General Sir Hugh Rose

Winner of impossible victories

I N THE STATES OF CENTRAL INDIA the Great Mutiny did not begin until June 1857 and was complicated by the participation of some of the princely rulers and their troops. Against this, others among the rulers remained staunchly loyal and the causes of unrest that had torn apart the Bengal army did not apply to the Company's Bombay and Madras armies to anything like the same degree. In fact, relations between the Bombay and Bengal armies were characterised by mutual dislike and jealousy. In the Bombay army, the question of caste was considered to be of far less importance and promotion was based on merit rather than seniority, and in consequence it was a far more efficient organisation.

The mutinies, both among the Bengal and state troops, involved the usual massacres of British administrators, officers and their families. Many of the rebels then headed north to Delhi, but the remainder were present in such overwhelming numbers that the scattered government forces could do little beyond consolidating their strength and containing the enemy as best they could. Even when consolidation had been achieved at Mhow, the breaking of the monsoon prevented active operations by the newly formed Central India Field Force for several weeks.

The commander of the field force was Major General Sir Hugh Rose. Born in 1801, he was the son of the British minister to the Prussian court and was educated at a Prussian military cadet school before entering the British Army in 1820. Now aged 56, Rose had seen active service during the Turkish-Egyptian war of 1841, but much of his subsequent career had been spent in diplomatic posts, first as consul-general in Syria, then as principal secretary to the British Embassy in Constantinople. Because of this background he had been appointed British Liaison Officer to the French headquarters in the Crimea, a difficult task which he had performed well. On the outbreak of the Mutiny he had volunteered for service in India, reaching Bombay on 19 September and being given command of the Bombay army's Poona Division. His appointment as Commander of the Central India Field Force on 16 December was not universally welcomed. He did not possess the fighting reputation of Sir Colin Campbell and as a field commander he had little experience. Furthermore, the snobbery between the Indian and Home establishments was by no means one-sided, for new arrivals in India were expected to spend their first year in the sub-continent learning the 'Indian' way of doing things. Again, his apparently poor physique suggested that he would be unable to withstand the rigours of a campaign. He was to surprise everyone, for not only was he a great deal tougher than he looked, he was intelligent, competent, vigorous, dashing and extremely determined. 'When your enemy is in the open,' he told his officers, 'go straight for him and keep him moving; and when behind ramparts, still go at him and cut off [his] chances of retreat if possible; pursue him if escaping or escaped.'

At Mhow he divided his force into two brigades, each of which was really a small battle group. The 1st Brigade, under Brigadier General Charles Stuart, consisted of half the 14th Light Dragoons, one troop of the 3rd Bombay Light Cavalry, two regiments of the Hyderabad Contingent Cavalry, the 86th Regiment (later the Royal Irish Rifles), the 25th Regiment Bombay Native Infantry, the 1st Troop Bombay Horse Artillery, two field batteries of the Hyderabad Contingent and some Madras Sappers and Miners. The 2nd Brigade, under Brigadier General Charles Steuart (confusingly), consisted of half the 14th Light Dragoons, part of the 3rd Bombay Light Cavalry, one regiment of the Hyderabad Contingent Cavalry, the 3rd Bombay European Regiment, the 24th Bombay Native Infantry, a battery of the Bombay Horse Artillery, a field battery of the Hyderabad Contingent, a company of Madras Sappers and Miners and a siege train.

With this small force, which, as can be seen, was particularly short of infantry, Rose took the field on 6 January 1858 against an enemy who outnumbered him many times over. His ultimate objective was the elimination of the rebels in the state of Jhansi, who posed a serious threat to British operations further north. Of more immediate urgency, however, was the relief of the garrison of Saugur, which had been besieged for seven months and had been only able to hold out because the 31st Bengal Native Infantry had remained true to their salt. Before this could be accomplished, the fortress of Rathgur, built on a hill overlooking the town of the same name, would have to be captured. On 26 January the siege train began battering away at its walls and three days later had created a breach. At this point a force commanded by the rebel Rajah of Banpur was observed closing in on the British rear with flags flying and bands playing. Rose instructed the siege guns to maintain their fire and detached a force of cavalry, horse artillery and infantry to meet the threat, but contact had hardly been made before the rebels took to their heels. The garrison of the fortress, witnessing the débâcle, slipped away during the night. Having been informed that they had joined the Rajah's men and were holding a position across the River Bina near a village called Barodia, some fifteen miles from Saugur, Rose set off after them with most of the cavalry, the horse artillery, the 3rd Europeans and the sappers. During the afternoon of 30 January he fought his way across the river and through the village, putting the enemy to flight.

Saugur was relieved on 3 February amid understandable scenes of jubilation. In this out-of-the-way place the inhabitants had become used to seeing individual white faces, but the sight of entire regiments of them was as much a source of wonder as were the huge siege guns drawn by elephants. Rose's next task was to clear the countryside east of the town, including the fortress of Garrakota, some 25 miles distant. This had been designed by French engineers and was so strong that, forty years earlier, a British force far larger than Rose's had failed to take it. It was now held by two mutinous regiments who had further strengthened the defences with outlying earthworks. Despite this, the rebels were in no mood to fight, for, after being worsted in an artillery exchange, they decamped during the night of 11 February, about 100 of them being cut down by the cavalry. It was a curious aspect of the Great Mutiny that, despite all that had happened, some of the rebels still took great pride in their former calling: one of those killed at Garrakota was found still wearing his scarlet sepoy jacket to which was pinned a British medal with two clasps.

Rose was anxious to advance on Jhansi, the epicentre of the rebellion in Central India. He had, however, to bide his time at Saugur until he was relieved by a column under Brigadier General George Whitlock that was marching by easy stages from Jubbulpur. Rose was infuriated by Whitlock's leisurely progress, but at least it gave him time to collect adequate supplies and put together sufficient transport. It also gave the rebels the breathing space they needed, for when the Central India Field Force renewed its advance on 26 February they had constructed strong defences in the passes through the mountain range lying across its path.

In particular, the Malthon Pass was so strongly held that any attempt to force it would obviously have resulted in heavy casualties. Rose decided to feint at the Malthon with a small force while he attacked the Madanpur Pass with his main body, hoping to gain access to the plateau beyond. The Madanpur was a narrow gorge between hills covered with dense jungle. The pass itself was commanded by guns on the heights and by batteries in the gorge, while the jungle was thick with rebel skirmishers. Thus when troops mounted their first attack on 4 March they were met by a storm of fire. Rose's horse was killed under him and there was a general retirement. The attack was renewed, and this time the 3rd Europeans and the Hyderabad infantry routed the enemy out of their positions and through the town of Madanpur itself. The effects of the victory were astonishing. The rebels holding the Malthon Pass, in danger of being outflanked, hastily abandoned it, as they did every fortified place between the pass and Jhansi save for the fort of Chanderi, which was taken by Stuart's 1st Brigade after a four-day siege.

Physically, few soldiers have ever been asked to endure the ordeal of the Central India Field Force. The temperature had already soared beyond 100°F in the shade, while strong winds sand-blasted faces with the grit thrown up by the marching columns, flaying the skin and making the eyes unbearably sore. The troops marched and fought in their shirtsleeves, with a neck protector known as a havelock attached to their white-covered forage caps. After dusk the temperature did not fall much, but for the lucky ones there might be a bottle of beer, wrapped in wet cloth to cool it by evaporation during the day's march.

Rose had reached a point only fourteen miles from Jhansi when he received positive orders to go the assistance of the loyal Rajah of Chark-

123

heri, who was being besieged by Tantia Topi, the ablest of the rebel commanders. Charkheri lay some 80 miles distant and Rose doubted whether he could arrive in time to be of any assistance. Furthermore, he considered that the capture of Jhansi would not only strike at the heart of the loose rebel confederacy in Central India but also destroy the prestige of its ruler, the Rani, who had done much to incite rebellion across a wide area. As the commander on the spot, Rose believed that, regrettable as might be the loss of an ally, Jhansi held the greater priority, and, having expressed his reasons in writing, he decided to disobey his orders. Happily, this demonstration of good rather than average generalship was accepted and approved by his superiors.

Even before the investment of Jhansi had been completed on 22 March, it was apparent that the fortress would prove a very hard nut to crack. The citadel, of massive construction, towered on a granite rock above the city, which was itself girdled by strong and well designed masonry walls with excellent fields of fire. These defences mounted 40 guns and were manned by a 12,000-strong garrison. It was true that the enemy's morale was shaky, but the Rani's formidable presence ensured that her men remained at their posts. Jhansi had become one of the Company's dependent native states in 1817, but when the Rajah died without issue in 1853 the young Rani requested that the succession should pass to her adopted son. As that was not permitted under the law of lapse, the state was formally annexed. Despite being awarded a handsome pension, the Rani remained extremely bitter towards the British in general and the Company in particular. When the 12th Bengal Native Infantry and the 14th Irregular Cavalry mutinied at Jhansi on 4 June 1857 she provided an active and charismatic leadership for them as well as disaffected elements across the whole of Central India. It was said that she had reneged upon a safe conduct granted to the Jhansi garrison's British officers and their families, who were savagely massacred within days of the mutiny, and that she personally mutilated her male prisoners in the most obvious way, but these may have been rumours generated in the overheated atmosphere of the times. Many British officers serving with the Central India Field Force had a sincere regard for her, enhanced by the fact that she dressed and fought as one of her own troopers. On Rose's approach she had asked Tantia Topi for his assistance.

Rose's siege batteries began firing on 25 March. The Rani conducted a vigorous defence, repairing the damage to the town walls by night and re-mounting guns which were thought to have been silenced. When a breach was finally made it was quickly closed with a stout stockade. Rose, worried by his rapidly shrinking supplies of ammunition, decided that he would have to mount an assault very shortly, but during the night of 30 March a large bonfire was observed some miles away. It announced the arrival of Tantia Topi, who, having captured Charkheri and received reinforcements, was marching to the Rani's relief with no fewer than 22,000 men and 28 guns.

The tiny Central India Field Force was now sandwiched between the defenders of Jhansi and Tantia Topi's horde. Rose dared not strip his siege lines lest the Rani's garrison fall on his rear, and he dared not retire since this would be tantamount to a defeat in the field. He decided to do what he had done at Rathgur, namely keep his siege guns firing and meet the relieving army with such force as he could muster. This amounted to only 430 men of the 3rd Europeans, 700 sepoys of the 24th Native Infantry and the Hyderabad Contingent, the 240-strong 14th Light Dragoons and 200 Hyderabad cavalrymen, plus sixteen field guns and three siege guns withdrawn from the lines—a total of about 1,500 men with which to oppose 22,000. It might be wondered, perhaps, why troops willingly accepted such odds during the battles of the Great Mutiny. The desire for revenge formed an obvious part of their motivation, but equally there was the understanding that while the rebels could afford numerous defeats, small columns like the Central India Field Force could not afford one. In the event of such a defeat, there was really nowhere for the survivors to go, as the nearest help lay many miles distant across a potentially hostile countryside. The will to win, therefore, was compounded by the will to survive to an even greater extent than usual.

Knowing that Tantia Topi would cross the Betwa River by the two fords closest to Jhansi, Rose further subdivided his slender resources by sending Stuart with a detachment to cover the lower of the two. By means of a feigned withdrawal, he enticed a large part of the enemy army across the upper ford during the afternoon of 31 March so that by dusk Tantia Topi had formed his first line of battle. The British slept on their arms, with a battery and two troops of the 14th Light Dragoons on the left, the

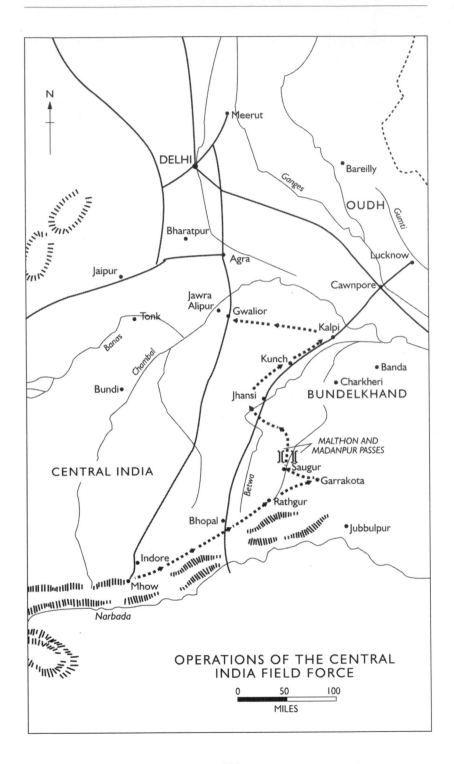

N

Meerut

DELHI

Bareilly

OUDH

Ganges

Bharatpur

Agra

Lucknow

Jaipur

Cawnpore

Jawra
Alipur

Gwalior

Kalpi

Tonk

Banas

Chambal

Kunch

Banda

Bundi

Charkheri

Jhansi

BUNDELKHAND

MALTHON AND
MADANPUR PASSES

CENTRAL INDIA

Saugur

Garrakota

Betwa

Rathgur

Bhopal

Jubbulpur

Indore

Mhow

Narbada

OPERATIONS OF THE CENTRAL
INDIA FIELD FORCE

0   50   100

MILES

infantry and three siege guns in the centre, and one troop each of Dragoons and Hyderabad Cavalry and a troop of horse artillery on the right.

Rose had intended to attack at first light, but in this the enemy forestalled him. As Tantia Topi's horde surged forward, covered by the fire of its guns, Rose ordered his infantry to lie down in dead ground. His own guns made little impression on the dense ranks but, at the critical moment, he ordered his whole line to charge. This was the last thing the enemy expected the little force to do, and its dramatic consequences are described by Corporal G. C. Stent of the 14th Light Dragoons:

> It was a glorious sight to see them thundering along, headed by the General and Captain Prettejohn, the latter of whom was bareheaded, and who fought and shouted like a demon. One minute, and they were among the enemy, and all that was to be seen was a confused mass of flashing swords and bayonets, struggling men and horses, and hoarse shouts of rage. From this seething, struggling mass our men emerged victorious. The rebels were thoroughly routed in this charge, and turned and fled; were rallied, formed up again, to be again charged and routed; and yet again, only to undergo the same infliction, losing all their guns, and finally bolting in the greatest confusion, pursued by our men, who cut up great numbers of them, stopping only at the River Betwa from sheer exhaustion. Many of the enemy who escaped our swords were drowned in attempting to cross the river; the whole of the ground passed over by our men was strewed [sic] with their bodies, and at the lowest estimate it was calculated that 1,500 of them must have been slain, and no doubt the wounded were at least as many more.

At the lower ford, Stuart had also counter-attacked, with similar results. The pursuit continued across the river until, in desperation, Tantia Topi set fire to the tinder-dry bush and escaped behind the flames. The decisive Battle of the Betwa had cost Rose nineteen killed and 66 wounded.

On 3 April the infantry stormed the breach in the walls of Jhansi. To British eyes, the massacre which had taken place in the town the previous year ranked second only in frightfulness to the horrors which had been so notoriously inflicted on their womenfolk and children at Cawnpore. No mercy was therefore shown during the subsequent three days of street fighting, those who attempted to escape being ruthlessly hunted down as they tried to break through the cordon of cavalry picquets. At the end of it, Jhansi had become a city of the dead, a vast charnel house that had been sacked, looted and virtually destroyed from end to end. There was little to choose between rebel atrocity and British revenge.

British casualties during the storming amounted to 343 killed and wounded. Of the Rani, who had taken an active part in the defence, there was no sign. During the early hours of 4 April Rose learned that at midnight she and her escort had left by the north gate and, using their local knowledge, worked their way through the picquets. Guessing that she was heading for Kalpi, 103 miles to the north-east, he sent a cavalry detachment under Lieutenant Dowker after her. The detachment caught up with her at Bhander, twenty miles from Jhansi, where her escort died almost to a man to cover her escape. During the running fight Dowker spotted her, riding a grey and surrounded by four bodyguards, and gave chase. He was gaining rapidly when he was unhorsed by a cut from one of the escort, receiving a severe wound that would have proved mortal had not his holstered revolver absorbed much of the blow's force. The Rani reached Kalpi the following evening after being twenty hours in the saddle, and was joined there by Tantia Topi.

Rose next intended marching on Kalpi, where the rebels had established a large arsenal capable of supporting them in the field indefinitely. Unfortunately, his men were exhausted by continuous marching and fighting under the Indian sun and were in urgent need of rest. This was a comparative term, for so unsettled was the area that daily sorties had to be mounted against the armed gangs that infested it. On the other hand, a steady stream of reinforcements was reaching India and his recent losses were made good by the arrival of several companies of the Highland Light Infantry. By the time he got moving again on 25 April the temperature had climbed to 117°F and was still rising. As the first part of the route passed through a wide zone of semi-desert, with wells eight to ten miles apart, men and animals began to suffer severely. Cases of heatstroke, sometimes fatal, began to increase rapidly.

Meanwhile at Kalpi, Tantia Topi and the Rani had been joined by Rao Sahib, the nephew of the Nana Sahib, the rebels' nominal commander-in-chief, and by the Nawab of Banda, who brought with them every man they could muster. The rebel army was re-organised, trained and disciplined to prevent another débâcle similar to that of the Betwa. It was decided, probably at the Rani's suggestion, to meet Rose at Kunch, 42 miles south of Kalpi, where a defeat with a desert at his back would almost certainly result in the destruction of the Central India Field

Force. The choice of Kunch offered the rebels an excellent chance of success, for the approaches to it lay through a difficult area of temples, woods and gardens, while the town itself possessed a wall in front of which additional entrenchments had been constructed. Despite the Rani's obvious abilities, she was not popular with her fellow leaders and command was once again given to Tantia Topi.

Having thoroughly reconnoitred the position, Rose formed the opinion that Tantia Topi had concentrated too much of his strength in the centre and that the enemy flanks could be turned by mounting converging attacks by both his brigades. Following a fourteen-mile approach march made under cover of darkness, these went in during the morning of 7 May and so unsettled the rebels that after an hour's fighting they were in full retreat along to the road to Kalpi. At first the withdrawal was orderly and covered by a mutinied regiment that remained perfectly steady, firing and retiring by sections as it had been taught. Such men evoked professional respect, and even a degree of admiration, but not pity. Three troops of the 14th Light Dragoons rode over them after making a difficult charge across ploughed ground, cutting them down almost to a man. A fourth troop dealt likewise with an attempt to form a fresh rearguard. The enemy column now became a jostling mob that abandoned its guns and was pursued ruthlessly for seven miles. Rebel losses during the battle were estimated at 600 killed and fifteen guns captured. British casualties amounted to 62 killed and wounded, but so exhausted were the men that Rose was compelled to allow them 24 hours' rest. He was himself so seriously affected by the heat that, while he had taken part in the pursuit, he had fallen from his horse four times during the day. The surgeon poured cold water over him and provided restoratives, enabling him to carry on. His dogged perseverance was noted and commented upon by the troops: 'He is a most determined, plucky fellow,' wrote one of his junior officers.

The march from Kunch to Kalpi was a nightmare. Heat exhaustion affected even the 25th Native Infantry, to the extent that at one time half the regiment had fallen out. The British infantry were in an even worse state, and even the cavalry suffered severely. 'The prostration of the whole force had become a matter of mathematical calculation,' wrote Rose. 'So many hours' sun laid low so many men.' To offset this he received reinforcements that had been operating with another column across the River Jumna. These included the 88th Regiment (The Connaught Rangers), and a Camel Corps consisting of 200 men of the Rifle Brigade and 100 Sikh policemen. Skirmishing was a regular occurrence. On 16 May the baggage train was attacked by a strong force of rebels including 1,000 cavalry, 4,000 infantry and several guns. The train consisted of thousands of bullocks, camels, elephants and mules, and hundreds of rickety country carts, all laden with ammunition and stores of every kind, including pontoon bridges and scaling ladders. It stretched for many miles, moved very slowly, and was encumbered with large numbers of sick in dhoolies or ambulances or making their way on foot. Despite the obvious advantages which the rebels possessed, the baggage guard commander, Major Forbes of the 3rd Bombay Light Cavalry, kept them at a distance with only 400 cavalrymen, 200 infantry and two guns at his disposal, facing them down repeatedly with aggressive movements.

Under the direction of the Rao Sahib a series of five defence lines had been constructed south of Kalpi. These were deliberately based on a series of ravines that ran down to the bank of the Jumna, the intention being that they would deprive Rose's artillery and cavalry of their mobility. If it had attempted to fight its way through such a defence in depth, the Central India Field Force would undoubtedly have sustained very serious losses. In the event, the rebels threw away their advantage by themselves attacking on 22 May. Believing that the British were prostrate with heat, they swarmed out of their trenches at 10:00, when the sun was climbing to its brazen zenith. Although also under fire from the column across the Jumna, they pressed their assault with such determination that at one point they were within twenty yards of the guns. The battle seemed lost when at this critical moment Rose brought up 150 men of the Camel Corps. They dismounted behind a ridge and, with the general at their head, charged with the bayonet down the forward slope and into the startled enemy, who gave way at once. Fighting continued until dusk, but this unexpected rebuff seems to have knocked all the heart out of the rebels, whose attacks elsewhere had been contained with less difficulty.

Morning revealed that the rebel army had gone. While the cavalry and horse artillery carried out a pursuit lasting eight miles, Rose entered the now deserted town. The arsenal, situated in the fort, contained an ordnance factory, some 60,000 pounds of gunpowder, heaps of ammunition manufactured to a high standard, a clothing store piled high with Company and British uniforms, and even a large quantity of band instruments. As it had now completed the tasks it had been set, Sir Colin Campbell, the Commander-in-Chief, decided to break up the Central India Field Force. On 1 June Rose bade his troops farewell in a general order:

> Soldiers! You have marched more than a thousand miles and taken more than a hundred guns; you have forced your way through mountain passes and intricate jungles, and over rivers; you have captured the strongest forts, and beaten the enemy, no matter what the odds, wherever you met him; you have restored extensive districts to the Government, and peace and order now reign where before, for twelve months, were tyranny and rebellion; you have done all this, and you have never had a check. I thank you with all my sincerity for your bravery, your devotion, and your discipline.

All of which was perfectly true, but a little premature, for the enemy's fortunes had undergone a remarkable transformation. Following their defeat at Kalpi the rebel commanders, squabbling fiercely among themselves, had led what remained of their following into the state of Gwalior. There, the Company's Gwalior Contingent had already mutinied and there were grounds for believing that the loyal Maharajah Sindhia's army would also change sides given the chance. With the exception of his bodyguard, this is exactly what happened when Sindhia led out his troops to meet the rebels on 1 June, forcing him to flee to Agra. Suddenly, Tantia Topi was once again in possession of a large army, a fortress, an arsenal and ample supplies. A real danger therefore existed that he would receive further reinforcements from wavering rulers.

When fugitives reached Kalpi with the news on 4 June, the Central India Field Force had actually begun to disperse. Rose, worn out, was about to depart on leave, the sick had been sent off to a healthier environment and the Hyderabad troops had started to march home. 'This is getting past a joke!' was the comment of one staff officer, indulging in the national habit of understatement. As it was important that the rebels should be decisively defeated before the monsoon made movement impossible, Sir Colin Campbell reacted quickly, ordering three columns to converge on Gwalior. One, with siege artillery, would march south from

Agra; a second, consisting of a brigade of the Rajputana Field Force under Brigadier General M. W. Smith, would close in from the south; and Rose's re-formed Central India Field Force would converge from the east.

Rose halted the Hyderabad Contingent's homeward march and deployed it to cut off the rebels' line of retreat to the south. He then despatched troops along the road to Gwalior as soon as they were ready to march. Even by the standards of Central India, the summer heat had now become intolerable, the thermometer in one officer's tent bursting when it reached 130°, so all movement was carried out at night. On 16 June the Morar Cantonments, five miles east of Gwalior, were stormed and the enemy was driven back towards the city. The next day Brigadier Smith's column made its presence felt. During a cavalry combat at Kotah-ke-serai a trooper of the 8th Hussars is believed to have either shot or cut down one of his opponents, little realising that he just killed the Rani of Jhansi. The only two certainties are that she was dressed as a man and that her body was burned by her retainers that night. Her loss was a hammer blow from which the rebels never recovered.

Meanwhile, Rose continued to close in on Gwalior. On 19 June he succeeded in turning the enemy's left flank under cover of a diversionary attack and was soon in possession of the high ground overlooking the city. Below, thousands of rebels could be seen flinging away their weapons as their ranks disintegrated in panic. By evening Rose was in possession of the new town that had been built outside the city walls and had set up his headquarters in the Maharajah's palace. Next morning the old town was found to be deserted save for a few diehards who perished in bitter hand-to-hand fighting for possession of the dominant fortress. Rose sent his cavalry and the 2nd Brigade, now commanded by Brigadier General Robert Napier* in place of Brigadier General Steuart, who had been sent home on sick leave, in pursuit of the rebels. On 22 June Tantia Topi, who had managed to rally some 4,000 men, was cornered at Jawra Alipur. There was no fight left in the enemy, for when Napier launched a dashing attack with a mere 560 cavalrymen and a battery of horse artillery, they broke and fled, leaving behind 25 guns, all their ammunition,

*Later Field Marshal Lord Napier of Magdala.

elephants, tents, carts, baggage and up to 400 killed, the last mainly cut down during the pursuit.

The battle put an end to the campaign in Central India. Rose handed over command to Napier and departed for a well-earned leave. The Central India Field Force was disbanded, its various elements being redeployed to hunt down the armed gangs that were all that remained of the rebel armies. Order was not completely restored until the following year, although across ever widening areas it became possible to hand over responsibility for law and order to the police. After Jawra Alipore, Tantia Topi remained at large until the following April, when he was betrayed by a former confederate, tried and hanged. The Rao Sahib tried to evade detection by assuming the life of an ascetic in the jungles of the Punjab, but in 1862 he too was betrayed, tried and hanged.

Although Sir Hugh Rose was arguably the most capable British general to take the field during the Great Mutiny, the astonishing achievements of his Central India Field Force have not always been given the credit they deserve. Indeed, in some accounts of the Great Mutiny they are mentioned but briefly or not at all. The most probable reason is that contemporary public attention at home was concentrated on the savage battles around Delhi, Cawnpore and Lucknow, and upon the deeds of such men as Sir Colin Campbell, Sir Henry Havelock, William Hodson, Sir Henry Lawrence, John Nicholson and Sir James Outram. To most people Rose was an unknown quantity and Central India seemed to lie on the fringe of greater events. By the time details of his successes were being reported in the press many readers had become used to victories won against impossible odds and were inclined to take them for granted. In the matter of prize money, the Central India Field Force received a niggardly 400,000 rupees for all its efforts. In contrast, General Whitlock's column, which had relieved Rose at Saugur, had done comparatively little fighting but had secured the treasury of the disloyal Raos of Kirwi, containing no less than 4,300,000 rupees and much else besides, amounting to the biggest prize money ever taken in India. This was obviously unfair and, with the support of the Governor-General, the Commander-in-Chief and the Prime Minister, Rose entered into expensive and protracted litigation on behalf of his men. That he lost merely confirms that the law and justice are not always synonymous.

If the public at large knew little of Rose, in the enclosed circle of the Army his worth was fully recognised. In 1860 he received promotion to lieutenant general and became Commander-in-Chief of the Bombay army. Fear and lack of understanding had induced the events of the Great Mutiny, a terrible aberration in the normally tolerant and even amicable Anglo-Indian relationship, but now they lay in the past. It could never be forgotten that both sides had performed acts of which they had good reason to be ashamed, but there was a general movement towards reconciliation. India was now ruled by the Crown instead of the Company, the Indian Army had been thoroughly reorganised and was now recruited solely from the sub-continent's martial races, and an amnesty was declared for all rebels who had not been complicit in the murder of British subjects. The Raj had now entered the form it would retain until the granting of Independence some eighty years later. Proof that the arrangement suited both sides is that a population of 350 million required only 250,000 troops, less than a quarter of them British, as contingency aid for the civil power, and of these a majority were always stationed on or near the volatile North-West Frontier. Furthermore, during the Second World War, with Independence in sight, no fewer than two million Indians volunteered for service in the armed forces of the Crown.

In 1861 Rose succeeded Campbell as Commander-in-Chief India. As might be expected, he became responsible for several small campaigns on the Frontier, although his principal achievements lay in improving the health and welfare of his troops. The advent of railways, for example, permitted quicker deployment than had been possible in the past, and this enabled him to close down a number of the less healthy cantonments. He also encouraged regiments to found libraries and what he called 'refreshment rooms' where the troops could buy hot drinks, ginger beer, bread rolls and cold meats as well as play dominoes, chess and backgammon, but not cards.

In 1865 Rose became Commander-in-Chief Ireland, where he was created the 1st Baron Strathnairn of Strathnairn and Jhansi in 1866 and was promoted to general the following year. In 1870 he retired from active military life, but he was awarded his field marshal's baton seven years later. He died in 1885.

Major General
Benjamin H. Grierson
*The Union Cavalry commander
who rode across the confederacy*

B ENJAMIN HENRY GRIERSON'S roots were not altogether typical of those from which the Union Army drew its officers during
the Civil War. He was the second son of Robert and Mary Grierson,
quiet, small-town folk who had settled in Jacksonville, Illinois, during
1851. He displayed an early aptitude for music, which he taught for a
while in his youth, then moved to Merediosa on the Illinois River, where
he opened a store. He apparently had no liking for horses, sharing the
view of those who believe them to be dangerous at both ends and un-
comfortable in the middle. When the war broke out, therefore, his decision to join the 6th Illinois Cavalry was all the more curious—unless, as
may well be the case, he was determined to overcome this difficulty. That
he succeeded there is no doubt, for he was to spend the rest of his working life as a cavalryman. Likewise, his profound belief in the need to
abolish slavery would be reflected in his career.

Grierson joined his regiment as a captain. He was a little older and
more mature than many of his fellow officers, possessed an intelligent,
logical mind, was a thoughtful tactician, looked after his men's welfare
and was careful with their lives. Above all, he possessed the quality of
leadership. Within a year, he had become the regiment's commanding
officer.

By now, although sabres were still issued, the cavalry on both sides
placed greater reliance on their firearms than did their European counterparts, and often fought as mounted infantry. In April 1863 the 6th
Illinois Cavalry, brigaded with two more cavalry regiments, the 7th Illinois and 2nd Iowa, was in southern Tennessee. The overall situation in
the western theatre of war was that General U. S. Grant was about to

commence the operations that would ultimately result in the capture of the Confederate fortress of Vicksburg on the lower Mississippi. The first phase would involve his army crossing from the west bank of the river to the east, and to facilitate this he requested a series of diversions elsewhere that would tie down the enemy's reserves. One of these was designed to destroy the Confederate railway system serving Vicksburg and so prevent large quantities of munitions and other supplies reaching the fortress before it came under siege. The basis of the plan is outlined in a letter from Major General S. A. Hurlbut, commanding XVI Corps, to the Assistant Adjutant General in Washington:

> As the spring opened, I was daily more and more impressed with the feasibility of a plan, long entertained, of pushing a flying column of cavalry through the length of Mississippi, cutting the Southern Railroad. By consent and approval of General Grant, I prepared a system of movements along my entire line from Memphis to Corinth for the purpose of covering this cavalry dash. At the same time General Rosecrans proposed to me to cover a movement of 1,800 cavalry from Tuscumbia down into Alabama and Georgia. This did not interfere with my plan, but simply required extra force to be developed from Corinth.

The task fell to Grierson, who assumed command of the brigade, handing over the 6th Illinois to Lieutenant Colonel Prince. At first light on 17 April, under cover of a diversionary attack arranged by the corps commander to assist its passage through the enemy screen, the brigade, reinforced with an artillery battery, left La Grange, Tennessee, and entered Confederate territory. The day's march was uneventful, but the afternoon of the second brought the first contact with the enemy. To conceal the size of his force, Grierson decided to cross the Tallahatchee River at three separate points. At New Albany a squadron of the 7th Illinois under Major Graham found the bridge defended and came under fire. Deploying, the squadron drove off the bridge guard, who made a hasty attempt to set the structure ablaze. The flames were quickly extinguished and, having replaced some of the decking that had been removed, the squadron crossed. Two miles upstream the 6th Illinois and the remainder of the 7th crossed by a ford, then proceeded south along the Pontotoc road, spending a rain-lashed night encamped on a plantation. The 2nd Iowa, commanded by Colonel Edward Hatch, forded the river four miles beyond. During the afternoon, near the hamlet of Chesterville, the regiment encountered a 200-strong band of rebels calling themselves Smith's Partisan Rangers, several of whom were killed, wounded or captured. The night was spent in an area approximately parallel to the rest of the brigade.

Now that his presence could no longer be kept a secret, Grierson strove to give the impression that his mission was to destroy various Confederate detachments nearby. During the morning of 19 April he sent squadrons back to New Albany and to the north-west, where a unit of Confederate cavalry was said to be encamped. An enemy force of about 200 men was encountered near New Albany, and again casualties were inflicted. At King's Bridge, however, the Confederates were nowhere to be found and were reported to have withdrawn westwards.

Hatch's regiment had some further skirmishing with the partisans during the morning but re-joined the brigade at noon. Once the diversionary parties had returned, Grierson set the brigade in motion for Pontotoc, which was reached at about 17:00. As the troops entered the town at the gallop they were fired upon by partisans, one of whom was killed while several more were wounded or captured. Pontotoc contained a large mill, quantities of Confederate equipment and 400 bushels of salt, all of which were destroyed. The brigade encamped five miles south of the town on the road to Houston. Here Grierson spent some time writing his only despatch to his immediate superior, Brigadier General W. S. Smith, who commanded at La Grange. From its tone it seems that he had already decided that after wrecking the railways in his path it would be safer to continue south to the Federal enclave around New Orleans and Baton Rouge rather than fight his way back through the forces he knew would be concentrated to pursue him, for he warned Smith not to worry if nothing further was heard from him during the next month.

Grierson does not seem to have had a high opinion of the 2nd Iowa, which he described as 'the least effective portion of my command', nor does he seem to have got on with Hatch, who was something of a moaner. At 03.00 on 20 April he handed his despatch to Major Love of the Second, ordering him to take 175 men and one gun and return immediately to La Grange. The column was to march in fours, thereby creating with its tracks the impression that the entire brigade was retiring within its own lines. Love was also ordered to detach a man to destroy the telegraph wires south of the township of Oxford, and he re-entered the Federal lines without incident. Hatch complained that this reduced the strength of his regiment to about 500 men. At 05:00 the brigade was on the move again. It bypassed Houston at about 16:00, halting for the night some eleven miles south of the town at a plantation on the Starkville road.

At 06:00 on 21 April the march continued. At 08:00 a halt was called at a road junction where a sign indicated that Columbus lay to the southeast. Here Grierson detached the 2nd Iowa and another gun, setting Hatch a number of objectives which included wrecking the Mobile and Ohio Railroad in the area of West Point, the capture of Columbus if possible and the destruction of Confederate war material, after which he was to return to La Grange by whatever route he thought best. In his own report Hatch complained that, when the brigade continued southwards, he was delayed for about three hours while his own regiment obliterated its tracks. The enemy had evidently formed the impression that Grierson's target was Columbus itself, deploying Smith's Partisan Rangers and other units in the 2nd Iowa's path. At about noon the regiment, now on the road to West Point, was ambushed from the flanks and rear as it was about to enter the village of Palo Alto. Hatch deployed to the rear and counter-attacked, forcing the enemy back for three miles in a protracted engagement that lasted until dusk. He now judged, correctly, that it was unlikely that he would reach the railway without heavy fighting, and the next morning, followed closely by the Confederates and sniped at the while with shotguns and sporting rifles by the country people, he commenced a fighting withdrawal northwards through Tupelo, burning a barracks and military stores at Okalona and destroying bridges over the Chiwapa Creek to foil the pursuit. When he reached La Grange on 26 April his men were down to ten rounds of ammunition apiece, having set out with 70. On balance, therefore, it seems as though Grierson's judgement of Hatch and the 2nd Iowa may have been somewhat harsh.

In fact Grierson was not worried whether Hatch's diversion achieved the objectives he had set, since on its own it would serve to distract the enemy's attention. The fight at Palo Alto, where the Confederates believed they were engaging the main body of the brigade, achieved this admirably, leaving Grierson undisturbed for the rest of the day. The brigade, now about 950 strong with two guns, passed through Starkville at 16:00, taking the Louisville road to the south-west. Some four miles beyond the town the road all but vanished into a swamp in which the troopers' mounts were often belly-deep in mud and sometimes compelled to swim across turgid streams. Camp was made in heavy rain as soon as reasonably dry ground was reached. As the Confederate Army was permanently short of footwear, Grierson despatched a squadron of the 7th Illinois to a nearby tannery, where it destroyed boots, shoes, stocks of leather and machinery to a total estimated value of $50,000 as well as capturing a Confederate quartermaster from Port Hudson who was purchasing supplies for his troops.

Next morning, 22 April, the march on Louisville was resumed. Most of the 28 miles consisted of an even worse swamp than that encountered the previous day. So isolated was the area that the few inhabitants encountered believed the soldiers to be Confederates. Progress, however, was slow, and it was dark when Louisville was reached. Some of the inhabitants, firmly believing that the approaching Yankees were little better than plundering savages, had already left with what they could carry. While the brigade passed quietly through, Grierson had the town picketed to prevent the remainder giving warning of his passage. Pleasant surprise was expressed by the citizens that none of the anticipated outrages had been committed.

Taking the road to Philadelphia, the regiments were forced to flounder through yet another girth-deep swamp. Because it was dark, several horses were drowned and a number of men narrowly escaped the same fate. At length, around midnight, the weary men and animals halted for a few hours' rest on dry ground ten miles south of the down.

The brigade moved off again at first light. Grierson was worried that the local people might destroy the bridge over the Pearl River, six miles north of Philadelphia. Such had been their intention, but on the approach of the advance guard their nerve had failed and they had fled to the woods. The brigade passed through the town at 15:00, pausing to feed and rest some five miles down the road to Enterprise. As Grierson was now within striking distance of his major objective, the Southern Mississippi Railroad, a word or two of amplification as to its construction and significance might be helpful.

139

On most American railways of the period ballast was not used on the road-bed, the sleepers (ties) being laid directly on to the bare earth. The rails were fastened to them by spikes, chairs only being used to connect adjoining rails to each other. The resulting track was of poor quality, and because of this trains rarely travelled at more than 25mph. Bridges were carried on timber trestles. Without railways, neither side would have been able to transport and supply the huge armies they had raised. In this respect the Confederacy was at a distinct disadvantage. Lacking much of a heavy engineering industry, it was chronically short of railway iron to manufacture rails and was almost unable to produce its own loco-motives. It was said that one locomotive was as important to the Confed-eracy as an infantry division, and rolling stock of every kind was nearly as valuable. Furthermore, although railways could be patrolled, their very nature meant that they were vulnerable to attack.

At the town of Meridian the north–south Mobile and Ohio formed a junction with the east–west Southern Mississippi. For Grierson, there-fore, the most important section lay west of Meridian, where the South-ern Mississippi line passed through Newton Station and on to Jackson and Vicksburg, At 22:00 on 23 April he despatched two squadrons of the 7th Illinois under Lieutenant Colonel Blackburn to proceed through the village of Decatur to Newton Station, following an hour later with the rest of the brigade. Blackburn galloped into the town at 06:00, quickly overwhelmed the slight opposition and took possession of the station and its telegraph. During the next 30 minutes two trains were snapped up. One, of 25 wagons, was loaded with sleepers and equipment for maintaining the railway; the other, of thirteen wagons, contained quarter-master's stores and ammunition, including several thousand shells. By the time Grierson arrived at 07:00 the work of destruction had been set in hand. The locomotive boilers were exploded and the wagons burned, as were 500 stands of arms and other military stores found in the town. A bridge half a mile east of the town was set ablaze, the telegraph was wrecked and long sections of track were destroyed by the usual method of laying rails across piles of burning sleepers and then bending them out of shape. A squadron of the 6th Illinois under Major Starr was sent east-wards along the line to the Chunkey River, where it burned three bridges and several hundred feet of trestles as well bringing down a two-mile stretch of telegraph line before re-joining. Parole was granted to the 75 prisoners taken.

The work of destruction complete, Grierson moved the brigade four miles south of the line to feed and rest. From captured telegraph signals he was aware that substantial Confederate forces were on his trail. The whole of Mississippi seemed to be in ferment, with enemy signals reporting him in various places at once. Thanks to his diversions, early reports suggested that his strength amounted to between 8,000 and 10,000 men, but gradually the figure stabilised at 2,000, although even before he detached the 2nd Iowa it had never amounted to more than 1,700. He was also concerned about the condition of his horses, some of which were showing signs of exhaustion after the forced marches they had made and would have to be replaced with captured stock along the way. All of this reinforced his decision to make for Baton Rouge.

After three hours' rest, the brigade set off south for Garlandville, where an unexpected form of resistance was encountered. As Grierson's narrative of the event reveals, he was a decent, humane man who disliked what the war was doing to innocent civilians:

At this point we found the citizens, many of them venerable with age, armed with shotguns and organised to resist our approach. As the advance [guard] entered the town, these citizens fired upon them and wounded one of our men. We charged upon them and captured several. After disarming them, we showed them the folly of their actions and released them. Without an exception they acknowledged their mistake and declared that they had been grossly deceived as to our true character. One volunteered his services as a guide and upon leaving us declared that hereafter his prayers should be for the Union Army. I mention this as a sample of the feeling which exists, and the good effect which our presence produced among the people of the country through which we passed. Hundreds who are skulking and hiding out to avoid conscription only await the presence of our arms to sustain them, and thousands who have been deceived upon the vindication of our cause would immediately return to loyalty.

The brigade encamped ten miles south-west of Garlandville, near Montrose. The following day, 25 April, Grierson decided to march by easy stages. During the morning he made five miles to the west then halted until 14:00, then made a further twelve to the south-west in the direction of Raleigh. At this point he learned from patrols and other sources that the enemy had hurriedly reinforced the garrisons of stations

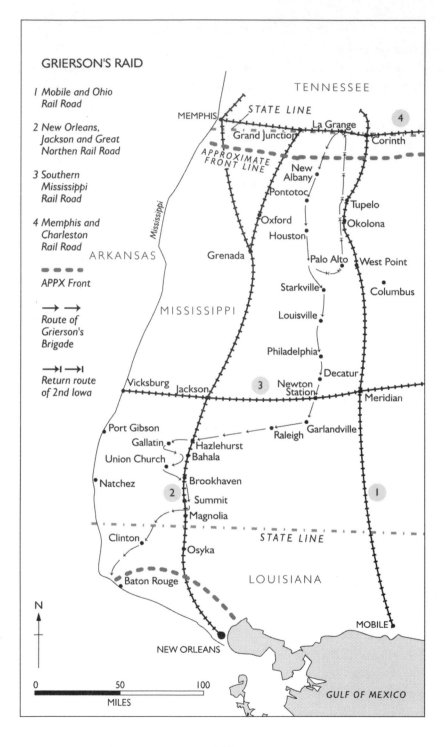

GRIERSON'S RAID

1 Mobile and Ohio
  Rail Road

2 New Orleans,
  Jackson and Great
  Northen Rail Road

3 Southern
  Mississippi
  Rail Road

4 Memphis and
  Charleston
  Rail Road

APPX Front

Route of
Grierson's
Brigade

Return route
of 2nd Iowa

TENNESSEE

STATE LINE

MEMPHIS
Grand Junction
La Grange
Corinth
4

APPROXIMATE
FRONT LINE

New
Albany
Pontotoc
Tupelo
Okolona

Oxford
Houston

ARKANSAS

Mississippi

Grenada

Palo Alto
West Point

Starkville
Columbus

MISSISSIPPI

Louisville

Philadelphia
Decatur

Vicksburg
Jackson
3
Newton
Station
Meridian

Port Gibson
Gallatin
Hazlehurst
Raleigh
Garlandville

Union Church
Bahala

Natchez
Brookhaven

2
Summit

Magnolia

STATE LINE

Clinton
Osyka

Baton Rouge
LOUISIANA

1

N

MOBILE

NEW ORLEANS

0   50   100

MILES

GULF OF MEXICO

on the Southern Mississippi from Jackson eastwards. Consulting his map (*Colton's Pocket Map of Mississippi*, a civilian publication and all that was available), he decided to cross the Pearl River and strike the New Orleans, Jackson and Great Northern Railroad at Hazlehurst.

A good night's rest benefited men and horses. At 06:00 on 26 April the brigade crossed the Leaf River, burning the bridge behind it to prevent pursuit. In Raleigh the county sheriff was captured and deprived of about $3,000 of government money left in his care. It began to rain heavily during the evening and two miles beyond Westville a halt was made for feeding, at the end of which Colonel Prince was sent ahead with two squadrons of the 7th Illinois to secure a ferry across the Pearl River. His arrival coincided with that of a Confederate courier carrying a warning of the brigade's approach and orders to destroy the ferry. Grierson came up two hours later with the main column. By 14:00 on 27 April the entire brigade was across. Meanwhile Prince and his two squadrons had again gone on ahead to Hazlehurst, where the townspeople, though armed, fled on the approach of the advance guard. In the station were a number of cars containing some 500 shells and other military stores. These were destroyed, as was as much of the track and telegraph as possible. In pouring rain, the brigade crossed the track and proceeded westwards to Gallatin, where a 64-pounder gun, its mounting and a wagonload of ammunition were captured on the road to Port Gibson. After the gun had been spiked and the carriages and ammunition destroyed, camp was made nearby.

On the morning of 28 April Grierson continued to move westwards for a while, detaching a squadron of the 7th Illinois under Captain Trafton to return to the railway at Bahala, south of Hazlehurst, and continue the work of destruction. Changing direction to the south-west, the brigade halted to feed at 14:00 near Union Church. Almost at once its picquets were heavily fired upon. The enemy consisted of three companies of Colonel Wirt Adams' Mississippi Cavalry, who had marched from Natchez. Grierson immediately formed a firing line and forced the enemy back through the town, in which he bivouacked for the night. Adams, reinforced by two more companies and two guns, intended attacking at first light but was unsettled by the return of Captain Trafton's squadron at 03:00 and withdrew westwards in the direction of Fayette.

Moving out of Union Church next morning, 29 April, Grierson followed up for a while with a diversionary force, wishing to give the impression that he intended attacking either Port Gibson or Natchez, then headed back towards Brookhaven on the railway. Adams was informed of the move and, guessing that Grierson's ultimate destination was Baton Rouge, marched to intercept him. At Brookhaven about 500 conscripts and citizens offered brief resistance but fled when charged. Over 200 prisoners were taken and paroled. A recruit training camp of several hundred tents, stores, arms and ammunition were all destroyed, as were more sections of railway, before the brigade moved off to encamp eight miles south of the town.

As Grierson relates in his report, 30 April was even more productive:

> We moved directly south, along the railroad, destroying all bridges and trestle-work to Bogue Chitton Station, where we burned the depot and 15 freight cars and captured a very large secession flag. From thence we still moved along the railroad, destroying every bridge, water tank, etc, as we passed, to Summit, which place we reached soon after noon. Here we destroyed 25 freight cars and a large quantity of government sugar. We found much Union sentiment in this town and were kindly welcomed and fed by many of the citizens. After resting two hours, we started southwest, on the Liberty road, marched about 15 miles and halted until daylight on the plantation of Dr Spurlark.

Grierson was now about to embark upon the most difficult part of his mission, namely re-entering the Federal lines at Baton Rouge through country now swarming with Confederate troops looking for him. The problem for the Confederates was that, thanks to his numerous changes of direction and interruption of telegraph communications, they were not sure where he was and were unable to co-ordinate their response. The despatch of Colonel R. V. Richardson of the 1st Tennessee Partisan Rangers gives some idea of the difficulties involved, as well containing elements of *opéra bouffe:*

> In obedience to orders dated April 28, 1863, I repaired at 9 p.m. of that day to the depot at Jackson, supposing the train of troops to accompany me was ready to start. When I got to the depot, I was chagrined and surprised to find that the three companies of the 20th Mississippi Mounted Infantry, who were to constitute a portion of the forces subject to my orders in the movement projected against the enemy, with horses, were just about to be placed on the train.
>
> About 2.30 a.m., April 29, 1863, the men and horse were all aboard. I inquired for the conductor and learned that he was in bed at his chamber. I sent an

order to get him up and proceed with his train immediately, or I would send for him a file of men. After a short time he came. He then inquired of the engineer whether he could pull the train, who replied that he could not, because there were too many cars. The conductor and engineer then said that three cars must be taken from the train. This was done. Now they said they had not wood enough to run the train to the next station, and they had no lamps. I inquired whether or not they had an axe to cut wood; they replied they had none. About daybreak they started with the train and did not reach Hazlehurst until 11 a.m. In spite of all efforts, these men were churlish and seemed to be laboring to defeat as far as possible the movement of troops. They claim their privilege of exemption from military service as employees of the railroad company. It should not be granted to men who are so unmindful of the public interests.

As we rolled into Hazlehurst a citizen approached us in an excited manner and said 1,000 Yankees were within a quarter of a mile of the place, approaching it. I did not much believe the report but as a measure of precaution I ordered the train to run back on the road about a mile. I then ordered the men to form on each side of the railroad and 20 horses to be taken from the train and sent out a scout in the direction of the reported advance of the enemy. The scouts returned in half an hour and the enemy not be found [*sic*] as reported.

I availed myself of every resource to get information as to the position and direction of movement of the enemy. He was reported to have been that Tuesday morning at Union Church and to have engaged Col. Wirt Adams' command there; also that he was making his way to Natchez. He had been seen the previous evening at Bahala by a detachment of 120 men which had gone west to Union Church. So far as I could judge, he was leaving the line of the railroad and going to Natchez. Colonel Adams seemed to be close after him. I could get no information of the locality of any other command which you [Lieutenant General J. C. Pemberton, Commanding the Department of Mississippi and East Louisiana] had ordered to report to me. It seemed that the proper direction for me to go, both for the purpose of reaching the enemy and gathering any portion of my command, except the three companies of the 20th Mississippi Regiment then with me, was Union Church. After feeding the horses, at 1 o'clock I started on the Natchez road for Union Church. I got there at 9 o'clock that night and learned that the enemy had left there at 8 o'clock in the morning for Brookhaven, and that Colonel Adams had camped the previous night within three or four miles of the enemy, but had gone that morning towards Fayette, believing that the enemy intended to go to Natchez.

On the morning of 1 May Grierson decided to avoid the townships of Magnolia and Osyka, where he believed the Confederates were present in strength, and headed south through woodland and along lanes and by-roads, emerging on the Osyka–Clinton road. Almost immediately the column found itself engaged with the 9th Louisiana Partisan Rangers, holding a bridge over the Tickfaw River. After capturing the enemy picquets, Lieutenant Colonel Blackburn and his men charged the bridge in the teeth of a heavy fire, causing the defenders to give ground. One man was killed, Blackburn was mortally wounded and four men were wounded in this encounter. The action is described by Major J. De Baun, the Rangers' commanding officer:

> At about 11.45 a.m. a volley in the direction of our rear guard warned me that the enemy was in the neighborhood. I immediately ordered the bridge to be dismantled and the men ambushed, posting men at the bridge to destroy it as soon as the rear guard would have reported. Some ten minutes had now expired, and the rear guard not reporting, Captain E. A. Scott went up the road to ascertain, if possible, the cause of the delay. I regret to say that he was captured by some of the enemy in the advance, wearing our uniform. At the bridge the road suddenly turns to the left, screening the road so the enemy could not be seen until they were at the bridge. A few minutes after the departure of Captain Scott, the enemy made their appearance at the bridge, delivering two volleys at the men there posted, without effect. Immediately my men opened a deadly fire upon them, killing and wounding 16 men and killing 15 horses. Lieutenant Colonel Blackburn is a prisoner, with three privates, all dangerously wounded. Besides them, five prisoners were captured. So deadly was our fire that the enemy, who had succeeded in crossing the bridge, were compelled to re-cross it. They, however, immediately opened fire on us with artillery, and were crossing the creek to our right. My command being small, not more than 90 men having been engaged, and fearing to be surrounded, I ordered a retreat in the direction of Osyka, which was executed in good order. My loss was one captain, one lieutenant and six privates; the lieutenant and men belonged to the rear guard; all captured. During the night cavalry reinforcement under Colonel R. V. Richardson, numbering 400 men, reached Osyka, when at 2 a.m. on May 2, we started in pursuit of the enemy towards Greensburg.

De Baun may have been over-optimistic in his estimate of casualties inflicted, but his resistance had been tough enough to convince Grierson that if he used the bridge he might be putting his head in a hornet's nest. Leaving the surgeon and sergeant-major of the 7th Illinois to look after the wounded, he crossed the Tickfaw by a bridge further south. Near Greensburg there was a brush with a squadron of Mississippi Cavalry under Major W. H. Garland, who were easily held off by the guns and one squadron of the 6th Illinois, without the need to halt the column.

Grierson was now fully aware that the Confederates were closing in from all sides. Just one major obstacle, the wide and fast Amite River, lay in his path. As only one bridge spanned the river, for several anxious hours he was a prey to worry that he should have to fight his way across.

Luck, however, was on his side for, incredibly, the bridge was unguarded, and the brigade crossed at midnight, some two hours ahead of the nearest pursuit. The march continued to Sandy Creek (Greenwell Springs in Confederate sources) where, at first light, the brigade surprised the camp of the 9th Tennessee Cavalry, taking a number of prisoners and scattering the only squadron present. Having set fire to the camp, which consisted of 150 tents, and destroyed arms, ammunition and stores, the brigade set off on the road to Baton Rouge. At Roberts' Ford on the Comite River it repeated the performance by surprising another cavalry camp, home to a squadron of Miles' Louisiana Legion. Its commander, Captain B. F. Bryan, somehow managed to escape and submitted the following rueful report.

> On the morning of May 2, at about 9 a.m., I was surprised by a body of the enemy, under command of Colonel Grierson, numbering upward of 1,000 men. They made a dash and surrounded me on all sides before I was aware that they were other than our own troops, their advance guard being dressed in citizens' garb. Most of my men being on picket, and having only about 30 of them immediately in camp, there was no possible chance of my making a stand; and, besides this, I had been on picket up to the eighth day, and my horses had had but one feed of corn within that time, and I necessarily had to graze them, hence their capture. My loss I beg leave most respectfully to submit in the following list: 38 men, 38 horses, two mules, one company wagon and harness, one borrowed wagon, 38 guns, 37 pistols, 2,000 rounds cartridges and our cooking utensils. I would state that I have six horses left by the enemy at the Comite Bridge.

Having rounded up their prisoners and booty, the brigade forded the river and entered friendly territory. Four miles short of Baton Rouge they halted to feed and smarten up. Word of their arrival soon reached Major General Christopher C. Augur, commanding the garrison, who sent out two companies of cavalry to meet them. At 15:00 Grierson's regiments marched into the town to the hearty cheers of Augur's men. Though balked of their prey, the Confederates were fair-minded in their acknowledgements:

> I found it impossible, to my great mortification and regret, to overhaul them [wrote Colonel Wirt Adams]. During the last 24 hours of their march in this state, they travelled at a sweeping gallop, the numerous stolen horses previously collected furnishing them fresh relays.

Colonel Richardson was even more generous in his praise:

From the best information I could get, the enemy's strength consisted of the 6th and 7th Illinois Regiments of Cavalry, the pride and boast of the United States Army, numbering in all about 1,100 picked men, well armed and mounted. It was not his desire to fight. He wanted to make observations, destroy railroads and telegraphic communications. It is said he pressed horses, the best he could find, to mount his men when a horse was jaded. He also captured mules and horses, negroes, forage, subsistence, and stole money and jewelry from the people in his course. He has made a most successful raid through the length of Mississippi and a part of Louisiana, one which will exhilarate for a short time the fainting spirits of the Northern war party.

On 5 May, having rested, Grierson sat down to write his lengthy report, concluding with a summary of the raid's achievements:

During the expedition we killed and wounded about 100 of the enemy, captured and paroled over 500 prisoners, many of them officers, destroyed between 50 and 60 miles of railroad and telegraph, captured and destroyed over 3,000 stand of arms, and other army stores and government property to an immense amount; we also captured 1,000 horses and mules. Our loss during the entire journey was three killed, seven wounded, five left on the route sick, the sergeant-major and surgeon of the 7th Illinois left with Lieutenant Colonel Blackburn, and nine men missing, supposed to have straggled. We marched over 600 miles in less than 16 days. The last 28 hours we marched 76 miles, had four engagements with the enemy and forded the Comite River, which was deep enough to swim many of the horses. During this time the men and horses were without food or rest.

The unseen results of Grierson's Raid were of even greater consequence. When, on 30 April, Grant crossed the Mississippi to begin the encirclement of Vicksburg from the south, Pemberton had already sent off his reserves in pursuit of Grierson, removing them from the vital sector at the critical moment. On 2 May Pemberton transferred his headquarters from Jackson to Vicksburg. The disruption of their vital rail supply network meant that during the siege of the latter the Confederates had insufficient ammunition for their guns to reply effectively to the sustained bombardment by Grant's artillery and the Federal gunboats on the river. When Pemberton surrendered on 4 July his troops had eaten their horses and many of the civil population were starving. The previous day, far to the north-east, General Robert E. Lee failed in his critical assault at Gettysburg. Although the year had begun well for the South, from this point onwards it would be thrown on to the defensive.

Grierson's spectacular achievement in riding right across the Confederacy resulted in his receiving personal commendations from General

Grant and President Lincoln, much popular acclaim and promotion to brigadier general. His comment that the interior of the Confederacy resembled a hollow shell was too modest, for, as we have seen, he outthought his opponents every step of the way. On 21 May his brigade was in action again, forming part of a force under Augur's command that defeated a small Confederate detachment at Plains Store. The effect of this was to close the last escape route of the enemy garrison holding Port Hudson, which was besieged by Major General Nathaniel P. Banks and surrendered on 9 July.

The entire length of the Mississippi was now in Federal hands, and the Confederacy was split in two. Grierson's brigade was shipped back to Tennessee. On 10 June the following year it formed part of a force under Brigadier General Samuel D. Sturgis that was roundly beaten by Major General Nathan Bedford Forrest, arguably the Confederacy's best cavalry commander, at Brice's Cross Roads, Mississippi. On 15 July Grierson, now serving under Major General Andrew Jackson Smith, had a measure of revenge when Forrest was defeated at Tupelo. Early in 1865 he was given the brevet rank of major general and appointed Commander of Cavalry Forces, Military District of West Mississippi. It was no mean achievement for a man who, four years earlier, had been a storekeeper. The last weeks of the war found him serving in Alabama. When the Confederacy finally surrendered his command was ordered to move south through the state to re-establish Federal authority. His despatch provides a sad picture of the South in the immediate aftermath of the war:

Almost the entire line of march was through country which had never been visited by Federal troops since the commencement of the war, and much of it was the richest portions of the State. The march of the various columns had a good effect upon the people. The entire distance marched was about 700 miles, and over 10,000 Confederate officers and soldiers were paroled. On the line of march we passed at least 300,000 bales of cotton, much of it [rebel] government property; also, considerable quantities of commissary and quartermaster's stores. Not deeming it good policy to destroy property when the close of the war was becoming so apparent, no cotton was burned, believing it would find its way to market and come under the control of the Government. Such Confederate commissary and quartermaster's stores as could not be made use of by the command, together with the unserviceable animals, were, by my direction, believing it would meet with approval, distributed to the poor, many of whom were suffering and entirely destitute. The country is filled with bands of armed marauders, composed mostly of deserters from the late rebel armies, who have returned to find their families suffering from the neglect and persecution of the wealthy leaders, at whose instigation they joined the rebel ranks. The poor people, including the returned Confederate private soldiers, are, as a general thing, now loyal; but the far greater portion of the wealthy classes are still very bitter in their sentiments against the Government, and clutch on to slavery with a lingering hope to save at least a relic of their favourite yet barbarous institution for the future.

Grierson elected to remain in the Army after the war, reverting to the substantive rank of colonel. The rest of his service was as remarkable as his first years had been. As many of the freed slaves were having difficulty in adjusting to their new life, the Army decided to form four regiments, the 9th and 10th Cavalry and the 24th and 25th Infantry, which would consist of black enlisted men and white officers. In 1866 Grierson was given the task of raising the 10th Cavalry at Fort Leavenworth, and he remained the regiment's commanding officer for the next 23 years. Throughout this period, in which racial prejudice was as rampant in the Army as elsewhere, he championed the rights of his troopers and insisted that they received the respect as soldiers that they undoubtedly earned. The black regiments were well-disciplined, good-humoured, enduring and generally recruited to strength, and suffered less from desertion than their white counterparts. In 1874 General Sherman publicly stated: 'They are good troops, they make first-rate sentinels, are faithful to their trust, and are as brave as the occasion calls for.' Yet, for all this, they were regarded askance by the rest of the Army and their white officers were looked down upon if not actually snubbed. None of this helped Grierson's career, nor did the fact that he was outside the fraternity of officers who had attended West Point—and nor did a personality clash with his superior, Lieutenant General Philip H. Sheridan. He was accused of being lax in his routine administration, but that was true of many men of action. He was also accused of imposing too lenient a discipline upon his regiment, although his accusers perhaps forgot that the 10th did not require a heavy hand. Its troopers not only were personally loyal to their commanding officer but also possessed a strong *esprit de corps* by virtue of their colour. As their chaplain put it, 'They are possessed of the notion that the coloured people of the whole country are more or less affected by their conduct in the Army.'

The United States had already begun to expand westwards, a process that would inevitably provoke a response from the Plains Indians. The Army's principal post-war task, therefore, became the protection of settlers moving out beyond the old frontier. In 1869 Grierson and his regiment were sent to found Fort Sill, Oklahoma, which lay beside a Kiowa and Comanche Indian reservation. Grierson and the Indian Agent, Lawrie Tatum, believed that the Indians would respond to decent treatment but were sadly disillusioned. In May 1871 General Sherman, now General-in-Chief of the Army, visited Fort Sill on a tour of inspection to discover whether reports of Indian depredations were justified. While he was there a chief named Satanta arrived with his band, boasting that he had just massacred a wagon train at Salt Creek Prairie, Texas, yet impertinently demanding arms, ammunition and guns with which to carry out further raids. This was too much even for Tatum, who demanded that Grierson arrest Satanta and two others, Satank and Big Tree, who were known to have been involved. A tense confrontation between Sherman and Grierson on the one hand, and Santanta and other chiefs on the other, took place on the veranda of the commanding officer's quarters. When Satanta again admitted the crime, Sherman told him that he would be placed under arrest. Satanta and others drew weapons, but immediately the building's shutters flew up to reveal the ranked faces of Grierson's troopers above levelled carbines. For a while the tension eased, but as tempers rose again an Indian named Stumbling Bear shot an arrow at Sherman. The result might have been fatal had not another brave deliberately knocked the bow off target. Simultaneously a man named Lone Wolf pointed his rifle at the general, only to be knocked flat and pinned down by Grierson. Once arrested and tried, Satanta and Big Tree were sentenced to death, commuted to life imprisonment. Satank attacked one of his guards and was shot dead before he could be brought to trial.

It was in the harsh, arid, semi-desert areas of the south and south-west that the Army chose to employ its black regiments, who were known to the Indians as Buffalo Soldiers and respected by them. Early in 1873 the 10th Cavalry moved to the Texan frontier with Mexico, spending much of its time at Forts Clark and Duncan. Its principal foes were renegade Apache war parties, noted for their ferocity, cruelty, cunning and apparently insensibility to hunger, fatigue, pain, intense heat or bitter cold and who were a menace to Americans and Mexicans alike. The protracted campaign that followed was one of raids, ambushes, riding to the rescue of settlers or detachments under attack and gruelling pursuits that told heavily on men and horses. A hot pursuit could lead across the frontier into Mexico. Sometimes the Mexican authorities would actively co-operate, sometimes they would simply turn a blind eye, and sometimes they would protest at the violation of their sovereignty; these were turbulent times for Mexico and much depended upon the stability of the central administration. Grierson finally out-thought the Apache in much the same way he had out-thought his opponents on his ride through Mississippi and Louisiana to Baton Rouge. Instead of embarking upon long and sometimes fruitless pursuits, he predicted which water holes the raiders were likely to use and posted troops to hold them. In this way he defeated the notorious renegade chief Victorio at Quitman Canyon on 30 July 1880. On 6 August Victorio, finding the water at Rattlesnake Springs similarly denied him, rode off to the east and ambushed a supply convoy bound for Fort Davis. The infantry escort held their own until Grierson's troopers arrived to drive off the raiders and chase them back across the border. Grierson also did much to expand the general knowledge of the area in which his regiment operated, adding to the accuracy of maps and so opening up fresh routes for transportation.

In 1890, shortly before his retirement, Grierson was promoted brigadier general. By then the West had largely been pacified and the world of his youth had changed beyond recognition. He was kindly remembered by the old soldiers who served under his command, but while the veterans' associations kept alive the spirit of comradeship they had known during the Civil War, the event itself was of such recent memory and so great a tragedy that the American public at large simply wanted to put it behind them; after all, more Americans had died in that conflict than in any previous or subsequent war. Grierson's Raid remained known only to military historians, although it did demonstrate the value of the indirect approach in war, which was itself to become an essential ingredient of the *Blitzkrieg* technique. It was not until the 1930s, when the last survivors of both armies were filmed on their old battlefields, shaking hands and agreeing that the other side were not such bad fellows after all, that interest in the Civil War began to grow, being further stimulated by the film *Gone With The Wind*. Grierson's Raid provided an ideal subject for a plot, although it was not until the 1960s that it found its way on to the screen in 'factional' form as *The Horse Soldiers*. The role of the brigade commander was played by the actor John Wayne, who was of similar build to Grierson but clean shaven, whereas the latter, like many senior officers of his time, sported a patriarchal beard. There were also some concessions to artistic licence. For example, the old gentlemen with shot-guns who tried to resist the brigade at Garlandville became cadets from a military school. In other respects the narrative follows the course of events closely.

Major General Lewis Wallace

Saviour of Washington

O F THE MILLIONS who have seen the film *Ben Hur*, the majority will recall that it was based upon the best-selling nineteenth century novel of the same name, written by a man called Lew Wallace. Fewer will know that Wallace served as a major general in the Union Army during the American Civil War, and fewer still that during the war he was first made a scapegoat for the errors of his then superior, the redoubtable Ulysses S. Grant, or that two years later Grant was to commend him warmly on a display of personal initiative that would lead to his being hailed as the saviour of Washington.

Lewis Wallace, a native of Indiana, was born on 10 April 1827. His father, a local politician, later became Governor of the State. After leaving school Lewis worked for a while as a clerk, but on the outbreak of the war with Mexico in 1846 he volunteered for service in the 1st Indiana, a state infantry regiment, and was awarded a second lieutenant's commission. His regiment saw little or no action, but while in Mexico he developed a lifelong fascination for the country and the Latin culture. On his return he studied for the Indiana bar, to which he was admitted in 1849, and in 1856 he followed his father into politics, entering the state senate.

When the Civil War began, Lewis's military career was meteoric, but not more so than others with previous military experience and strong political connections. Offering his services as soon as he learned that the Confederates had bombarded Fort Sumter, he was immediately appointed Adjutant-General of Indiana. Eleven days later, on 25 April 1861, he became colonel of the 11th Indiana. During this period, when ideals were at their highest, states vied with each other to raise the largest number of regiments possible from their available manpower, with too little thought being given to their adequate training, supply or reinforcement. Likewise, many of the political appointees to high rank were quite unfamiliar with the techniques of handling large bodies of men in the field, let alone strategy or tactics. Fortunately for them, their opponents were similarly handicapped, and during a skirmish at Romney, Virginia, Wallace's regiment drove a smaller number of Confederates off the field. As a result of this, Wallace received promotion to brigadier general of volunteers on 3 September 1861. The following February he assumed command of the 3rd Division of Major General U. S. Grant's Army of the Tennessee, the headquarters of which were based at Cairo, Illinois.

A key element in the Union strategy was the need to secure control of the entire course of the Mississippi, effectively cutting the Confederacy in two and rendering its most important eastern states vulnerable to invasion not just from the north but from the west as well. Before this could be put into effect, however, it would be necessary to capture the two neighbouring rebel fortresses of Fort Henry and Fort Donelson, lying on, respectively, the parallel Tennessee and Cumberland rivers, both of which flowed into the Ohio, itself a tributary of the Mississippi. Together, the two fortresses were the cornerstone of the cordon defence the Confederates hoped to establish in the western theatre of war, and they also posed a threat to the flank of any Union advance down the Mississippi.

Early in February 1862 Grant's army, some 15,000 men strong and accompanied by a flotilla of river gunboats, commenced its advance from Cairo. Fort Henry, badly sited on low ground, fell to the fire of the gunboats on 6 February. While they descended the Tennessee and made their way up the Cumberland, Grant marched most of his army the eleven miles across country to Fort Donelson, encircling the landward side of the fortress on 13 February. During the night the gunboats arrived, bringing with them an additional 6,000 men. Lewis Wallace's division also came in from Fort Henry, bringing Grant's strength up to 27,000. Next day the gunboats, commanded by Commodore Andrew Foote, attempted to repeat their success at Fort Henry. On this occasion, however, the Confederate gunners, better emplaced, quickly found the range and inflicted serious damage, forcing them to break off the attack.

Early in the morning of 15 February Grant went aboard the flotilla's flagship to confer with Foote, who had been wounded in the engagement. The two were still discussing their plans for the day when, at 05:00, the Confederate garrison, which had been concentrated for a breakout attempt, smashed through the extreme right of the Federal siege lines, held by Brigadier General John McClernand's 1st Division. Though taken by surprise, shaken by the force of the rebel attack and compelled to give ground, McClernand managed to form a firing line that prevented his division from being completely rolled up. Wallace, in the centre of the Union siege lines, read the battle correctly and sent up reinforcements as well as wheeling some of his own units to the right to meet the threat. This halted the Confederate advance, although the unexpected turn of events had caused considerable confusion and dismay in the Federal ranks.

A further surprise was to follow. By now the Confederates were in control of the road to Nashville. Two options were therefore open to their commander, Brigadier General Gideon Pillow: he could either break out in the direction of Nashville or he could inflict a defeat on Grant's already disorganised army. Inexplicably, he lost his nerve and chose neither, deciding instead to withdraw into his own lines. Grant, returning to the field, ordered Wallace and McClernand to follow up. Examining the packs of the Confederate casualties, he discovered that they contained three days' rations, from which he deduced that Pillow regarded Fort Donelson as a trap and had actually been trying to break out. That being the case, he concluded, most sectors of the defences would have been stripped of men to assemble the necessary force. He ordered Brigadier General Charles Smith's division, on the extreme left of the siege lines, to mount an attack on the fortifications opposite, and, as he had hoped, it secured a lodgement within the fort's defences.

This was too much for the senior Confederate commanders. Leaving the only professional among them, Brigadier General Simon Buckner, a former West Point classmate of Grant's, to superintend the surrender of the fortress, the majority escaped up-river by steamer, taking about 2,000 men with them; a notable exception was Colonel Nathan Bedford Forrest, who led his cavalry and a few infantrymen to safety through the Federal lines in the pre-dawn darkness of 16 December. The loss of Fort Donelson was the first major defeat to be sustained by the Confederacy. Of the 21,000 men who had formed its garrison, about 2,000 were killed or wounded in the fighting and 15,000 became prisoners of war. This was not the sort of loss the South, critically short of men, could afford, any more than it could the capture of 48 guns and tons of accumulated war material. Grant's losses amounted to 2,832 men killed or wounded. Lewis Wallace was among those divisional commanders who received promotion to major general following the battle, and he seemed set to pursue a promising military career.

The army continued its advance southwards along the Tennessee river. At one stage Grant fell foul of his immediate superior, Major General Henry Halleck, responsible for the western theatre of war, and was relieved of command, only to be reinstated following the personal intervention of President Abraham Lincoln. The next Union objective was the town of Corinth, Mississippi, a strategically important railway junction from which lines radiated to the north, south, east and west. By the end of March Grant's Army of the Tennessee, now consisting of six divisions and numbering almost 47,000 men, had reached Pittsburg Landing, some 22 miles north-east of Corinth, while marching to join him from Nashville was Major General Don Carlos Buell's 50,000-strong Army of the Ohio. Simultaneously the Confederates, anxious to restore their fortunes in the west, had begun to concentrate in Corinth itself, forming the 41,000-strong Army of the Mississippi under General Albert Sidney Johnston, one of their ablest commanders. Johnston's plan was to strike hard and decisively at Grant before Buell could join him, thus throwing the Federal plan of campaign into disarray.

The terrain to the south and west of Pittsburg Landing was rolling and heavily forested, intersected by numerous creeks and streams and punctuated here and there by large open areas that had been cleared for agriculture. It was sparsely inhabited, although about two miles southwest of Pittsburg Landing was a tiny Protestant meeting house named Shiloh that would give its name to the ensuing battle. The bulk of Grant's army was encamped across the area partly because the road network was suited to a continued advance on Corinth, partly because ample supplies of wood and water were readily to hand and partly because the cleared fields provided good training grounds for the newer divisions. As no attack on the encampments was anticipated, no steps were taken to render them defensible. Nor were the roads to Corinth patrolled, and although cavalry vedettes were put out they were too close to the camps to provide adequate warning. Lewis Wallace's 3rd Division was placed in reserve, approximately five miles to the north of the main body of the army, its three brigades and supporting arms strung out along a road leading west from Crump's Landing. Grant's headquarters were even further away, upstream in the town of Savannah. None of his divisional commanders had been given the authority to assume temporary command of the army in his absence, so that when the time came they would all be compelled to fight their own battles in isolation.

Johnston began his approach march from Corinth on 3 April. Despite being slowed down by atrocious weather and overcrowded roads, it went undetected. The Confederate plan of attack had been drawn up by Johnston's second-in-command, General Pierre Beauregard, and involved isolating Grant's army from its principal source of supply at Pittsburg Landing, then driving it into the difficult swampland to the north. The rebels struck at 05:00 on Sunday 6 April, achieving complete tactical surprise. Four of the five Federal divisions were driven out of their camps and pushed steadily back throughout the day. The nature of the terrain made it a difficult battle for both sides. Amid the dense woodland and underbrush, the fighting took place at close quarters, while troops attempting to cross the cleared areas in close order were mown down. Apart from those Federals who had seen some fighting at Fort Donelson, both armies were completely raw. Never having seen the effects of concentrated firepower before, they were shaken by the sights and sounds of the battlefield as well as the number of casualties they were sustaining. The surprised Federals were worst affected, fugitives from their ranks converging on Pittsburg Landing by the hundred. On the other hand, their artillery distinguished itself, fighting to the muzzle time and again as it covered the withdrawal. For senior commanders, exercising control was a nightmare. The Confederates had adopted the corps system and therefore enjoyed the benefit of an intermediate level of command, but until Grant reached the field at about 08:30 the Federal divisional commanders could only fight their own battles and struggle to conform with their immediate neighbours. Thereafter, stubborn knots of resistance slowed down the Confederate advance. Nevertheless, at 14:00 victory seemed to be within Johnston's grasp, but shortly afterwards he was mortally wounded while directing the breakthrough that he hoped would bring him to Pittsburg Landing. By the time Beauregard assumed command, Grant had put together a new line of defence and the chance had gone. At 17:00 the first elements of Buell's Army of the Ohio began reaching Pittsburg Landing from across the river. Thirty minutes later the final Confederate attack was broken up by the fire of two gunboats. Gradually firing died away along the front.

Lewis Wallace's division had played no real part in the day's fighting. It has to be said that while Wallace had already shown signs of being a competent general, he was not a lucky one. As soon as the sounds of battle reached him, Grant abandoned his breakfast and, sending a message to Buell urging him to hurry towards the scene of the action, he embarked on a steamer at Savannah. On his way up to the fighting, he had stopped briefly at Crump's Landing and ordered Wallace to place his division on standby. Wallace sent instructions to his brigade commanders to assemble their troops at a central point. Shortly before noon he received imprecise orders to bring the division forward. No guides were available, and the two regiments from another division which had been positioned to form a link between him and the rest of the army had long since been sent forward to join the firing line. Nevertheless, he set off through the heavily wooded country on what he believed to be the correct heading, crossing Snake Creek above instead of below its confluence with Owl Creek. Suddenly he realised that he was marching southwest, leaving the battle far to his left, and was on the wrong side of Owl Creek. It took time to turn round three infantry brigades, two artillery batteries and two cavalry units, counter-march them and set them on the right route. The division, having been on the march for six-and-a-half hours and covered fifteen miles instead of five, did not arrive on the army's right flank until 19:15, and by then the crisis was long past.

Next morning Grant, having been reinforced by Buell, counter-attacked. Now it was the turn of Beauregard to retire under pressure, covered by his artillery. By 16:00 his rearguard had disengaged and the battle was over. Federal casualties amounted to 13,047 men killed, wounded or missing, while Confederate losses totalled 11,694. Both sides, shocked by the carnage, recognised that a long, bitter struggle lay ahead. Although he had won a victory, Grant came under sharp criticism for the laxity that had allowed his army to be surprised. He was never to repeat the same mistakes. Still angry with Lewis Wallace because of his lacklustre performance during the first day's fighting, he dismissed him from his command, so providing a scapegoat for the disaster that had almost overtaken the army. When Wallace subsequently defended himself on the grounds that his orders were imprecise, Grant retorted in his *Memoirs*: 'I never could see and do not now see why any other order was necessary further than to direct him to come to Pittsburg Landing, without specifying by what route. His was one of three veteran divisions that had been in battle, and its absence was severely felt.' The probability is that there was wrong on both sides, although during the second day's fighting the division had acquitted itself as well as any.

Wallace was to spend the next two years in a sort of military limbo. He again offered his services to the Governor of Indiana, and, when the Confederates mounted a counter-invasion of Kentucky later in 1862, he assumed temporary command of a regiment, notwithstanding his rank. As the high-water mark of this invasion began creeping towards the Ohio River, he organised a largely civilian defence force to hold the city. Once the threat had receded he sat on the commission which examined Buell's tardy reaction, recommending his dismissal, and on various other boards. In March 1864 he was appointed commander of the Middle Department and VIII Corps, with his headquarters in Baltimore, Maryland. The post was primarily administrative and the troops under his command were largely a floating population *en route* to or from the front. In such a backwater it began to seem as though he would never see active service again.

Meanwhile Grant's star had continued to ascend. Now a lieutenant general, on 9 March 1864 he was appointed the Army's General in Chief and immediately decided that the only way to bring the war to a speedy conclusion was by imposing a brutal policy of attrition on the Confederacy. He personally accompanied Major General George Meade's Army of the Potomac during a series of bloody battles against General Robert E. Lee's Army of Northern Virginia, preventing the latter from disengaging by constantly sliding past his right flank, so forcing him to remain between Meade and Richmond, the Confederate capital. Attrition, however, is a two-edged weapon. The casualties sustained by the Army of the Potomac were so high that he was forced to bring forward the Heavy Artillery regiments manning Washington's defences to serve as infantry. These regiments had never expected to serve in the field and their arrival was greeted gleefully by Meade's troops, who innocently enquired whether they had brought their fortifications with them! Their departure meant that although Washington was surrounded by a ring of forts, the only troops left to man them were companies of the Veteran Reserve Corps, consisting of men so badly wounded or ill that they were unfit for service in an active unit. They were badly armed, and their usual duties included guarding prisoners or working in the city's military hospitals. They were certainly in no condition to offer determined resistance to veteran troops, and, for the moment, the capital of the United States was, for all practical purposes, undefended.

By the middle of June the effects of constant attritional fighting had become even more apparent in Lee's army. Lee desperately needed some relief from the pressure, and, recalling that in the past the Shenandoah Valley had been used twice as a back door into the Federal heartland, generating panic in Washington, he decided to do the same again, detaching Lieutenant General Jubal Early's II Corps for the purpose. The alarm created by Early's appearance would, he reasoned, force Grant and Meade to send substantial numbers of troops hotfoot back to Washington and provide the breathing space he so badly needed. At this stage Lee, unaware that Washington was virtually defenceless, merely instructed Early to 'threaten' the city.

Early's march began on 12 June. He advanced steadily up the Valley, brushing aside resistance, and on 5 July crossed the Potomac into Maryland. His troops wrecked stretches of the Baltimore & Ohio Railroad and demolished an aqueduct of the Chesapeake and Ohio Canal, but one of their most pressing concerns was the looting of shoe stores, for many of them were marching barefoot. From the citizens of Hagerstown Early extracted $20,000 in exchange for a promise that the town would not be burned. His progress was now being screened by a single Union cavalry regiment, the 8th Illinois, whose commander, Colonel David Clendenin, telegraphed regular reports to Wallace's headquarters in Baltimore.

Wallace knew that Grant had promised to send back a corps for the defence of Washington if Early invaded Maryland. The question was,

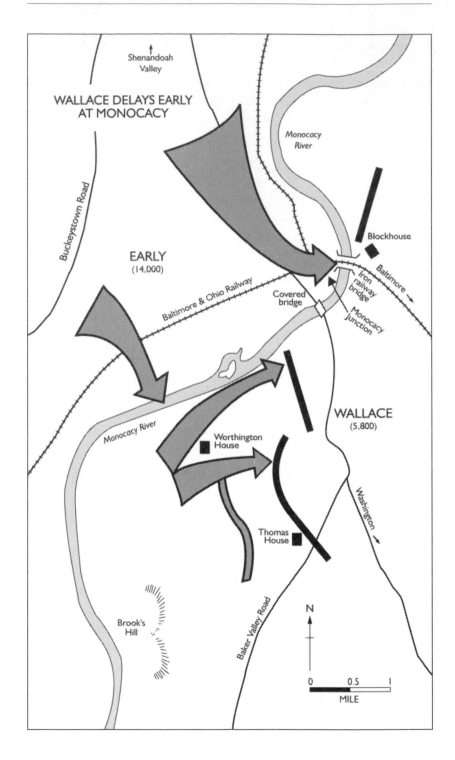

would it arrive in time? Although his primary responsibility was the defence of Baltimore, two other courses of action were open to him. He could either assemble such troops as he was able and take them to Washington, or he could use them to impose a delay on Early, so buying time for the promised corps to arrive. He was entirely without instructions from his superiors and dependent on his own initiative. Against this, he appreciated that his own stock could not be much lower than it already was, whatever decision he took. He decided to fight Early and began directing the nearest troops to join Clendenin, whose regiment was now holding a ridge between Hagerstown and Frederick, covering the routes to both Washington and Baltimore. The troops themselves were a very mixed bunch, including the 3rd Maryland Potomac Home Brigade and contingents from the 159th Ohio Mounted Infantry and the Loudon County Rangers, followed by the 1st Maryland Potomac Home Brigade, two 90-day volunteer regiments, the 144th and 149th Ohio National Guard, the 14th New Jersey Infantry and Alexander's Baltimore Battery, the last a unit of re-enlisted bounty men who enjoyed a comfortable life close to home.

On 6 July Wallace left his headquarters and travelled by train to the front. Observing the movement of Confederate cavalry to the south of the ridge, he telegraphed Washington at 20:00 that evening to the effect that the enemy had begun moving towards Washington by way of Urbana and, that being the case, he intended withdrawing immediately from Frederick to a position from which he could cover the Washington road. He fell back during the night to Monocacy Junction, where the high ground south of the Monocacy River not only covered all approaches from the north-west but also offered a natural refused left flank where the river swung south. In the centre of the position was an iron railway bridge and a covered wooden bridge, while further bridges and fords existed up and downstream. Aware that Early possessed greatly superior numbers, Wallace expected him to use these to outflank the position, but his sole concern was to buy the time needed for the corps promised by Grant to reach Washington. While his men were settling in he received a message telling him that he would also receive reinforcements.

The first of these, the 10th Vermont, came in by train on 8 July. Wallace ordered the regiment to march round and round a hill, like a stage army, to convince the watching Confederates that his force was much stronger than it was. The rest of the 3rd Division of the experienced VI Corps arrived during the night. The division, commanded by a regular officer, Brigadier General James Ricketts, consisted of only two brigades and did not, therefore, add greatly to Wallace's numbers. On the other hand, it was the best asset he had and he deployed it along the refused left flank, covering the road to Washington.

For a man supposedly in a hurry, Early had taken his time. He had allowed Wallace to remain unmolested in his first position because many of his men were foraging and driving in cattle from the surrounding countryside. He had not attacked at Monocacy on 8 July because he was extracting a $200,000 ransom from the town of Frederick—a sum of money that took hours to assemble. By the following morning, however, he was ready to pit his 14,000 men against the 5,800 Wallace had emplaced on the heights and in outposts.

The battle commenced at about 08:00. Early launched a series of converging attacks, all of which, to his surprise, were beaten off. Throughout the day the *ad hoc* Federal force, facing odds of almost three to one, put up the roughest resistance imaginable, inflicting unexpectedly heavy loss. Wallace remained cool throughout, adjusting the position of his guns and re-positioning his troops as he thought necessary. Nevertheless, by 15:30 Early's superior numbers and his ability to manoeuvre against the flanks had begun to tell. At 16:00 Wallace gave the order for a general withdrawal along the Washington road. Early did not press his pursuit, commenting later that he did not wish to be encumbered with prisoners. Confederate losses amounted to between 700 and 900 men killed and wounded. Wallace's casualties included 676 killed and wounded, plus 1,317 missing, the majority being taken prisoner when cut off from their units during the disengagement or captured when the Confederates overran his field hospital.

Wallace had lost the tactical battle, although he had won a strategic victory. Early's approach had caused no end of fluttering in the political dovecotes of Washington, but the 24 hours' delay imposed on him by Wallace at Monacacy enabled the rest of the Union VI Corps to reach the capital in the nick of time. Early reached the suburbs of Washington during the afternoon of 11 July. Within sight of the dome of the Capitol, his guns exchanged fire with those of Fort Stevens, which was manned by a scratch garrison of artillerymen, men of the Veteran Reserve Corps and government clerks hastily armed for the occasion. It was, however, too late to start an attack, and that very evening VI Corps began streaming ashore from its steamers. Early mounted another abortive probe next morning, notable in that the fighting was witnessed by President Lincoln from the ramparts of the fort. Bullets were striking the parapet and nearby a man was struck down. The story has it that an officer named Oliver Wendell Holmes, a future US Supreme Court Justice, did not recognise the President and shouted 'Get down, you damned fool!' Lincoln took no notice, refusing to take cover until Major General Horatio Wright, the commander of VI Corps, threatened to have him removed by force.

Whether Early ever intended to capture the capital is a matter for speculation. He decamped almost immediately and by 14 July had retreated across the Potomac. Be that as it may, to grateful politicians and citizens alike Monocacy became 'the battle that saved Washington' and Wallace was its hero. Even Grant decided to let bygones be bygones, commenting that Wallace had acted 'with commendable promptitude'. Although Wallace was never to command troops in action again, he was now a highly respected figure, a man whose opinions were sought and deferred to. In 1865, following Lincoln's assassination, he was a member of the military commission that tried and sentenced the conspirators. He was also president of the court martial that tried Heinrich Wirz, commandant of the notorious Confederate prisoner-of-war camp at Andersonville. Wirz, found guilty of cruelty and personally killing prisoners, was hanged.

Throughout the war Wallace had retained his interest in Mexico, where, in 1863, the machinations of Napoleon III had resulted in the Archduke Maximilian of Austria being installed as Emperor. Naturally, the Mexican people resented the imposition of a foreign monarch upon an artificially created throne. A rising, led by Benito Juarez, swept the country. French troops contained this, forcing Juarez to seek refuge in the United States for a while. Wallace, having resigned from the Army in November 1865, offered to raise funds and recruits for the cause, and in return Juarez awarded him the title of major general. In the event his services were not required as diplomatic pressure from the United States, coupled with the threat of direct intervention, resulted in the withdrawal of French troops, without whom Maximilian could not hope to survive.

Wallace's career in public service still had some years to run. He served as Governor of New Mexico Territory and as US Minister to the Ottoman Empire. In parallel he pursued a literary career, sometimes drawing on his own experiences for his plots. He is best remembered for *Ben Hur: A Tale of the Christ*, published in 1880, a copy of which could be found in most Victorian households. By the time of his death on 15 February 1905 few remembered, or even cared, that he had induced the Battle of Monocacy.

Lieutenant
Walter Hamilton VC

The fight to the death at the Kabul Residency

W HEN, AT THE END of the First Sikh War, the Punjab became a British protectorate, it brought the Honourable East
India Company an entirely fresh set of problems in that it
came into permanent contact with the fierce Pathan tribes inhabiting the
tangled mountain terrain beyond the Indus. In this area, which would
become known to history as the North-West Frontier, not even the writ
of the warlike Sikhs had extended far beyond the walls of Peshawar. Fortunately, when it came to restoring order and establishing a viable administration in the new protectorate, the hour produced the men in the
form of excellent officers, including the Lawrence brothers, Henry, John
and George, Herbert Edwardes, John Nicholson and William Hodson.
All were vigorous men of action with strong personalities who believed
that the end justified the means and, thrown entirely upon their own resources, were prepared to take whatever steps were necessary to achieve it.

The first Company administrators to serve in Peshawar were George
Lawrence and his assistant, Lieutenant Harry Lumsden of the 59th Bengal Native Infantry. Neither felt that they could rely on the loyalty of
their Sikh troops, still resentful of their defeat in the recent war, when it
came to dealing with the tribes. In December 1846 Lawrence ordered
Lumsden to raise an irregular unit which was to include 'trustworthy
men who could at a moment's notice act as guides to troops in the field
and collect intelligence beyond as well as within the border'—an onerous
burden to place upon the shoulders of any 25-year-old subaltern. Initially, Lumsden raised two companies of infantry and a troop of cavalry
locally, but during his journeys among the mountains he recognised that
the Pathan hill men were what he was looking for, on the basis that poach-

ers make the best gamekeepers. He made it clear that he was recruiting hard cases, 'men notorious for desperate deeds, leaders in forays, who kept the passes into the hills and lived amid inaccessible rocks'. Amused, such men came in to look him over, soon found themselves in awe of his formidable presence, and enlisted. Somehow his forceful personality and insight turned them into a disciplined body in which his authority went unquestioned. He demanded initiative, daring and, above all, that they should be true to their salt. This last quality they were to demonstrate during the Second Sikh War of 1848–49, after which the Punjab was formally annexed, and again during the Indian Mutiny. At first they wore their own clothes dyed to the colour of mud for concealment. After a few years, when they became part of the establishment, they became the first unit in the British or Indian Armies to be issued with khaki uniforms. Like the soldiers of today's SAS, they were engaged in active, and often covert, service to a much greater extent than conventional troops and can be regarded as one of the forerunners of modern special forces. Such were the results they produced and the reputation they established that competition to join was intense, and selective recruitment was applied across the entire Indian Army. The ultimate sanction against a man who had let his comrades down was to order him to hand in his weapons and uniform, a fate involving such loss of honour and standing that the threat was sufficient to reduce strong men to tears. They were never a regiment in the usual sense of the word, since their establishment continued to include both infantry and cavalry. Officially they were designated the Corps of Guides, in recognition of the purpose for which they had originally been raised , although as general familiarity with the Frontier increased their guiding function soon ceased. In 1876 Queen Victoria conferred the honorific 'Queen's Own' upon them.

Just as the Guides were selective in recruiting their rank and file, so were they in choosing their British officers, for in their life-and-death business on the Frontier there was no place for those who simply sought a place in an élite unit. This was particularly important, for, as with every regiment of the Indian Army, the number of British officers was small and their responsibilities consequently greater than elsewhere. One of those who offered himself as a candidate in the late 1870s was a young Irish officer, Lieutenant Walter Richard Pollock Hamilton. After passing through Sandhurst, Hamilton would have gone through the usual selection procedure, serving for a while with a British regiment in India while he familiarised himself with local conditions and brushed up on his Urdu, the Indian Army's *lingua franca*. In due course his request to join the Guides would have been acknowledged with an invitation to visit the Corps' depot at Mardan, close to the Frontier. He would have spent several days there, during which he would have met all the British officers who were not on leave or engaged in duty elsewhere. After he had gone the entire Mess would have voted on whether or not he was what they were looking for, and especially whether he would fit in. Evidently they had liked the look of him, for Hamilton, slim, dark haired, well above average height and with an erect carriage and a pleasant, open face, was offered a place in the Guides Cavalry. On arrival he would have spent some time in the Mess of the unit's Risaldars and Jemadars, who were known as VCOs (Viceroy's Commissioned Officers). The VCOs were highly respected figures, being experienced, long-service professionals who had risen through the ranks. In British Army terms their status lay between that of the warrant officers and the commissioned ranks, and they were entitled to a salute from Indian soldiers. Part of their responsibilities lay in instructing newly arrived British subalterns in the ways of the regiment and, particularly in the Guides, giving them a detailed insight into the customs and personalities of the Frontier tribes they would encounter.

In 1877 relations between Great Britain and Afghanistan declined with dramatic speed. Britain wished to preserve Afghanistan as a buffer state between the expanding Russian Empire and India, but Sher Ali, the unstable Amir (King), while seemingly wishing to maintain a position of non-alignment, made the mistake of welcoming a Russian military mission to Kabul. The mission was withdrawn, but when the British decided to send a mission of their own it was forcibly halted in the Khyber Pass. An ultimatum was sent to Sher Ali, demanding that he receive the mission or face the consequences. No reply was received and on 20 November 1878 British troops crossed the frontier. When his requests for Russian assistance met with no response, Sher Ali fled. On his death in February 1879 his son Yakub Khan succeeded to the throne.

Three British columns had invaded Afghanistan. In the south was Lieutenant General Sir Donald Stewart's Kandahar Field Force; in the centre was Major General Frederick Roberts' Kurram Field Force, of which more in the next chapter; and in the north the Peshawar Valley Field Force, commanded by the one-armed Lieutenant General Sir Sam Browne, inventor of the famous cross-belt, fought its way through the Khyber Pass to advance on Jalalabad. The Guides formed part of the last, the Guides Cavalry being commanded by Major Wigram Battye, a member of a prominent Indian Army family with long associations with the Corps.*

Browne's advance was contested by Afghan regular troops and tribesmen, but he succeeded in taking Jalalabad. However, in late March 1879 he found further progress towards Kabul barred by tribal gatherings and sent out columns. The Guides formed part of a 1,500-strong column commanded by Brigadier General Charles Gough, consisting of four cavalry squadrons, one and a half infantry battalions and four guns. On 2 April found he found the enemy occupying a strong position near Futtehabad. There were about 5,000 of them, drawn up on the edge of a plateau behind stone breastworks with both flanks protected by crags. Attack had generally proved to be the best course of action when faced with this kind of opposition, but on this occasion Gough realised that his heavily outnumbered troops would be advancing uphill against a prepared position and almost certainly sustain heavy casualties. On the other hand, if he retreated, this would be taken as a sign of weakness and probably provoke a full-scale tribal rising. He decided, therefore, to try and lure the Afghans out of their position and, concealing his infantry and three squadrons of cavalry among broken ground to the right, he sent the remaining squadron forward with the guns to within a mile of the enemy. The guns fired a few rounds and then, as though their commander had suddenly realised the strength of the opposition, were limbered up with every sign of apparent haste and driven back the way they had come. The tribesmen took the bait and triumphantly surged down the hill in

---

* Wigram was one of four brothers: Lieutenant Quintin Battye was killed while serving at Delhi during the Indian Mutiny; Major Legh Battye, 5th Gurkhas, was killed during the Black Mountain Expedition of 1888; Lieutenant Colonel Frederick Battye, Commandant of the Guides, was killed during the Chitral Campaign of 1895; and two years later, Legh's son, Lieutenant Richmond Battye of the 6th Bangal Cavalry, was killed during the Tirah Campaign.

pursuit. As soon as they had advanced far enough Gough ordered his infantry to attack them in flank from the nullah in which they lay concealed. Temporarily halted, the Afghans soon realised that they had only a small force to deal with and a fierce close-quarter fight developed. At the precise moment that the enemy were fully committed to the struggle, Gough launched the three concealed cavalry squadrons in a charge into their left. Battye, riding at the head of the Guides, was shot dead. Hamilton, the only remaining British officer, came to the fore, cheering his men on and yelling for them to avenge their commanding officer. As the charge struck home, the Afghans broke and fled in the direction of their breastworks. However, they were far from being cowards and those who were overtaken fought back savagely until they were cut down. In the mêlée, one of the Guides' horses was killed, pinning its rider down. Three Afghans immediately began slashing at him. Seeing his plight, Hamilton, who must have been a very competent swordsman, galloped to his rescue and disposed of all three. The infantry now joined in the pursuit and the guns were lobbing shells into the running mob, which did not pause to rally. Gough's column sustained the loss of six killed and 40 wounded; Afghan casualties amounted to some 300 killed and perhaps as many as 900 wounded, most being inflicted by the cavalry. Two days later Gough reached the stronghold of the tribe most involved, the Khugianis, and blew up its walls and towers. For the leadership he displayed during the action of 2 April, and for saving the life of the trooper, Hamilton was awarded the Victoria Cross. He was already a hero, but these were not the deeds for which he would be remembered.

Shortly afterwards, Yakub Khan decided to negotiate. On 26 May a treaty was concluded at Gandamak, under the terms of which the Kurram Valley and the Khyber Pass became British territory, Afghan foreign policy passed under British control and a British Resident was to be accepted in Kabul. In return, the British recognised Yakub as Amir, agreed to pay him an annual subsidy and promised their protection for his country. It seemed as though the Second Afghan War was over; in fact, its more serious phases had yet to begin.

The man who negotiated the Treaty of Gandamak was Major Pierre Louis Napoleon Cavagnari, a naturalised Englishman who was the son of an Anglo-Irish mother and one of Napoleon Bonaparte's generals. He had served as an infantry subaltern during the Mutiny but in due course had decided that brighter prospects were to be found in the political service. While serving as deputy commissioner for Kohat and later Peshawar he had conducted numerous skilful negotiations with the hill tribes, and for his expertise at Gandamak he was rewarded with a knighthood. That he was a man of great intelligence was generally recognised, although some found him rather too overbearing, volatile and quick-tempered for their liking. As he seemed to have got on so well with Yakub he was the obvious choice for British Resident in Kabul, just as Hamilton was the obvious choice to command his escort. Also present in Kabul would be Cavagnari's secretary, Mr William Jenkins, and Dr Ambrose Kelly. Before they set off, Major General Roberts gave a farewell dinner for the mission, during which he was struck by an uneasy feeling that he would never see any of them again.

The mission reached Kabul on 24 July 1879 and was accommodated in a large building known as the Bala Hissar, the lower part of which had been reserved as a Residency, conveniently situated only 250 yards from the Amir's palace. The escort commanded by Hamilton consisted of just 25 men of the Guides Cavalry and 50 men of the Guides Infantry, it being considered that anything larger would be seen as provocative by the Afghans, added to which the conventions of diplomacy made Yakub responsible for the safety of the Residency and those within. However, Cavagnari's only reliable means of communication with the outside world was by mounted messenger to Ali Khel, 60 miles distant, and thence by telegraph to India, so for all practical purposes he would be completely isolated in the event of serious trouble. Furthermore, British troops had already begun to withdraw from Afghanistan. Although Cavagnari continued to put a good face on the situation, he was seen by the Afghans as the source of their humiliation and heartily disliked, while support for Yakub had declined because of his easy acceptance of the terms of the Treaty of Gandamak. For the moment, therefore, while Kabul remained peaceful, there were pressures building up beneath the surface that threatened to explode at any moment.

That moment arrived late in August when six Afghan regular regiments from Herat marched into Kabul on routine relief. They were owed several months' arrears of pay and were beyond the control of their officers. They jeered at the Kabuli regiments that had been beaten by Browne and Roberts, wanted to know why the British mission had been allowed to remain in Kabul and demanded to be led against it. Cavagnari was warned of all this by a retired risaldar-major of the Guides, Nakhshband Khan, who lived just outside the city, but his only comment was that barking dogs do not bite.

'But these dogs do bite,' replied Nakhshband Khan.

'Well,' said Cavagnari, 'they can only kill the handful of us here, and our death will be avenged.'

On 2 September he despatched the short message 'All well.' By the time it was delivered to Lord Lytton, the Viceroy of India, at Simla, he was dead.

Early in the morning of 3 September the mutinous regiments paraded without arms to receive pay. When they were given less than their entitlement, such discipline as they retained broke down completely. When someone shouted that the British had money they swarmed towards the Residency. It was true that Cavagnari possessed funds with which to assist the Amir if the need arose, but he was not inclined to part with them in these circumstances. Thwarted, the mutineers made to loot the building, but were quickly dissuaded when the escort fired several shots. Now inflamed with murderous fury, they rushed off to collect their own weapons.

All now depended upon 22-year-old Lieutenant Walter Hamilton and his Guides to defend a compound that was not defensible since it did not even possess a perimeter wall and consisted of a series of flat-roofed buildings surrounding a courtyard that was overlooked from several directions. A sullen roar announced the return of the mutineers, accompanied by the Kabul mob. Fire was opened on the Residency and promptly returned. As to the course of events, we are dependent upon outside witnesses, notably former Risaldar-Major Nakhshband Khan, and such evidence as could be subsequently collected, for with three exceptions those within died to a man. The old soldier recalled:

> I myself saw the four European officers charge out at the head of some 25 of the garrison. They drove away a party holding some broken ground. When chased, the Afghan soldiers ran like sheep before a wolf. Later, another sally was made by a detachment, with but three officers at their head. Cavagnari was not with

them this time. A third sally was made with only two officers leading, Hamilton and Jenkins; and the last of the sallies was made by a Sikh jemadar [Jewand Singh] bravely leading. No more sallies were made after this.

Nakhshband Khan's evidence was obviously given with a heavy heart. Unfortunately, he gives us no time scale, for the fight raged on throughout the day until evening. It is known that, one after the other, three men were sent to thread their way through the Bala Hissar to ask the Amir for help. All got through but were detained under guard by Yakub, a fact to which they owed their lives. In other respects the Amir, knowing that he had lost popular support, was in a difficult situation, for few Afghan kings died peacefully in their beds and although he had 2,000 troops at his disposal he was not willing to test their uncertain loyalty in a fight against his own people. Instead, he sent a cryptic message to Hamilton saying, 'As God wills; I am making preparations.' He also sent one of his generals to restrain the mutinous troops, but the man was promptly pulled from his horse and beaten up.

Meanwhile the Guides were taking a fearful toll of their attackers. At about noon the Afghans succeeded in forcing the gates and swarmed into the compound, setting fire to the main building of the Residency. Hamilton is said to have been killed, sword in hand, while leading what seems to have been a successful counter-attack, for the survivors of the garrison were able to maintain their position on the roof and in a detached building. Yells of derision greeted Afghan suggestions that if the Muslims among them surrendered their lives would be spared. Inevitably, as thousands of bullets rained in upon the compound, the Guides' numbers began to fall steadily. Towards dusk the fire completed its work. The roof collapsed, and amid the holocaust the few survivors were swamped in savage, deadly little struggles. To the end, the Guides had remained true to their salt and kept faith with each other. In and around the Residency were strewn some 600 Afghan bodies; perhaps twice that number of wounded hobbled or were carried away from the scene of the massacre by their friends.

The news reached Simla on 5 September. At home the stand of Hamilton and his men aroused pride, fierce anger and calls for revenge. The withdrawal of troops to India was reversed and the war was on again—with a vengeance. Yakub lost his nerve and fled to Roberts' camp, claiming that he wished to abdicate and that he would rather cut grass for the British than rule Afghanistan; few trusted him. Having defeated an Afghan army at Charasia on 6 October, Roberts reached Kabul four days later. On 11 October he visited the ruins of the Residency, the dismal scene being described by Howard Hensman, an eye witness:

> Our first view was of the rear wall, still intact, but blackened on the top, where the smoke had swept across. At each angle where the side walls joined were seen the loopholes from which the fire of the little force on the roof had been directed at the overwhelming numbers attacking them.* Every square foot round these loopholes was pitted with bullet marks, the balls having cut deeply into the hard mud plaster. The courtyard of the Residency is about 90 feet square and at its northern end, where formerly stood a three-storey building, are nothing but bare walls, blackened and scarred by fire, and a huge heap of rubbish, the ruins of the roof and walls which fell in as the woodwork was destroyed. Portions of the partition walls still remain, jutting silently, sullenly out of the mass of debris. The whitewashed walls on the left are here and there bespattered with blood, and on the raised basement on which the building stood are the remains of a large fire, the half-charred beams still resting in the ashes in the middle of the chamber, and near them were two skulls and a heap of human bones, still fetid. It would seem as if a desperate struggle had taken place in the room, the blood stains on the walls and floor being clearly discernible.†

A few days later the accidental explosion of a powder magazine symbolically completed the destruction of the Bala Hissar. The Kabulis remained hostile and sullen and expressed no remorse whatever for the massacre of Cavagnari and his escort. Roberts therefore decided that a degree of terror would concentrate their minds effectively, hanging every one of those known to have been implicated in the deed. Evidence was taken from the seven Guides who had either been detained by Yakub or were absent from the Residency on duty, and from many other sources. Among the first to hang was the Mayor of Kabul, who had contemptuously had the bodies of the Guides thrown into the ditch of the Bala Hissar, where they became carrion. Another was a man known to have stuck Cavagnari's head on a pole on the ridge above the city. Nominal rolls of the disbanded Herati regiments enabled more of the ringleaders

---

* As these loopholes did not exist previously, Hamilton or his VCOs must have given orders for them to be knocked through, which cannot have been an easy task in the circumstances.
† Howard Hensman, *The Afghan War of 1879-80*, London, 1881.

to be rounded up in the villages around Kabul. Altogether, about 100 were hanged in batches of ten.

After the commission appointed to enquire into the attack on the Residency had completed its work, consideration was given as to how those who had fought in its defence should be honoured. At the time Indian soldiers were not eligible for the Victoria Cross, but the entire escort was awarded the Indian Order of Merit, an older award of similar standing that had been introduced in the days of the Company's rule. In addition, the Guides were authorised to wear the battle honour 'Residency, Kabul' on its colours and appointments. In their depot at Mardan the Guides erected a memorial to Lieutenant Walter Hamilton and his men, inscribing upon it a sentence from the commission's report: 'The annals of no army and no regiment can show a brighter record of bravery than has been achieved by this small band of Guides.' Few would wish to argue with that.

Well over half a century has passed since India and Pakistan attained their independence, time enough for the public memory of the many battles fought together by British and Indian soldiers to have faded into the blur of long ago and far away. Yet some things remain. The Corps of Guides became part of the Pakistan Army and is still regarded as an élite. The Raj itself remains the subject of considerable interest—witness the success of M. M. Kay's novel *The Far Pavilions*, which was adapted for television and contains a factional reconstruction of the defence of the Kabul Residency, accurate insofar as some of the facts can never be known.

General
Sir Hector Macdonald

'Fighting Mac'

TO THE NORTH-WEST of Inverness is the town of Dingwall, near which is a hamlet called Rootfield, a community so tiny that it fails to find a place in the average road atlas. In Rootfield is a small, whitewashed farmhouse, no different from many hundreds of others across Scotland, which was once the home of William Macdonald, crofter and stonemason, and his wife Ann. Above Dingwall itself is Mitchell Hill, on which stands an imposing granite tower, 100 feet high, dominating the town. Croft and tower are separated in distance by only a few miles, and in time by 54 years. They are linked by the career of Hector Archibald Macdonald, who was born at Rootfield on 13 April 1853, and whose many achievements are commemorated by the memorial tower, erected in 1907, three years after his death.

It is rare even today for a private soldier to rise to general's rank, but in Queen Victoria's army such an event was almost inconceivable. Nevertheless, there were men of unusual ability who achieved that distinction. One such was William Robertson, who eventually became a field marshal and Chief of the Imperial General Staff. Another was Hector Macdonald, a soldier's general who led from the front, universally known as 'Fighting Mac'.

William and Ann Macdonald had five sons. Supporting a large family on William's income cannot have been easy, but it says much for the value they set on education that young Hector was not sent out to work until he was aged 14. He was at first apprenticed to a draper in Dingwall but soon joined a larger organisation, the Royal Clan Tartan and Tweed Warehouse in Inverness, although this meant living away from home. However, as were many young Scots of his age, he was driven by the

177

urge to be 'o'er the hills and far away'. Every week a recruiting sergeant in the full dress of the 92nd Gordon Highlanders visited Inverness. Impressed by what the sergeant had to say, Hector volunteered, but was told he would have to wait until he was 18. He protested that he hadn't far to go and the sergeant, seeing a strong, healthy, well set-up lad with plenty of potential for growth, decided not to apply the strict letter of the law.

Hector Macdonald was a natural soldier and the type of recruit to be welcomed by any regiment. He was educated, intelligent and of smart appearance, and he paid attention to detail. Immensely strong, he more than held his own in the rough and tumble of barrack-room life. Both his comrades and his superiors recognised that he possessed the indefinable quality of leadership, so that he rose steadily through the ranks of the non-commissioned officers. Throughout his life he emphasised the importance of drill, not simply as a means of instilling discipline and teamwork but also, in an era when soldiers still fought in close order, as a means of getting them exactly where they were wanted in the shortest possible time. His word of command could be heard well beyond the parade ground.

When the Second Afghan War broke out in 1878 Macdonald had attained the rank of colour sergeant, in itself a remarkable achievement after only eight years' service, especially as he was still a comparatively young soldier. The 92nd Highlanders moved up to the Frontier from the regiment's peacetime stations at Sitapore and Benares, but, apart from the usual sniping and small-scale actions, the regiment did not become engaged in serious operations until the following year, when it formed part of a column advancing on Kabul from the south, via the Shutagardan Pass. During the subsequent campaign the Gordons, consisting of fully acclimatised, long-service professionals, fought in the Battle of Charasia, took part in the dangerous operations around Kabul, formed part of the force which made the epic march from Kabul to Kandahar in 1880 and fought in the decisive Battle of Kandahar. To tell their story in full would be to tell much of the story of the war itself, for which there is insufficient space; nor would it be entirely relevant, as Colour Sergeant Macdonald was not yet in a position to influence events at that level.

The war, nonetheless, marked a turning point in his fortunes. Towards the end of September 1879 the regiment was encamped at

Shutargardan with C Company, in which Macdonald was serving, detached to hold Karatiga Fort. Shortly after the company's arrival tribesmen cut the telegraph wire to the fort, then ambushed a party of Sikhs sent out to repair it, killing four of them. As the hills were now swarming with men, a much stronger party was needed to complete the task. Those detailed included eighteen men of the 92nd under Macdonald and a 45-strong detachment of the 3rd Sikhs commanded by a native officer who was himself an Afghan. Seeing how few men Macdonald had with him, the tribesmen mounted a fierce attack, charging down a hillside towards the little group. Many of them, both in the North-West Frontier Province and in Afghanistan itself, were Muslim religious fanatics known as Ghazis who believed they would go straight to heaven if they killed or were killed in battle by unbelievers such as the British or the Hindus. Once launched on an attack, they took a great deal of stopping, and for this reason the Army had adopted the accurate Martini-Henry rifle, which fired a heavy .45in calibre bullet that would drop a man in his tracks. Macdonald, who had assumed overall command and positioned his men carefully, waited until the enemy were within 300 yards, then gave the order for rapid fire. The enemy's leading ranks were bowled over. Some 30 of the Afghans were killed, a similar number were wounded and the rest were chased back over the hill. It says much for the way his men regarded Macdonald that on their return to the fort one of them shouted, 'We'll mak' ye an officer for this day's work, sergeant!' 'Aye,' added another, 'and a general too!' The words were half-joking, but they were to prove prophetic. Roberts commented that 'The manner in which the colour sergeant and the native officer handled their men gave me a high opinion of them both.'

Macdonald was to distinguish himself twice more during the campaign, during the Battle of Charasia on 6 October and on the Sher Darzawa Heights in December 1879. On the former occasion tribesmen crowded on to hills on either flank to watch the assault on the enemy's principal position. Some of them began sniping at the picquets, making such a nuisance of themselves that it became necessary to dislodge them. A party of Gordons under Lieutenant Grant and Colour Sergeant Macdonald mounted an attack, climbing a bare hillside so steep that at times they were on all fours, under fire the while. On reaching the summit, breathless, they were counter-attacked by superior numbers. As one account recalls:

> The Ghazis again and again threw themselves on the group of Gordons led by Colour Sergeant Macdonald. Using his immense strength, he parried and lunged and, at last, by sheer force drove the enemy from their position. None fought more bravely than Macdonald.

The result of these actions was that when the army reached the fortified encampment at Sherpur, Kabul, Roberts offered Macdonald the choice between a battlefield commission or the Victoria Cross. Both were signal honours, but Macdonald shrewdly calculated that commissioning in the field was actually a rarer event than the award of the supreme decoration for valour. He accepted the commission and is said to have commented that there would be time for the Victoria Cross later, becoming one of a tiny handful of men known to have refused the award. When his promotion was officially announced in the *London Gazette*, the men of his company carried him shoulder high behind a piper through the cheering lines of the regiment to the officers' quarters, where each of them took it in turn to salute him. The officers later presented him with a suitably engraved sword to commemorate the event, and the sergeants gave him a dirk. Thus while the transition from the Sergeants' to the Officers' Mess can sometimes be difficult, on this occasion Macdonald's worth was clearly recognised throughout the regiment and it was not so. Only later, when he came into contact with those to whom airs and graces were important were his accent, direct manner and humble origins the subject of snide comment, always delivered behind his back and, significantly, never to his face.

On the conclusion of the Second Afghan War the Gordons moved to South Africa, where they immediately found themselves involved in another war. Once the Zulu menace had been contained, the Boers of the Transvaal made it clear that they resented the annexation of their country by the British and in 1880 they declared themselves to be an independent republic. As the small British garrisons scattered across the Transvaal were thought to be in some danger, a relief column under Major General Sir George Colley was sent to get them out. The problem was that Colley fatally underestimated the fighting qualities of the Boers. They fought neither like European armies nor like the native armies the British had become accustomed to dealing with. As farmers surrounded by potentially hostile tribes and wild animals, they were of necessity crack shots, and they were also adept at fieldcraft and concealment, capable of taking advantage of every scrap of cover. On 28 January 1881 they inflicted a sharp reverse on Colley at Laing's Nek. He decided to render their position untenable by occupying the nearby Majuba Hill, 2,500 feet high. On the night of 26 February he led a 650-strong scratch force, including 180 Gordon Highlanders and detachments from the Northamptonshire Regiment and The King's Royal Rifle Corps, plus a party of seamen, in the long climb to the summit. With them went 2nd Lieutenant Hector Macdonald's platoon, which was to hold the western flank of the defences. Perhaps 'defences' is an inappropriate word, as Colley, supremely confident, rejected every suggestion that the position should be entrenched.

When dawn revealed to the Boers the presence of scarlet coats on Majuba Hill, they mounted an immediate counter-attack while Colley and his men were still sleeping. The slopes of the hill contained numerous false crests and were covered with boulders, enabling them to approach undetected. Before those on the summit understood what was happening, the Boers were within killing range, their specially selected marksmen picking off anyone who dared to show himself. In a fight lasting just one hour Colley's troops were driven off the hill with the loss of 93 killed, 133 wounded and 58 taken prisoner. Colley paid for his over-confidence with his life. The Boers sustained the loss of one man killed and five wounded.

Macdonald's platoon was gradually whittled away until only he and a lance corporal remained, reduced to hurling rocks when their ammunition ran out. As the firing died down they found themselves surrounded by Boers, one of whom made a grab for Macdonald's sporran. Outraged, Macdonald kicked the man the stomach, sending him winded to the ground. A second Boer clapped a rifle to the officer's head, but on recovering his breath the first man knocked it away, commenting that Macdonald was too good a man to kill. The two of them laid into him, only to find that he was too much for them, for by now he was berserk with fury. In the end it took four Boers to restrain him and he was still cursing them fluently in Gaelic. He was brought before their commander, General

Petrus Joubert, who examined the sword which had been presented to him when he was commissioned. After reading the inscription, Joubert handed it back to him with the comment, 'A man who has won such a sword should not be separated from it.' Macdonald was held prisoner in the camp at Laing's Nek for a few days, then released. His bout of fisti-cuffs with his captors had earned him the nickname 'Fighting Mac', and it would stick. His chivalrous treatment by Joubert was typical of the Boers on that occasion. Colley's aide, the then Lieutenant Ian Hamilton, who would command at Gallipoli during World War I, was so seriously wounded that he was released at once. During his brief captivity he had pondered aloud on the reasons for the defeat. 'What else can you expect when you choose to fight on a Sunday?' asked the Boers, a scrupulously devout people. The battle won the Transvaal its independence, although the terms of the peace treaty were such as to render another war inevitable.

In 1883 Macdonald was on leave in Edinburgh. Socially he was in something of a limbo, for as an officer in a Highland regiment some of the simpler forms of enjoyment he had been used to while serving in the ranks were no longer appropriate, yet he was on no more than nodding terms with the gentry. He began taking long solitary walks, and it was during one of these that he met Christina Duncan. In the spring of 1884 the two were married according to the old Scottish style, which amounted to little more than a declaration sworn on the Bible. Legally binding, this form of marriage ceremony was not revoked until 1940. It was used in this case because Christina's family did not approve of Macdonald and their marriage remained a secret known only to a very few. This was to have a baleful effect on his later career.

Great Britain had now become involved in Egypt and the Sudan. In 1885 Macdonald took part in the expedition to rescue General Charles Gordon, who was besieged by the dervish army in Khartoum, serving as garrison adjutant at Assiut. When the expedition proved abortive it was decided to withdraw altogether from the Sudan and concentrate on the defence of the Egyptian frontier as well as holding the port of Suakin on the Red Sea. In addition, the decision had already been taken that, as the old Egyptian Army, an indifferent organisation of poor morale, had been reduced to a constabulary, Britain would be responsible for creating a new one. Twenty-five experienced British officers of proven ability would be seconded for the purpose, being given ranks two grades above those which they held in the British Army. Among those selected was Hector Macdonald who, now that he had a wife to support, was doubtless grateful for the additional pay.

Given decent conditions of service and fair treatment, the Egyptians made good soldiers, as did the Sudanese recruits, who, mainly former slaves or fugitives from the Khalifa's savage rule, were formed into their own battalions. To Macdonald's amusement, they loved drill for its own sake and would even drill each other in their spare time. A fine linguist, he was quickly able to communicate with his troops. In due course he would raise and train the 11th Sudanese. His training methods pushed the men to their limits but paid off in battle. One story has it that while on a gruelling route march he overheard three grumbling soldiers vowing to shoot him in the back when they next went into action. Halting the column, he formed it into a square and confronted them.

'Now, you three fellows are going to shoot me when we are next fighting, are you?' he said. 'Why wait so long? Why not do it now? You have your rifles, so why not use them? Here I am—shoot me!'

Guffaws of laughter spread along the ranks. Eyes downcast and shamefaced, the three embryo assassins began shuffling their feet in the dust. The march continued.

For a while Macdonald served under Colonel Horatio Kitchener at Suakin. Kitchener possessed a bleak, humourless personality and, a bachelor himself, he did not care for married officers, which gave Macdonald another reason for preserving the secrecy of his own nuptials. The hinterland of Suakin was home to the fierce Hadendowa tribesmen, the original 'Fuzzy Wuzzies', who were led by Osman Digna, the best of the dervish generals. The battles around the port, therefore, while small in scale, were fought with unparalleled ferocity, with quarter rarely being expected or given by either side. Macdonald took part in the battle of Gamaizah, was present when a dervish force crossed the Egyptian frontier in 1889, only to be defeated at Toski with heavy loss, and was present at the capture of Tokar. Shortly after this, he was awarded the Distinguished Service Order.

The British decision to reconquer the Sudan was taken partly because the Italian Army had sustained a severe reverse at the hands of the

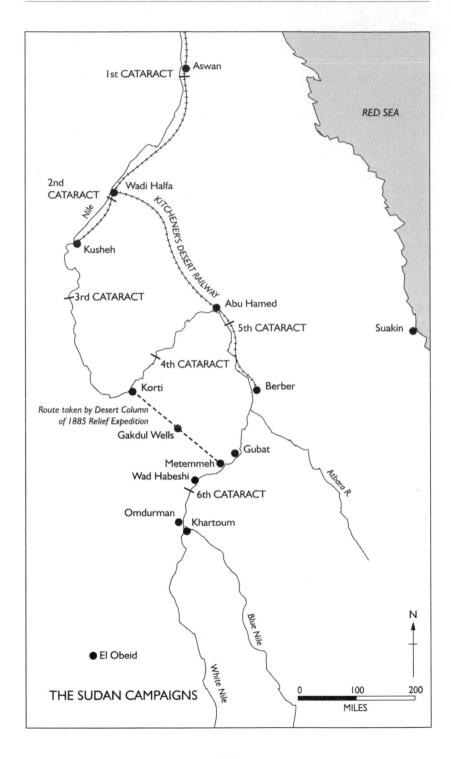

1st CATARACT
Aswan

RED SEA

2nd CATARACT
Wadi Halfa

Nile

KITCHENER'S DESERT RAILWAY

Kusheh

3rd CATARACT

Abu Hamed

5th CATARACT

Suakin

4th CATARACT

Korti

Berber

Route taken by Desert Column
of 1885 Relief Expedition

Gakdul Wells

Gubat

Metemmeh

Wad Habeshi

Atbara R.

6th CATARACT

Omdurman

Khartoum

N

El Obeid

Blue Nile

THE SUDAN CAMPAIGNS

White Nile

0   100   200

MILES

Abyssinians in 1892, the result being to lower European prestige across Africa, but mainly because other powers, notably France, were showing an unwelcome interest in establishing control of the upper reaches of the Nile. Kitchener, who had been appointed Sirdar (Commander-in-Chief) of the Egyptian Army in 1892, was ordered to plan and execute the campaign. As we shall see, although he was far from being a notable tactician, he was an extremely efficient organiser. The campaign he planned would consist of a slow, step-by-step advance, during which his strength would be increased steadily until he was in a position to fight the final, decisive battle under the very walls of the Khalifa's capital, Omdurman.

The first major action of the new campaign took place on 7 June 1896, when the dervishes' advance post at Firket was stormed by three Egyptian infantry brigades. Macdonald, still a major, commanded the 2nd Brigade, which, having shot flat a mounted counter-attack, fought its way right through the position. More dervish outposts fell with varying degrees of fighting as the advance progressed, these local successes doing much to raise the Egyptians' morale. On 21 September Dongola was captured, and here Kitchener took the bold decision that was to win him the campaign, namely to build a railway across the 235 miles of arid desert separating Wadi Halfa from Abu Hamed, so forming an arc across the great bend in the Nile's course. Work began on 1 January 1897. By the end of October the line had reached Abu Hamed and was being extended still further southwards. The continued advance of Kitchener's army, accompanied by hard-hitting gunboats on the river and supported by a sound logistic infrastructure, rendered Osman Digna's position near Suakin untenable and he withdrew to join the Khalifa's main army at Omdurman. Too late, the Khalifa recognised the menace inherent in his opponent's implacable progress. He sent out an inadequate force to contest it, but by now Kitchener's army had been reinforced by a British brigade and at Atbara on 5 April 1898 the dervishes were roundly defeated.

Five months later Kitchener, who had been joined by a second British brigade, was within striking distance of Omdurman. On 1 September, while his gunboats battered the town, the army began constructing a huge half-moon zareba, both flanks of which rested on the Nile, around the village of El Egeiga, seven miles to the north. Outside the zareba lay a wide, featureless plain, bare of cover but intersected here and there by a shallow depression. Approximately two miles to the south-west was a rocky feature known as Jebel Surgham, about 250 feet in height, while a similar distance to the north-west were the low Kerreri Hills. The British held the left of the line and the Egyptians the right. Macdonald's brigade, consisting of the 2nd Egyptians and the 9th, 10th and 11th Sudanese, was positioned on the extreme right. Macdonald himself, who had risen to the rank of lieutenant colonel by the time of the Atbara battle, had recently been promoted to full colonel.

The Khalifa was unable to resist the challenge. At dawn he led out his army, over 60,000 strong, swinging round behind Jebel Surgham for an immediate assault on the zareba. The tossing banners, the sun sparkling on thousands of spear-points and sword-blades, the groundswell of chanting as the dervishes roused themselves into a killing frenzy—all induced a universal feeling of awe. At 06:25, with the enemy 2,700 yards distant and closing, Kitchener's artillery opened fire, followed by the gunboats and then the Maxim machine guns. Bayonets fixed, the infantry made ready. At 06:35, with the range down to 2,000 yards, firing commenced on the British sector, and within ten minutes the whole of Kitchener's line was ablaze. Although their leading ranks were continually shot to tatters, the dervishes came on with an astonishing courage that provoked sincere admiration. On the British sector few got closer to the zareba than 800 yards, but against the slower-firing Egyptians they managed to close the gap to within 400 yards. Then, at about 07:30, recognising the impossibility of their task, those of them that could turned and began walking slowly away.

Kitchener now made the most serious mistake of his professional career. He seemed unaware that the Egyptian cavalry and the Camel Corps had provoked about one-third of the dervish army, under an emir named Osman Sheikh el Din, into pursuing them across the Kerreri Hills. The cavalry had disengaged neatly and re-entered the zareba by making for the river, as did the slower-moving Camel Corps, although the latter got into difficulties from which it had to be rescued by the gunboats. Balked of his prey, Osman began retracing his steps to the battlefield with no fewer than 20,000 men at his disposal. Concurrently Kitchener, believing the battle to be over, ordered the army to leave the zareba and, wheeling left across Jebel Surgham, commenced a general advance on Omdurman.

Being on the extreme right, Macdonald's brigade had furthest to go, and it also had to strike more deeply across the battlefield, now littered with the enemy's dead, dying and wounded. The brigade was deployed in line, facing roughly west, and actually engaged with a heavy counterattack made by the sullenly retreating dervish force commanded by the emir Ali Wad Helu. At that moment Osman's force came streaming into view across the Kerreri Hills, hell-bent on blooding its spears. The implications were immediately apparent to Macdonald. If his brigade were swamped by this fresh attack, the dervishes would charge on into the rear of the advancing army, now about a mile distant, and do immense damage. At just that moment he received orders telling him to catch up with the advance on Omdurman.

'I'll no do it!' he snapped, pointing to the advancing enemy. 'I'll see them damned first. We maun just fight!'

Now engaged on two fronts, he coolly redeployed the brigade so that it resembled an 'L', shifting battalions from the left flank to the right across the inner angle. His calm was so icy that he rebuked the 9th Sudanese for their sloppy drill. Then his regiments opened a tremendous fire, supported by the brigade's Maxims and attached artillery, the last having to resort to case shot. Even so, the dervishes managed to close to within 30 yards of the line. For a moment Kitchener was stunned by this unexpected development, then he despatched reinforcements from every quarter of the battlefield. The Camel Corps came up, extending Macdonald's line to the right, followed by the Lincolnshire Regiment. The 4th Egyptian Brigade, left behind to guard the zareba, marched towards the action, around the eastern edges of which the Egyptian cavalry was already hovering. Finally, the 1st British Brigade, hurrying back across the battlefield, fell on the dervish flank and the attack shredded away into the desert. It had been a very near run thing indeed, for by the time the first reinforcements arrived Macdonald's men were down to six rounds of ammunition apiece. The brigade's losses, amounting to eleven killed and 121 wounded, were higher than those of any other formation in the army, although the 21st Lancers suffered the highest regimental loss during the famous charge in which Winston Churchill took part, sustaining 71 casualties.

MACDONALD'S REDEPLOYMENT OF HIS BRIGADE
TO MEET TWO DERVISH ATTACKS

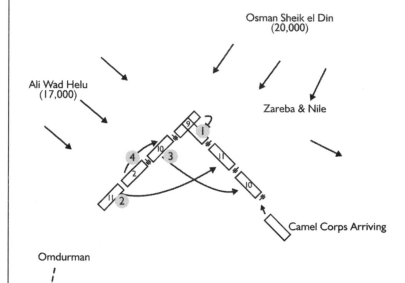

Kerreri Hills

Osman Sheik el Din
(20,000)

Ali Wad Helu
(17,000)

Zareba & Nile

Camel Corps Arriving

Omdurman

1 Three Companies of 9th Sudanese wheel
   right to meet new attack

2 11th Sudanese move across to their right

3 10th Sudanese move to extend right flank

4 2nd Egyptians take ground to their right, extending
   left flank of 9th Sudanese Sections of artillery
   battery to conform to these movements

N

Macdonald's own version of these events, described in the following extract from a letter he wrote shortly after the battle, is as modest as it is professional:

> Their [the enemy to the west's] advance was very rapid and determined and though they appeared to be mowed down by the artillery and maxims they still pressed on in such numbers and so quickly that I brought up the infantry into line with the guns, but in spite of the hail of lead now being poured at effective ranges into their dense masses they still pressed forward in the most gallant manner until between 300 and 400 yards when they practically melted away, leaving the Khalifa's black flag flying alone within 250 yards of Jackson's battalion. A fine performance, truly, for any race of men. You can well imagine how anxiously I watched during the progress of this attack the movements of the enemy on my right [north], whom I now saw advancing in huge masses. I was just in time to bring the battery on to the new front and complete at the double the movement of each battalion [to this] before I moved the next, as the remnants of the first attack were still hanging around, and the Camel Corps prolonged to my right. During this movement the enemy cavalry charged home to death—not one got away as far as I am aware. They could not have been more than 100 in all; a heroic deed if ever there was any. The enemy pressed on in two columns densely packed, but were disposed of as the first attack was and slunk away to the west. A couple of companies of Maxwell's brigade returned while this was going on and Lewis turned his brigade about and came up on my left. The 1st British Brigade also arrived and I placed the Lincolns on the right. The remainder went to the left but by now the action was over and the enemy in full flight. I confess I was thankful to see them go. It was hard work, especially for the artillery. In the first attack's second phase they fired from 1,100 yards to case and in the second attack's second phase 800 yards to case and were engaged thus for over two hours without ceasing, a tremendous physical strain on any set of men. The infantry on average fired 71 rounds per man. The 11th fired 105 rounds per man. Lots of men had not a round left. The fire discipline of the brigade under very trying circumstances was markedly good and I cannot but feel proud of the splendid discipline of the troops who enabled me to make a complete change of front by moving whole battalions in strings of fours from one flank of the line to the other in the face of a persistently aggressive enemy.

By 11:30 the battle was over. The army resumed its march on Omdurman, which fell that afternoon. The power of the Khalifa, now a fugitive who would be hunted to death, was broken for ever. The battle was Kitchener's victory, but its hero was Macdonald—a fact that the Sirdar generously acknowledged in his despatch: 'Macdonald had handled his troops with masterly skill, and had snatched victory from the jaws of peril.'

On his return home 'Fighting Mac' was lionised wherever he went. He was the toast of London and honoured all over Scotland. The University of Glasgow awarded him a Doctorate of Law. Promoted to brigadier general, he served briefly as Aide de Camp to Queen Victoria and then, in 1899, departed for a new command in the Sirhind district of India.

During the same year the Second Boer War broke out. Its early stages were marked by serious incompetence on the part of the local British commanders, resulting in a number of humiliating defeats. In particular the Highland Brigade, consisting of the Black Watch, the Argyll and Sutherland Highlanders, the Seaforth Highlanders and the Highland Light Infantry, sustained needlessly high casualties and was mishandled in action to the point that, demoralised and unhappy, it had begun to hate some of the generals. In the opinion of many, it would respond only to 'Fighting Mac', and he was sent for. Promoted to major general, he assumed command at the end of January 1900 and was immediately into everything. He visited all four battalions, meeting every officer personally and as many of the NCOs and men as possible, probing into every aspect of regimental life from the cookhouse to recreational facilities. Having served in the ranks himself, he knew how soldiers thought. On occasion, while carrying out formal inspections, he would dismount to question individual soldiers in his blunt, no-nonsense way, and he would listen carefully to their answers. The impression he left with them was of a commander who knew his business and could be trusted. His message was always the same. The past was over and done with, so they should stop feeling sorry for themselves and smarten up. Furthermore, Lord Roberts was on his way to take command of the army, with Kitchener as his chief of staff; from now on, therefore, there would be a radical change in the way the war would be conducted. The result was that, once again, the brigade became the formidable fighting force it had always been.

Having already familiarised himself with the situation before he arrived, Roberts was able to put his plans into effect immediately. Under cover of a feint attack, to be delivered by the Highland Brigade, he intended redeploying the army in secret and outflanking the Boer defences on the Modder River. For the operation Macdonald would be reinforced with two cavalry squadrons and an artillery battery.

The diversion began on 3 February. The Highlanders marched to a ford known as the Koodesberg Drift, which was found to be undefended. Macdonald promptly pushed the Seaforths across to entrench the Koodesberg hill itself as well as adjacent high ground while the rest of the brigade pitched camp on the south bank of the river. With great satisfaction, Macdonald noted that the move had been watched by Boer scouts, who galloped off with the news. By 6 February it was apparent that a large Boer force had been drawn to the area. The following morning the Seaforths were attacked in strength. Macdonald sent up two companies each of the Black Watch and the Highland Light Infantry to support them, with the result that the attack was beaten off with severe loss. On 9 February the brigade, having achieved what it set out to do, marched back to its base camp, where it received Roberts' personal congratulations for a neatly executed operation.

The rest of the army's secret redeployment had now been completed. General Piet Cronje, commanding the Boer forces on this sector, suddenly found himself in danger of being cut off from Bloemfontein, the capital of the Orange Free State, and began to withdraw eastwards along the Modder. His retreat, however, was slow, being restricted to the pace of the ox wagons used by his men's families. On 18 February he was encircled at Paardeberg Drift by the faster-moving British, and entrenched himself along the banks of the river. Roberts, suddenly taken ill, temporarily handed over command to Kitchener, who decided to launch an attack.

Unfortunately the area across which the Highland Brigade advanced was flat and completely featureless, offering no cover of any kind. The Boers waited until they were within 100 yards, then opened fire. The Highlanders sustained casualties, but this time they were not required to execute vain, suicidal charges. Though pinned down and unable to advance throughout the day, they returned the fire, making careful note of all the enemy positions, details of which were later passed to the artillery. Macdonald was hit in the left foot, just below the ankle, but the bullet passed through cleanly. While his wound was being dressed his horse was shot dead beside him. As soon as he was able he borrowed a horse and visited each of his battalions in their bivouacs, hobbling among the men with the aid of a walking stick. The brigade's morale remained unaffected by its ordeal.

The abortive attack had cost the army 320 men killed and 942 wounded. Roberts, less than pleased, hurried forward to resume command. To avoid further useless casualties he resorted to sustained bombardment by his artillery, recognising that the Boers, close to starvation, could not hold out for long. On 27 February Cronje and his 4,000 men surrendered. For Macdonald, the date had a special significance as it was the anniversary of the débâcle on Majuba Hill, which had been celebrated by Boers ever since. If, however, that particular ghost had been laid to rest, there was little jubilation. The Boer laager was a scene of desolation, strewn with graves, smashed wagons, dead horses and oxen. In particular, the presence of women and children on the battlefield was something the troops found alien to their nature, albeit in circumstances that were beyond their control.

Kimberley had already been relieved. Far to the east, General Sir Redvers Buller's army finally broke through to Ladysmith the day after Cronje's surrender. On 13 March Roberts' troops captured Bloemfontein and began marching north towards the Transvaal. Success now followed hard on the heels of success. After a siege of seven months, Mafeking was relieved on 18 May. Johannesburg fell on 31 May and Pretoria, the capital of the Transvaal, was entered on 5 June. When the two armies of Roberts and Buller met at Vlakfontein on 4 July, all formal resistance had been crushed and it seemed that the war was over.

Not all Boers were inclined to accept the verdict of the battlefield. Some of their commandos, seeing that the British lines of communication were dangerously strung out, had already begun to resort to guerrilla tactics. General Christian de Wet's men were particularly active, capturing two convoys escorted by detachments from the Highland Brigade. In contrast, the brigade fought a successful action against a Boer force at Brantford, north of Bloemfontein, putting it to flight and capturing 270 oxen and 31 wagons containing artillery and small arms ammunition, dynamite, blankets, food and clothing, mainly of British origin. Some Boers were indeed faltering in their resolve, notably those under Commandant General Marthinus Prinsloo of the Orange Free State. In August Prinsloo, cornered in the Brandwater Basin by a force which included the Highland Brigade, decided to surrender. His commandos, each 300 to 500 strong, came in over a period of several days, bringing with them five field guns, until the number of prisoners actually exceeded that of those taken at Paardeberg.

Although Roberts departed for home, leaving Kitchener in command, the war was far from over. It became a different kind of war as the die-hard Boers escalated their guerrilla campaign. It became a war of sudden raids, blockhouse lines and cordon-and-search operations, absorbing huge manpower resources, and it took another two years to bring it to its conclusion. In such a war the formal battlefield formation had no place. When the Highland Brigade was broken up in February 1901 Macdonald was left with genuine sadness. He told the assembled troops:

> I shall always look back with pride on having had the honour of commanding you. Commanding the Highland Brigade is the highest ambition of every Highland soldier, and I am proud and happy in the conviction that your record in South Africa has added fresh lustre to the already glorious annals of the Highland regiments. With soldiers so well disciplined, enduring and humane, the burden of command has been easy and success certain, and it is with deepest regret and feelings of profound admiration for your many sterling qualities that I now bid you farewell.

He was now at the pinnacle of his career and he received a knighthood. It was thought that, after years of arduous campaigning, he deserved a pleasant, undemanding posting. In 1902 he was appointed General Officer Commanding Ceylon. This proved to be a disaster, for the island's Governor, Sir J. West Ridgeway, was devious, politically ambitious and an outright snob. Naturally, the two men disliked each other on sight, but before discussing the course of events it is worth examining the nature of colonial society, where a strict pecking order existed. At the top were those who were considered socially acceptable by Government House, including the local military and naval commanders, the heads of the civil administration and the colony's most important British citizens; then came the officers of the army and navy and executive officials of the civil service; below them were the officers of the police force, engineers and planters; and at the bottom of the pile were the 'box wallahs', who were directly engaged in trade. This hierarchy was paralleled exactly by that of their wives, the memsahibs. Of all those ex-patriots who peopled the colonies it is the mems, with some notable exceptions, who are least fondly remembered. With servants to attend their every need, they sometimes had little to do but gossip over the teacups, and if the chatter revolved around the destruction of someone's reputation, so much the better.

Governor Ridgeway's influential circle of friends included tea planters who had made a great deal of money and liked to think it was they who ran the island. In Macdonald they were confronted by a man who was blunt and straightforward and spoke with a pronounced Scottish accent. They were outraged that that they had been sent someone they considered to be of such 'low breeding'. Furthermore, as his marriage still remained a secret, surprise was expressed at his still apparently being a bachelor.

He ran into trouble almost immediately, while presiding over a review of the island's garrison. To a soldier the parade ground is almost sacrosanct, not to be crossed or entered upon save on duty, and never by a mere civilian without invitation from the parade commander. On this occasion, however, one of the Governor's cronies, who evidently considered himself to be no end of a chap, casually strolled on to the field and began poking about among the troops. It was too much for Macdonald. The former drill sergeant rose within him and his furious word of command shook spectators and troops alike.

"*You, Sir! Get off the field this instant! Yes, you, Sir!*"

Red-faced, the man retreated into the crowd, but the general had made a mortal enemy. The more poisonous of the mems, furious that one of the Governor's charmed inner circle had been publicly humiliated, wasted no time in hitting back. A few days later the following letter appeared in the gossip column of the *Times of Ceylon:*

> Dearest Mab,
>
> Do you really mean to say that, besides yourself, three ladies (all up-country ones, too) were the only ones who went to see our new General arrive? Then, dear, you know we heard a rumour that *he does not like ladies*, and possibly may have been pleasantly surprised to find he had dropped on a spicy little isle where ladies are few and far between.

The implication was obvious. Ridgeway, wanting Macdonald off the island, began encouraging further malicious stories, which were soon forthcoming. One was that he had urinated from the door of a railway carriage within sight of children—but then so did every man in Ceylon, as the carriages were not equipped with toilets. Far more damaging was the suggestion that he had formed an unhealthy friendship with a school-boy, the son of a wealthy Sinhalese family. Having got what he needed, Ridgeway summoned Macdonald to his office and confronted him with the various allegations. Macdonald had never backed away from a fight in his life, but now it was vicious whispers that were being fired at him rather than honest bullets and, simple, honourable soldier that he was, he was out of his depth. He defended himself fiercely, commenting that Ridgeway was in no position to judge him. The Governor silkily responded that Macdonald's way out of the dilemma was for him to leave the island, the only alternative being a court martial.

Macdonald travelled to London, where he obtained an audience with King Edward VII. The King, a noted connoisseur of other men's wives, would doubtless have taken appropriate steps had Macdonald faced similar charges, but, with the trial of Oscar Wilde still fresh in the public memory, this was not an area in which he wished to become involved. He suggested that Macdonald should return to Ceylon, with the proviso that the evidence should be examined *in camera* to determine whether there was a case to answer, prior to any advance notice of a pending court martial.

Macdonald agreed. In March 1903 he set off along the favoured route, which would take him across France to a Mediterranean port, from which he would sail to Port Said and there pick up a steamer bound for the Far East, the advantage being that this cut several days off the journey and avoided the unpleasant passage of the Bay of Biscay. In Paris, feeling unwell, he decided to rest for a few days at the Hotel Regina. He was unaware that Ridgeway, having learned that he was on his way back to Ceylon, had vindictively released the entire unsupported story to the world's press, knowing full well that some of the mud, once thrown, would stick. Thus, when Macdonald came down to breakfast one morning he was thunderstruck to discover from his newspaper that he was to be made to answer what were described as 'grave charges'. He immediately returned to his room and, preferring death to dishonour, shot himself.

There were few in England willing to accept the slur on 'Fighting Mac', and even fewer in Scotland. The government, astonished by the discovery that the general had a wife and son, offered Lady Macdonald a hero's funeral. She was, however, a very private person and declined, earning the resentment of many Scots who wished to commemorate the occasion fittingly; she incurred further resentment when, on 30 March 1903, she interred the general's body at Dean Cemetery, Edinburgh, in a lonely, pre-dawn ceremony. By the coming of light, word of the burial was out and a crowd estimated to number 30,000 had assembled to pay their last respects; during the weeks that followed many thousands more from across the world arrived to say their farewells. Such, indeed, was the public anger at the manner in which Macdonald had been treated that the government appointed a six-man commission to examine the background to the affair. Its report, published on 29 June 1903, clearly indicated that a number of Ridgeway's supporters had hurriedly changed their minds:

> We, unanimously, find absolutely no reason or no crime whatsoever which could create feelings such as would determine suicide, in reference to conviction of any crime affecting the moral and irreproachable character of so brave, so fearless, so glorious and unparalleled a hero; and we firmly believe the cause which gave rise to the inhuman and cruel suggestions of crime were prompted through vulgar feelings of spite and jealousy in his rising to such a high rank of distinction in the British Army; and while we have taken the most reliable and trustworthy evidence from every accessible and conceivable source, we have without hesitation come to the conclusion that there is not the visible, not the slightest particle of truth in foundation of any crime.

The depth of popular feeling can be judged by an extract from a letter written by the novelist Marie Corelli to the Reverend William Macdonald, the general's brother: 'It is hoped and prayed for that, through the unerring justice of God, those who so wickedly hounded a fine soldier to untimely death may meet with lifelong remorse and well-merited punishment.' In the end, there was justice of a kind, for the ambitious Ridgeway, deserted by his influential friends, had become *persona non grata*, remembered only for his vicious attempt at character assassination. In contrast, Macdonald's memorial tower, erected by public subscription in 1907, still stands proudly above Dingwall and has recently been restored. Lady Macdonald died four years later. The general's only son, another Hector, took after his mother in valuing his privacy; he became an engineer and died in 1951.

It might be thought that when all the tumult and the shouting had died away, that was the end of the matter, yet it had the most bizarre sequel.

For many years the story persisted that Macdonald's suicide was rigged. He had, it was said, gone to Germany, where he had assumed the identity of a German officer named August von Mackensen, who was dying of cancer. In fact, Mackensen, also a major general, was in excellent health and at the time of Macdonald's death was commanding an infantry division in Danzig. He was originally an officer of the famous Death's Head Hussars, whose uniform he continued to wear throughout his life. As a full general he won a series of spectacular victories on the Eastern Front in 1915 and was awarded his field marshal's baton. He retired from the army in 1920 but remained a staunch monarchist, being the only one of Imperial Germany's senior officers to attend the former Kaiser's funeral in 1941. He died on 8 March 1945, aged 96, and was buried with full military honours.

Macdonald and Mackensen were indeed of comparable age, and, their differing styles of moustache apart, they could almost have passed for each other, so similar were their features and expression. Mackensen was apparently proud to claim that there was Scottish blood in his ancestry, and, although he denied this on the outbreak of the First World War, the fact was that his caste of features was undeniably Scottish rather than Teutonic. As to why Macdonald/Mackensen chose to serve exclusively on the Eastern Front during the war, the myth had it that he refused to fight against his former countrymen.

The origins of the story are nearly as strange as the story itself. One version puts the source as being a leaflet dropped on British trenches during the war, boasting that Mackensen was really Macdonald and giving details of the latter's career. Superficially the document, if it existed, was a clever piece of propaganda that played upon the British regard for 'Fighting Mac', but the more closely the alleged quotations from it are examined the less convincing they become. Macdonald would never have sanctioned the use of such phrases as 'Scottish peasant', 'common soldier' and 'fell into disgrace'; nor would Mackensen, scion of one of Germany's military families, have permitted such tampering with the truth of his own career. Taking all the circumstances into account, therefore, it is difficult to accept the Macdonald/Mackensen connection as amounting to anything more than an inspired piece of journalism that continued to sell newspapers and magazines to successive generations of those who enjoy an apparent mystery.

A century and more has passed since Hector Macdonald fought his battles and met his tragic end. For most people, the man and his achievements have faded into history, but in Scotland he is still regarded as one of the nation's heroes. In particular, his memory is kept fresh and alive in Dingwall, his home town, where his memorabilia dominate the museum's military room and are a popular tourist attraction. Likewise, his regiment, the Gordon Highlanders, remains proud of the man who joined as young private, was commissioned in the field and went on to become a major general. He has, too, an honoured place in the story of his parent clan, Clan Donald, whose centre on the Isle of Skye is visited every year by thousands of Macdonalds from all over the world.

Major General
Sir Charles Townshend

A hero fatally flawed

CHARLES VERE FERRERS TOWNSHEND was born into a
noble family with military traditions. One of his ancestors, in fact,
had fought at Culloden, succeeded to command when Wolfe was
killed at Quebec and become a field marshal. Despite this, over the years
the family wealth had been dissipated, so that when Charles first saw the
light of day on 21 February 1861 it was in a modest house in unfashionable Southwark. His father, Charles Thornton Townshend, was a cousin
of the third Marquis Townshend and had expectations of inheriting the
title from the fifth marquis until the latter produced an heir. Charles
Thornton had always supported himself, working as a civil servant and a
clerk with a railway company, but his earnings were meagre and he made
little progress. Nevertheless, the fifth marquis looked kindly upon him,
paying for his two sons' education at public school. When Charles Vere
emerged from Dartmouth in 1881 with a subaltern's commission in the
Royal Marine Light Infantry, he also made him an allowance to supplement his junior officer's pay.

The principal elements of Charles Vere Townshend's character had
already become apparent. He was driven, even obsessed, by the need to
succeed in life where his father had failed. To this end, he would throughout his career importune anyone and everyone he thought might assist
his advancement. His features might have been considered handsome
but already contained a hint of self-indulgence. He was good company
and witty, enjoyed every aspect of good living and was popular with
women. He also enjoyed the company of theatre folk and took part in
amateur theatricals, relishing the applause his performances generated.
Professionally, he was a keen student of military history and the lessons it

taught, and he appreciated, correctly, that promotion came most easily to those who sought active service.

In 1884 he was posted to Suakin in the Sudan, where he underwent his baptism of fire and earned a mention in despatches during the skirmishes around the port. He began lobbying for a transfer to the cavalry, but in 1885 found himself in the Camel Corps that formed part of Lord Wolseley's expedition up the Nile to rescue General Charles Gordon from Khartoum. As speed was essential, Wolseley divided his force, forming a Desert Column that would traverse the Bayuda Desert from Korti to Gubat, following a track which cut a cord across the arc formed by the great curve in the Nile's course, and a River Column that would follow the Nile itself. The idea was that once the Desert Column reached Gubat, Gordon's steamers would transport reinforcements into Khartoum, so that the city could hold out until the spring, when the Nile would rise, enabling the River Column to complete the relief. It was a high-risk strategy, fraught with potential dangers, but the only one that stood the slightest chance of getting Gordon out alive.

The Desert Column, commanded by Brigadier General Sir Herbert Stewart, was 2,000 strong and included the Camel Corps, although its strength would be reduced by the need to guard wells and supply depots along the route. It left Korti on 9 January 1885, plodding steadily deeper and deeper into hostile territory. Awaiting it were no fewer than 12,000 dervishes, ordered by the Mahdi to permit Stewart to advance to a point from which escape would be impossible once his little force had been defeated. On 17 January their local commander, considering that such a point had been reached at Abu Klea wells, launched 5,000 of his men in a frenzied attack. By now, Stewart's strength had fallen to 1,500 men, three guns and a Gardner machine gun. He formed a hollow square with the camels hobbled down in the centre. Disciplined firepower kept the dervishes at bay until the Gardner, sited at a corner, jammed. A dervish rush overran it, smashing through the corner into the interior of the square. For the few long minutes it took to restore the situation, Townshend found himself engaged in savage hand-to-hand fighting, sword against sword, bayonet against stabbing spear. With the intruders despatched and its ranks re-formed, the square continued to blast the dervishes at close quarters until, recognising that the attack had failed, they turned and walked off, leaving 1,100 dead behind them. Stewart's casualties amounted to 76 killed and 82 wounded.

The Desert Column resumed its march but was again attacked two days later, near Abu Kru. This time the dervishes were held off at a distance and again sustained heavy casualties before withdrawing. The column sustained the loss of 23 killed, including Stewart, and 98 wounded. Now commanded by Colonel Sir Charles Wilson, it reached the Nile that evening, drank its fill and began constructing a fort for itself. On 21 January Gordon's steamers arrived. Three days later Wilson embarked a token force aboard two of them and set off for Khartoum.

By this time Townshend was escorting a convoy of wounded back along the desert track to the intermediate base established at Gakdul Wells. Shortly after his return to Gubat it was learned that Khartoum had fallen and Gordon was dead. After a series of hair-raising adventures, Wilson and his party managed to reach safety, but now the whole purpose of the expedition had been lost. The Desert Column retraced its weary way to Korti and, with the exception of the Suakin garrison, British troops were withdrawn north of the Egyptian frontier. Townshend, now ill with enteric fever, was sent on leave to England.

A year earlier he had applied for a transfer to the Indian Army, believing that this offered better promotion prospects. His request was granted in January 1886 and he joined the Central India Horse. For the next few years he was employed on regimental duty, seeing minor action on the North-West Frontier. Growing bored, he applied for a return to the Egyptian Army, without result. In 1891 he was sent on a detached posting to Kashmir, where he was given command of a locally raised regiment and took part in the Hunza-Nagar campaign of the same year. Townshend received promotion to captain on 1 February 1892. He resumed his regimental duties, but when trouble broke out in the neighbouring state of Chitral the following year his request for a return to northern Kashmir was granted. Here a word of explanation is necessary.

Chitral, about the same size as Wales, consisted of a remote mountain valley squeezed into the corner where the frontiers of India, Afghanistan, Russia and China converge. It was of no value in itself, but its position made it a player in the Great Game, the nineteenth-century equivalent of the Cold War in which Great Britain interpreted Russian expansion into central Asia as a threat to India and reacted accordingly. In 1876 the ruler of Chitral, known as the Mehtar, had formally placed his country under the protection of the Maharajah of Kashmir, who was in turn under the protection of the government of India. British involvement in the internal affairs of Chitral therefore became inevitable. The Chitralis themselves, while universally regarded as a charming and friendly people, had nevertheless developed treachery and assassination to the point that they had become acceptable social skills. If an individual's quest for power involved him flinging his father, uncle or brother over a precipice, then so be it. Thus, when the reigning Mehtar died in 1892, there ensued the usual murderous scramble for his throne. To recount its convoluted course would absorb many pages and become tedious. Suffice it to say that the only candidate acceptable to the British was a ten-year-old boy named Shujah-ul-Mulk, which quickly became corrupted to 'Sugar and Milk'. Unfortunately, the boy's uncle, Sher Afzul, also wanted the throne. With Afghan assistance, he assembled an army of sorts and early in 1893 began advancing against the state's capital, also called Chitral, which was little more than a village with its own fort. The fort, soon to become the focus of press attention, is described as follows:

> The Chitral Fort is 80 yards square, with walls 25 feet high and about eight feet thick. At each corner there is a tower some 20 feet higher than the wall, and outside the north face on the edge of the river is a fifth tower to guard the waterway. On the east face a garden runs out for a distance of 140 yards, and 40 yards from the south-east tower is a summer house. On the north and west faces are stables and other out-houses. The fort is built of rude masonry kept together, not by cement or mortar of any description, but by a cradlework of beams of wood placed longitudinally and transversely, so as to keep the masonry together. Without this framework of wood the walls would fall to pieces. The fort is situated on the right bank of the Chitral river some 40 or 50 yards from the water's edge. It is commanded from nearly all sides, for mountains close by the river rise above the valley bottom. The fort is so situated for the purpose of maintaining its water supply and at the time of its construction breech-loading rifles were not in possession of the people of the country, so that the fort could not then be fired into.

Within the fort were Shujah-ul-Mulk and a few followers, plus its garrison of Imperial troops. The British officers present were Surgeon Major G. S. Robertson, the British Political Agent; Captain C. Campbell, Inspecting Officer of the Kashmiri Imperial Service Troops; Captain Charles Townshend, commanding the Agent's escort; Captain Baird of the 4th Kashmiri Rifles; Surgeon Captain Whitchurch; Lieutenant B. E. M. Gurdon, the Agent's assistant; and Lieutenant H. K. Harley of the 14th Sikhs. At their disposal were 301 men of the 4th Kashmiri Rifles and 99 men of the 14th Sikhs. The Kashmiris were armed with old Snider rifles and the Sikhs with modern Martini-Henrys, for which 280 and 300 rounds per man, respectively, were available. The garrison's artillery consisted of two 7-pounder guns lacking sights, and 80 rounds of ammunition. There were also in the fort about 160 non-combatants, including 52 Chitralis, who would have to be watched carefully.

At 16:30 on 3 March 1895 Robertson received warning that Sher Afzul was approaching with a large force. Campbell, the senior combatant officer, decided to make a reconnaissance in force and, accompanied by all the British officers save Harley, took out 200 Kashmiris. Two miles down the valley they came under intense fire. It was immediately apparent that they were heavily outnumbered. In a very short time Campbell and Baird were both wounded and two of the native officers were killed. The Kashmiris, encumbered by the long coats they were wearing because of the cold, became unsettled when the enemy began working round their flanks. Something like a panic retreat to the fort began, a massacre only being avoided by the onset of dusk and the appearance of Harley and his Sikhs, who covered the final stages of the withdrawal with their steady fire. Even so, the garrison had sustained the loss of 23 killed and 33 wounded in the foray; in addition Whitchurch, Baird and several sepoys were missing, presumed dead. Some time after the gates had been closed there were calls for them to be opened again and the missing party, completely exhausted, staggered in. Whitchurch had led them, carrying the sorely wounded Baird, through the darkness in a wide detour back to the fort, a feat for which he was subsequently awarded the Victoria Cross. Several of the sepoys undoubtedly owed their lives to his efforts, but Baird died the following morning.

As Campbell's kneecap had been shattered he was unable to exercise effective command, and the defence of the fort therefore became Townshend's responsibility. It was immediately apparent that the only troops upon whom he could rely were Harley's Sikhs, for after their defeat the Kashmiris had, for the moment, degenerated into an armed rabble. Tak-

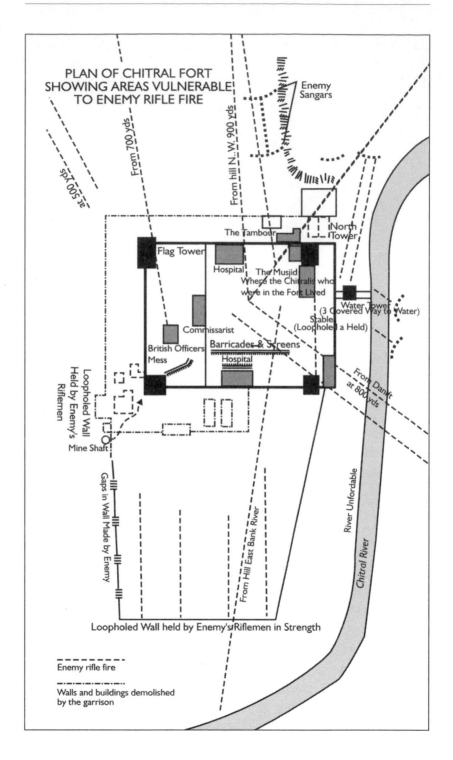

PLAN OF CHITRAL FORT
SHOWING AREAS VULNERABLE
TO ENEMY RIFLE FIRE

Enemy
Sangars

at 500 yds

From 700 yds

From hill N.W. 900 yds

The Tambour

North
Tower

Flag Tower

Hospital

The Musjid
Where the Chitralis who
were in the Fort Lived

Water Tower
(3 Covered Way to Water)

Stable
(Loopholed a Held)

Commissarist

British Officers
Mess

Barricades & Screens

Hospital

Loopholed Wall
Held by Enemy's
Riflemen

From Danin
at 800 yds

Mine Shaft

Gaps in Wall Made by Enemy

From Hill East Bank River

River Unfordable

Chitral River

Loopholed Wall held by Enemy's Riflemen in Strength

- - - - - - - - - -
Enemy rifle fire

- · - · - · - · - ·
Walls and buildings demolished
by the garrison

ing stock, he placed everyone on half rations, calculating that this would enable the fort to hold out for two and a half months; these were supplemented when the officers later decided to kill and eat their horses. His principal anxieties, however, arose from the fact that the fort was overlooked from all sides. Using planks, doors, boxes, sandbags and even piled saddles, he created protection for the troops' backs while they fired from the parapets, and cut up carpets and curtains with which to mask internal doorways and passages, reasoning that the enemy's snipers, unable to see their targets, would soon grow tired of firing at the screens. He also had a covered way dug across the 30 yards separating the water gate from the river and cleared as much ground around the fort as possible to deprive the enemy of cover. The non-combatants he organised into water-carrying and fire-fighting parties.

The enemy quickly established himself in sangars (breastworks built from rocks) all round the fort and began sniping, particularly at the water parties. Townshend retaliated by authorising 30 rounds a day to be fired at the house in which Sher Afzul was known to have taken up residence, but, given the shaky morale of the Kashmiris, he decided against mounting sorties. Several attacks on the east face of the fort were beaten off. However, as all communication with the outside world had been severed, the garrison, uncertain whether the authorities were aware of their predicament, began to suffer increasingly from a sense of isolation. Playing upon this, on 15 March Sher Afzul disclosed that a routine supply convoy on its way to the fort had been ambushed and that a force sent to its rescue had been all but wiped out. As a result of this, he was holding two British officers as hostages, one of whom was produced to verify his story. A hint that the garrison would be given safe conduct if they withdrew from the fort was wisely ignored. Robertson, unsettled by the lack of a Union flag, had one made and run up.

On 7 April the enemy made a determined attempt to destroy the Gun Tower at the south-eastern corner of the fort, piling up bundles of brushwood against its base and setting them ablaze in the hope that the fire would destroy the structure's timber framework and bring it down. Townshend was prepared for this, although it took five hours to bring the flames under control. Of necessity, the fire fighters had to expose themselves above the parapet to drop water and soil on to the fire, nine of them, including Robertson, being wounded by sniper fire. Further attacks on the water point were beaten off on 10 and 11 April.

On 12 April large numbers of the enemy were seen moving off, suggesting the presence of a relief column in the area. In fact, two relief columns were on their way. One, commanded by Major General Sir Robert Low, had assembled at Peshawar and consisted of 15,000 men supported by over 30,000 animals; the other, starting from Gilgit, was commanded by Lieutenant Colonel James Kelly and consisted of just 382 men from his own regiment, the 32nd Punjab Pioneers, two mountain guns, and some 200 reinforcements he was able to pick up along the way. Both Low and Kelly were involved in heavy fighting and forced to traverse difficult mountain terrain, the latter crossing the 12,000-feet high, snow-covered Shandur Pass in arctic conditions.

Meanwhile Sher Afzul had decided to make one last attempt to capture the fort. A mine was started from the summerhouse, the sound of digging being masked by the beating of drums. At midnight on 16 April, however, a sentry noticed the thud of picks close to the walls. Clearly, little time remained before the tunnel was complete and the charges laid that would bring down a section of the defences. Townshend began preparing his counter-measures at once. At 16:00 that afternoon the garden door was opened and Harley led a charge of 40 Sikhs and 60 Kashmiris across the intervening space to the summerhouse, covered by fire from the walls. During the ensuing fight 35 of the enemy were bayoneted as they emerged from the tunnel, 25 more were shot and two were taken prisoner. Harley then blew out the mine with his own demolition charges and returned to the fort. His casualties came to eight killed and thirteen wounded.

The besiegers became less evident during the next few days, and on 20 April Kelly's little column marched in. The siege had lasted forty-six days and cost the garrison 42 killed and 62 wounded. Among the honours awarded, Robertson was knighted, Townshend became a Commander of the Order of the Bath and was promoted to brevet-major, Campbell received the Distinguished Service Order and promotion to brevet-major, and Gurdon and Harley also received the DSO. All ranks of the garrison were rewarded with six months' pay. Kelly, like Townshend, became a CB, was promoted to full colonel and made an ADC to the Queen, all of which was modest enough when one considers his achievements.

Townshend left for some overdue home leave. Arriving in London, he found himself the man of the hour. His defence of the little ramshackle fort on the edge of the world had caught the public imagination in a way that the Herculean efforts and Kelly and Low had not. Now he was known to all and sundry as 'Chitral Charlie'. He dined with Queen Victoria, and the Prince of Wales offered to support him if he requested a transfer to the Guards. He was a welcome guest at influential dinner tables and held intimate dinner parties of his own at the Savoy, where those he thought might benefit his career were introduced to his theatrical friends. Early in 1896 he received an invitation from Sir Herbert Kitchener to join the Egyptian Army, in which he would be given command of a battalion. He accepted with alacrity, although this meant severing his long connection with India. In itself this provides an interesting insight into one aspect of his character which would become more evident as the years passed. Most British officers retain a sentimental attachment to the regiment in which they have served for years, but Townshend was an exception. Rather, in the theatrical terms he would have understood, the regiment and its men were there to provide the backdrop and setting for his own career.

He reached Egypt in February 1896 and assumed command of the 12th Sudanese, serving for a while under Hector Macdonald. His battalion played a full part in the long advance up the Nile, particularly distinguishing itself during the Battle of Atbara on 8 April 1898 when it mounted a dashing attack on the dervish zareba, of which Townshend has left us his own vivid account:

> We advanced with bayonets fixed, drums beating and colours flying: it was a grand sight! The dervish riflemen opened a biting fire from the trenches. The ground was perfectly open and descended in a gentle slope towards the dervish position, putting us up against the skyline, as it were. I soon opened fire in return, using independent fire instead of volleys. After a short fire, I advanced again, myself leading in the centre, Lieutenant Harley leading the right wing, and Captain The Hon. C. E. Walsh the left wing. Captain Fort-Hutchinson, my second-in-command, was in charge of the two companies in reserve, in rear of centre. My orders to him were to keep the two companies in hand at all costs, for I knew that when we rushed the zareba the confusion would be very bad.

Alternately firing and rushing forward, I rapidly approached the dervish position. The men were dropping fairly fast. Walsh had been shot and the fire got very hot. I led each rush myself, sounding the 'cease fire' on my whistle, which the men obeyed very well. Then I dashed through the ranks, leading the battalion about thirty yards ahead, the men following excellently. General Hunter [the commander of the Egyptian Division] was riding along in the front rank of the battalion, cheering them on. A lot of men were firing as I called on the 12th to charge. They broke into a rush with cheers and we swept into the position through the zareba. How it was I wasn't hit I don't know, for the dervishes must have been firing at me. I was well ahead and the bullets were cutting the ground all about me. They did not run till we were about thirty yards from them. Harley was shot just behind me, just as I started the charge.

The disorder was great when we had got through the zareba, a bickering fire was kept up on us from the interior trenches. All companies were mixed up except the two reserve companies. Sergeant Hilton, my drill instructor, was hit in the arm but went on all the same. It was a splendid charge. We were in first by a long way. The day before I had determined in my own mind to be first in and to show everyone that the 12th were second to none. I had the chance (as I had had at Chitral) and I took advantage of it. When we entered the zareba my sergeant-major heard General Hunter order Kincaid to ride to the Sirdar and tell him the 12th were in the enemy's position. I now collected a crowd and rushed the second line of trenches, after keeping up a short hot fire on them. Two or three mines exploded on us: one of our men had the top of his head blown off: this makes me think that they must have been a sort of *fougasse* loaded with stones. We kept surging on through the crowd, carrying two or three lines of trenches by rushes, and arrived on the river bank. The men were drunk with excitement and fight. I had lost my voice. The men crowded round shaking and kissing my hand and said that I should be a Pasha, and now lead them to Omdurman! I was helpless and could do nothing but whisper. I got on my horse, the men all round me offering me flags and loot. Desultory firing was still going on, some of our men lining the river banks firing at the fugitives crossing the river and at the dervishes hiding under the precipitous bank.

The scene in the trenches was awful: dead and dying dervishes, all black riflemen, like our own men . . . After forming up the battalion I took them back through the position to the ground whence we had started. The Sirdar and his staff rode up and said, 'Townshend, I congratulate you.' He addressed the battalion, telling them that he was proud of them. He called for the sergeant-major and promoted him to be second lieutenant on the spot. I have never had a prouder day, nor felt more elated in my life. It had been a proud day for me when the Queen pinned on my CB at Osborne. Today was prouder, for I had been congratulated by the commander-in-chief on the field of battle.

The reference to Chitral is interesting and, later in life Townshend would again be influenced by this episode, with baleful consequences. Nevertheless, Atbara was undoubtedly a high point in his career. At

Omdurman his battalion again performed well, although Macdonald's handling of the battle's crisis eclipsed all else. With the war in the Sudan almost over, he resigned from the Egyptian Army on 12 September 1898, reverting to his Indian Army status. On 22 November that year he married Alice Cahen d'Anvers, the daughter of a French nobleman.

One of the more unpleasant aspects of his character soon became evident. Obsessively ambitious himself, he was spitefully jealous of the advancement of others, even his superiors. Winston Churchill, who had charged with the 21st Lancers at Omdurman, asked him to read the manuscript of his history of the campaign, *The River War*. Townshend thought that would be 'best', generously offering to devote 'some morning before lunch' to the exercise. In the same letter he commented that the campaign had been 'a job well done and well rewarded—not to say over-rewarded, and the consequence is that the Sirdar, Hunter, Macdonald and Co. get a reputation—perhaps greater than they can uphold.'

His marriage and the birth of a daughter apart, the next fifteen years of his life were to prove arid. During the Boer War he served on the staff of the Military Governor of Bloemfontein and saw no action. The rules were bent to allow him to serve as a major in the Royal Fusiliers, but he did not enjoy the experience. Despite his constant pesterings for advancement, none of his appointments seemed to satisfy him, except that of Acting Military Attaché in Paris. Since his father's death he had been heir apparent to the family title and a modest increase in fortune, but even this ambition was threatened when the sixth Marquis Townshend, apparently a confirmed bachelor, unexpectedly married in 1905. When World War I broke out he had reached the rank of major general and was serving in India. Feeling that opportunities for promotion and further glory were passing him by, he promptly despatched a flurry of letters to all and sundry, requesting a transfer home so that he could serve in France. By now, everyone was tired of him and they were ignored. The Fates, however, had their own ideas about his future.

When Great Britain declared war on the Ottoman Empire on 5 November 1914 one of the primary concerns was to maintain the Royal Navy's supply of fuel oil. This meant securing the oil terminal and refinery situated on the island of Abadan on the Persian side of the Shatt al

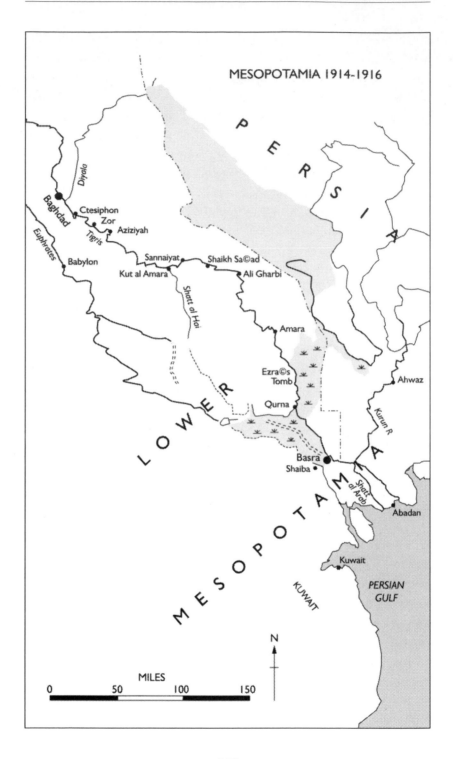

MESOPOTAMIA 1914-1916

PERSIA

Baghdad
Diyala
Ctesiphon
Zor
Aziziyah
Tigris
Euphrates
Babylon
Sannaiyat
Shaikh Sa©ad
Kut al Amara
Ali Gharbi
Shatt al Hai
Amara
Ezra©s Tomb
Ahwaz
Qurna
Kurun R
LOWER
Basra
Shaiba
Shatt al Arab
MESOPOTAMIA
Abadan
Kuwait
KUWAIT
PERSIAN GULF

N

MILES

0   50   100   150

Arab waterway. The Shatt al Arab was the route followed by the combined waters of the Rivers Tigris and Euphrates on the final stage of their journey to the Persian Gulf. Upstream, both rivers flowed through the Turkish province of Mesopotamia, known today as Iraq. An expeditionary force, already at sea when war was declared, quickly secured not only Abadan but also the city of Basra. The Turks could hardly be expected to accept the *status quo*, nor the implicit threat to Baghdad, and began moving troops into the area. In this way what had been intended as a purely local venture developed into a new war front, to which Townshend was directed as a divisional commander.

By early 1915 the front had moved north of Qurna. The British commander, Lieutenant General Sir John Nixon, had two infantry divisions, Townshend's 6th Indian Division and Major General George Gorringe's 12th Indian Division, plus a cavalry brigade and supporting arms at his disposal, as well as the close co-operation of several naval gunboats. Towards the end of May Nixon ordered Townshend to continue the advance up the Tigris with the object of capturing Al Amarah. The Turkish position north of Qurna was located in swampland in which the only areas above water level were in enemy hands. This meant that Townshend would have to prepare a series of amphibious operations to secure a breakthrough. The naval resources at his disposal were three sloops, four armed tugs, two horse-boats armed with 4.7in guns, two gun barges with 5in and 4in guns, and an assortment of steamers and rafts carrying mountain artillery and machine guns. The infantry would follow in *bellums*, flat-bottomed local canoes like punts, which could be paddled or poled along. No fewer than 500 of these craft had been assembled, those forming the assault wave being fitted with armoured shields.

The attack began at 05:00 on 31 May. The naval vessels, supported by artillery, smothered every objective with their fire. The Turks were at a fatal disadvantage, for not only had they been unable to dig deep trenches because of the high water table, they lacked timber or other material with which to revet such as they had been able to dig. Consequently, most of their trenches were wide, shallow scoops offering no protection against high explosive or shrapnel, and they suffered severely from the shellfire. Furthermore, in some areas they were unable to see the swarms of infantry *bellums* poling their way through the dense reed beds towards them.

Many simply faded away in their own boats while others surrendered as soon as the infantry appeared.

Having taken the enemy's outpost line, Townshend assaulted their main position, two miles upstream, the following morning, only to find it completely deserted. When it became apparent that the Turks were retreating up the Tigris as fast as they could go, he decided to exploit the situation to the full. Ordering an infantry brigade to embark on three paddle steamers and follow with all possible speed, he went aboard the sloop *Espiegle* with his staff and a small escort and set off in pursuit with the rest of his gunboats. As expected, the Turks had mined the navigable channel. However, the officer responsible was now a prisoner, and, travelling in the bows of the leading armed tug, he diligently ensured that no one came to any harm. Below Ruta the Turks had also sunk two lighters as blockships, but they were badly positioned, leaving just sufficient room to squeeze past.

This strange pursuit of a beaten army by warships of the Royal Navy would become known ever after as 'Townshend's Regatta'. The general, climbing to the crow's nest on the *Espiegle*'s foremast, keenly observed the way ahead. In the distance, two moving smudges of smoke indicated the enemy gunboat *Marmaris* and the steamer *Mosul*, both towing lighters crowded with troops. Visible, too, were the numerous white sails of local *mahelas*, all heading for imagined safety upstream. The dun, featureless desert slid past on either bank, only the blue-domed Ezra's Tomb, surrounded by palm trees, providing some relief from the monotonous landscape. Gradually, the gap narrowed until by early evening the sloops were within range and opened fire. Both Turkish captains promptly cast off their tows, leaving them to make for the bank as best they could. Dropping off the sloop *Odin* to round up the fugitives, Townshend steamed on until darkness made further progress impossible.

At first light on 2 June the flotilla got under way again. After six miles had been covered the *Marmaris* was sighted, aground, burning and abandoned by her crew. Further on, in response to a single round of gunfire, the *Mosul* heaved to and ran up a white flag. As the river was becoming too shallow for the sloops, Townshend and the senior naval officer, Captain Nunn, transferred to the armed tug *Comet*. With more tugs towing gun-armed horse-boats, the chase began again. More white flags fluttered at every village passed, save at Qal'at Salih, where a force of cavalry and infantry was dispersed by shellfire.

The following morning's progress was similar. Townshend, uncertain as to the Turkish strength at Al Amarah, prudently sent the armed tug *Shaitan* to scout ahead while the rest followed. Incredibly, with just 100 bluejackets and soldiers aboard, the tug's captain bluffed the entire garrison into surrendering. By no means all the Turks accepted this willingly and the situation remained potentially explosive even after the rest of the flotilla had arrived. However, the next day, 4 June, infantrymen of the Royal Norfolk Regiment began coming ashore from their paddle steamers, resolving the issue once and for all.

Townshend's Regatta had succeeded in punching a hole deep into the enemy's hinterland. Its results included the destruction of a gunboat, the capture of two steamers, many smaller craft and large quantities of military supplies, and the taking of 2,000 prisoners, all at trivial cost. Townshend's achievement was undeniably brilliant and a tonic to a general public at home that was becoming disappointed by the lack of progress in France and at Gallipoli. It was recalled that he was the same 'Chitral Charlie' who had so successfully defended the isolated little fort on the North-West Frontier twenty years earlier. It was also good to know that the Army possessed one general who could get things done, and in some style too. Townshend accepted the plaudits as his due. He did not even care that his fellow divisional commander, Gorringe, another veteran of Omdurman whom he considered to be a deadly rival in his quest for promotion, had captured An Nasiriyah on the Euphrates.

After a short spell of sick leave in India, Townshend returned to find that Nixon had decided he should capture Kut al Amara, 120 miles further upstream, possession of which he felt would guarantee the security of the enclave around Basra. Barring the way were 6,000 Turks and 30 guns under the command of Nur-ed-Din Bey, who had taken up an extremely strong position in what became known as the Hanna Defile, some miles downstream from Kut. Here the negotiable ground on the left bank of the Tigris was restricted to a narrow corridor between the river and a broad area of seasonal lakes and marshes. The right bank was also heavily fortified, and, to prevent another breakaway by the gunboats, an effective obstruction was placed across the river itself.

Once again Townshend made thorough preparations. On 27 September he made a feint attack against the apparently more vulnerable entrenchments on the right bank, forcing Nur-ed-Din to commit his reserves to contain it. After sunset, two brigades crossed a bridge of boats six miles downstream, then carried out a night march to fall on the flank of the Turkish positions on the left bank at dawn. After a hard fight the trenches were taken and held against repeated counter-attacks. The Turks withdrew during the night, abandoning Kut as they retreated north.

Kut, a grubby little town of winding alleys situated on a peninsula, was not much of an acquisition, but the press could announce that 'Chitral Charlie' had done it again and in Nixon's mind its capture opened the road to the glittering prize of Baghdad itself. He obtained qualified permission for an advance on the city and was surprised when Townshend expressed serious reservations, some of which he confided to his diary:

> We are now some 380 miles from the sea and have only two weak divisions, including my own, in the country. There is my division to do the fighting and Gorringe's to hold the line of communications from Kut to the sea. There is no possible support to give me if I receive a check and the consequences of a retreat are not to be imagined. Thus, I feel it my duty to give my opinion plainly to the Army Commander, whether he likes it or not!

He informed Nixon of his likely problems, stressing that the seasonal fall in water level would make river transport extremely difficult. He went on to suggest that 'on all military grounds' the consolidation of the position at Kut offered a more sensible alternative. He also offered his considered opinion that an advance on Baghdad in anything less than corps strength would be attended by 'great risk'. Unfortunately, while Townshend possessed much the clearer strategic insight, Nixon had already made up his mind. The 6th Indian Division would be reinforced by the cavalry brigade, it was going to Baghdad, and that was that.

Townshend spent five weeks preparing for the continued advance. Even as his columns began trudging north, intelligence sources reported to Nixon that 30,000 good-quality Turkish troops under the command of Khalil Pasha, one of the best generals in the Sultan's service, were converging on Baghdad, and that the German Field Marshal von der Goltz had been appointed the enemy's overall commander in Mesopotamia. It was now clearly apparent that Townshend's single division was marching steadily into terrible danger, but Nixon, blinded by his own optimism, declined to recall it.

At Ctesiphon, 30 miles from Baghdad, Nur-ed-Din had again constructed entrenchments on both banks of the Tigris. The gunboats were unable to provide much support because of high floodbanks and, as the ground on the right bank was impassable in places, Townshend was compelled to mount a frontal attack on the two lines of trenches which had been dug opposite. Commencing on 22 November, the battle continued for two days and resulted in the Turks being ejected with the loss of 6,200 casualties. For the 6th Indian Division, however, the hard-won victory was crippling. Of the 11,000 men engaged, 4,600 were killed or wounded, and the ammunition reserves were seriously depleted.

On 25 November air reconnaissance revealed that fresh Turkish formations were streaming out of Baghdad. Townshend, incapable for the moment of fighting another battle, decided to retreat. The shocking plight of his wounded exposed the complete breakdown of the medical services in Mesopotamia, generating a huge scandal. Days after they had been transported from the Ctesiphon battlefield in jolting carts they reached Basra aboard the steamer *Mejidieh* and two barges she was towing, the dead, dying and living packed tightly together, lying in their own accumulated excreta.

On 1 December Townshend fought a sharp rearguard action at Umm-al-Tubal, sustaining 500 casualties but inflicting thrice that many. Against this, his fears regarding the falling level of the river proved entirely justified, as several of his gunboats had to be abandoned after they had run fast aground. Two days later he was back in Kut.

Although, throughout his career, he had demonstrated that he was a capable, efficient officer, he now took a decision which was to have fatal consequences for many, and for this his soaring ambition must be blamed. Until Ctesiphon, he was everyone's favourite general and his promotion seemed assured. As he had sustained a reverse he must therefore find a way to restore his fortunes—and what better way was there than as the heroic commander of a besieged garrison? It had worked for him at Chitral, and it had worked for Colonel Robert Baden-Powell at Mafeking. He decided to allow himself to become besieged in Kut, which possessed no value in itself, despatching the deliberately theatrical signal to Nixon,

'I intend to defend Kut as I did Chitral.' Chitral Charlie, it seemed, was about to become Townshend of Kut. It would have made better sense to retire to the Hanna Defile, where a stronger defensive position existed and where he would not have been isolated. It has been suggested that the exhaustion of his infantry rendered a protracted halt, and therefore a siege, inevitable, yet hardly had the troops arrived than they dug six miles of trenches across the Kut peninsula. Again, the time factor militates against the argument. The Turks did not finally invest Kut until 7 December; when Townshend sent the cavalry brigade out the previous day it experienced no serious difficulties in re-joining the army. Townshend could, therefore, have easily continued his retreat down-river, had he chosen to do so. Perhaps the most criminal aspect of his decision was his knowledge that, as we have seen from the diary extract quoted above, Nixon's resources were so limited as to render an early relief impossible.

A Turkish attempt to storm the town on 24 December was so sharply rebuffed that von der Goltz decided to starve the garrison into surrender, concentrating his efforts on blocking attempts at relief. His position at the Hanna Defile became almost impregnable when heavy rain caused the river, marshes and canals to expand their bounds, so restricting the frontage on which the relief force could attack. Townshend deliberately added drama to the situation by stating that he had only one month's rations in hand; in fact, the situation did not become critical until the early days of April 1916. The government, though far from pleased that the Mesopotamian venture had become a new war front, could not ignore Townshend and began pouring reinforcements into the area. Nagged by Nixon, Lieutenant General Sir Fenton Aylmer, commanding the relief force, mounted a premature attempt to break through. It failed, as did every subsequent attempt.

Inside Kut there were curious parallels to the siege of Chitral. Townshend refused to make sorties that might have assisted the relief force, and, just as he had once favoured the Sikhs over the Kashmiris, he now favoured the British rather than the Indian soldiers of his division, visiting casualties in the field hospital to entertain them with his banjo. There is no doubt that at this period his men thought the world of him. Yet, throughout the siege, he continued to absorb valuable signals time with repeated requests for promotion. When his rival, Gorringe, was promoted lieutenant general on his appointment to succeed Aylmer as commander of the relief force, Townshend burst into tears in front of the startled subaltern who had brought him the news.

By 15 April ration stocks had indeed reached a dangerously low level. For the first time in history, an attempt was made to supply a besieged garrison by air. The daily requirement was set at 5,000lb but the actual lift capacity was only 3,350lb. Even worse, the severe heat badly affected the performance of the aircraft available, so there was always a shortfall. Total deliveries made amounted to 16,800lb, some of which consisted of inedible items such as rifle pull-throughs. 'I shall fight house by house till my ammunition and food are exhausted,' signalled Townshend. On 24 April the supply ship *Julnur*, manned by a volunteer crew, made a last desperate attempt to break through but came under heavy fire and was driven aground.

There was no more to be done. As the relief force had incurred 23,000 casualties attempting to break through to a garrison half that number, it would have been madness to persist. On 26 April Townshend was authorised to open surrender negotiations with the enemy. As von der Goltz had succumbed to cholera some days earlier, these were conducted with Khalil Pasha. Townshend offered £1 million in gold in exchange for the garrison's parole and the surrender of its guns. Khalil was tempted, but Constantinople wanted the famous General Townshend and his men as trophies and declined, even when the offer was doubled. The most the Turks would agree to was the exchange of 345 hospital cases for an equal number of fit prisoners, although they did promise that the garrison would be treated as 'honoured guests'. This apart, the surrender, concluded on 29 April, was unconditional. Townshend, bitterly critical of the relief force, commented, 'I must go into captivity with my troops, even though the heat will kill me.'

He did not go into captivity with his troops, who were herded off on a death march to their prison camps. During their years of captivity, 7,000 of the 'honoured guests' died of malnutrition, disease or brutal indifference on the part of their guards. Of those who survived, the health of many was damaged beyond repair. In sharp contrast, Townshend was treated like visiting royalty when he arrived in Constantinople. He spent the rest of the war in a luxurious villa on an island in the Sea of Marmara, with a yacht at his disposal. He was allowed to visit Constantinople under escort and dined regularly with local society. The Turks even told him that his wife would be welcome to share these pleasures. She lobbied hard to be allowed to join him but the British Government was emphatically against the idea. When she took her case as far as Prime Minister Herbert Asquith, the latter replied in a curt note, 'This matter is not one in which I feel able to interfere.' At about the same time Townshend learned that his expectations of inheriting the family title were doomed, the Marchioness Townshend having given birth to a son. Against this, in October he received a knighthood, presumably for his earlier victories rather than for the siege of Kut. He commented, 'I do not suppose anyone will grudge me my KCB. It has not been awarded *too* soon!'—this from a general whose egocentric decision to allow himself to be besieged had resulted in the death, wounding or ruined health over 30,000 men.

When the war ended he expected to be welcomed home as 'The Hero of Kut', and was once hailed as such during a visit to the theatre. His friends were pleased to see him, but the official attitude was one of frigid indifference, the tone being set by King George V in a comment to Field Marshal Earl Haig:

> His Majesty then went on to tell me how General Townshend of Kut fame should have remained to share the fate of his fellow prisoners, instead of taking his liberty in order to help the Turks to get a satisfactory peace. Townshend, he thought, was 'an advertising sort of fellow.' I agreed, and a semi-lunatic as well!

It never seems to have occurred to Townshend that he had done anything wrong or that his conduct had fallen below acceptable standards. He claimed that he had saved thousands of lives by persuading Turkey to request an armistice when she did, although the real reasons were the collapse of her ally Bulgaria and the virtual destruction of her own armies in Mesopotamia and Palestine. His incessant lobbying of the War Office and those with influence began as soon as he returned. He demanded promotion, honours and appointments in Ireland, Egypt and Poland, but he was met with blank refusals. Sitting briefly as Member of Parliament for The Wrekin in Shropshire, he found the world of politics quite beyond him. Equally, his self-appointed task as a sort of honest broker between Great Britain and the new Turkey presided over by Kemal Ataturk was not especially welcomed by either. When he died in May

1924 neither the British Government nor the War Office sent representatives to his funeral.

Difficult as it is to imagine now, the fall of Kut was as much of a shock to contemporary opinion as was that of Singapore in the Second World War, although its significance was by no means as profound. Today, few can point directly to the town on the map, let alone recall the career of Major General Charles Townshend. Perhaps Townshend was the last of his kind, for in the era of total, machine-age warfare involving huge armies confronting each other on fronts hundreds of miles wide, the chances of a single individual's actions at the tactical level influencing the outcome of a battle or campaign have become astronomically remote. That, of course, is by no means the same as suggesting that the day of the hero is over.

Select Bibliography

Anglesey, the Marquess of, *A History of the British Cavalry: Vol. II, 1851–1871,* Leo Cooper, 1975

Barker, A. J., *Townshend of Kut,* Cassell, 1967

Barthorp, Michael, *The North-West Frontier: British India and Afghanistan,* Blandford, 1982

Barthorp, Michael, and Embleton, G. A., *Napoleon's Egyptian Campaigns 1798–1801,* Osprey, 1978

Braddon, Russell, *The Siege,* Jonathan Cape, 1969

Cannan, John, *The Antietam Campaign,* Combined Books, 1994

Catton, Bruce, *A Stillness at Appomattox,* Doubleday, 1953

Chandler, David, *Dictionary of the Napoleonic Wars,* Simon & Schuster, 1993

Churchill, Winston S., *The River War,* Four Square, 1960

Cork, B. J., *Rider on a Grey Horse: A Life of Hodson of Hodson's Horse,* London 1958

Edwardes, Michael, *Battles of the Indian Mutiny,* Batsford, 1963

———, *Red Year: The Indian Rebellion of 1857,* Hamish Hamilton, 1973

Farwell, Byron, *Queen Victoria's Little Wars,* Allen Lane, 1973

Featherstone, Donald, *Victorian Colonial Warfare: India,* Cassell, 1992

Forbes, Archibald, *The Afghan Wars 1839–42 & 1878–80,* Darf, 1987

Gruber, Ira D., (ed.), *John Peebles' American War 1776–1782,* Sutton Publishing/Army Records Society, 1998

Hamilton Williams, David, *Waterloo: New Perspectives,* Arms & Armour Press, 1993

Harris, John, *The Gallant Six Hundred,* Hutchinson, 1973

Haythornthwaite, Philip J., *The Napoleonic Source Book,* Arms & Armour Press, 1990

———, *The Colonial Wars Source Book,* Arms & Armour Press, 1995

Hibbert, Christopher, *The Destruction of Lord Raglan,* Longmans, 1961

Hofschroer, Peter, *1815: The Waterloo Campaign,* Greenhill, 1999

Hofschroer, Peter, and Fosten, Bryan, *The Hanoverian Army of the Napoleonic Wars,* Osprey, 1989

Howarth, David, *Waterloo: A Near Run Thing,* Collins, 1968

Katcher, Philip, *The American Civil War Source Book,* Arms & Armour Press, 1992

————, *Lethal Glory: Dramatic Defeats of the Civil War*, Arms & Armour Press, 1995

————, *Great Gambles of the Civil War*, Arms & Armour Press, 1996

Kennedy, Frances H., *The Civil War Battlefield Guide*, Houghton Mifflin, 1990

Ketchum, Richard, *The Winter Soldiers: George Washington and the Way to Independence*, Macdonald, 1973

Kruger, Rayne, *Good-Bye Dolly Gray: The Story of the Boer War*, Cassell, 1959

Leasor, James, *Mutiny at the Red Fort*, Werner Laurie, 1956

Ludlow, J. M., *The War of American Independence 1775–1783*, Longmans, 1895

Naylor, John, *Waterloo*, Batsford, 1960

Nevill, Captain H. L., *North-West Frontier*, Tom Donovan, 1992

Packenham, Thomas, *The Boer War*, Weidenfeld & Nicolson, 1979

Pemberton, W. Baring, *Battles of the Crimean War*, Batsford, 1962

————, *Battles of the Boer War*, Batsford, 1964

Perrett, Bryan, *Desert Warfare*, Patrick Stephens, 1988

————, *At All Costs*, Arms & Armour Press, 1993

————, *Gunboat*, Cassell, 2000

Robson, Brian, *The Road to Kabul: The Second Afghan War 1878–1881*, Arms & Armour Press, 1986

Rogers, Colonel H. C. B., *The Confederates & Federals at War*, Ian Allan, 1973

Swinson, Arthur, *North-West Frontier*, Hutchinson, 1967

Symonds, Craig L., *A Battlefield Atlas of the American Revolution*, Nautical & Aviation Publishing Company of America, 1986

Tarleton, Banastre, *A History of the Campaigns in the Southern Provinces of North America*, London, 1787

Utley, Robert M., *Bluecoats and Redskins: The US Army and the Indian 1866–1891*, Cassell, 1973

Various, *The War of the Rebellion*, Vol. XXXVI, Government Printing Office, Washington, 1895 (official reports submitted by Federal and Confederate commanders relating to Grierson's Raid)

Warner, Philip, *Dervish: The Rise and Fall of an African Empire*, Macdonald, 1973

Woodham-Smith, Cecil, *The Reason Why*, Constable, 1953

Ziegler, Philip, *Omdurman*, Collins, 1973

DESIGNATED WEBSITES OF RELATED INTEREST ACCESSIBLE BY KEYWORD
Benedict Arnold
Major General Benjamin Grierson
The King's German Legion
Major General Sir Hector Macdonald
The Battle of Marengo and Kellermann's Charge
Victoria Cross Reference
Major General Lewis Wallace and the Battle of Monocacy

Index

Arnold, Benedict: early career, 16; at capture of Fort Ticonderoga, 16–17; at Quebec, 17–18; at Freeman's Farm, 22; quarrels with Gates, 23; wounded at Bemis Heights, 23; appointed military governor of Philadelphia, 25; charged with fraud, 25–6; appointed commandant of West Point, 26; offers to surrender West Point, 26; escapes to British lines, 26; operations in Virginia and Connecticut, 26–7; subsequent career, 27.

Baring, Major George: service with King's German Legion, 67; ordered to hold La Haye Sainte, 69; dispositions in La Haye Saint, 71–2; descriptions of French attacks on, 73–5, 77–80; is forced to abandon La Haye Saint, 80, 82; reflections on battle, 83; subsequent career, 84.

Bonaparte, Napoleon, 53–7, 57–63, 68, 72, 74, 75, 77, 81

Burgoyne, Major General John, 17, 18, 21–2, 23–5;

Campbell, General Sir Colin, 88, 90, 93, 117, 118, 131

Cardigan, Major General the Earl of, 86, 87, 91, 97, 100–1, 102

Cavagnari, Major Pierre, 171–2, 173

Clinton, General Sir Henry, 22, 26, 27, 32, 36–9, 41, 43, 44

Cornwallis, Major General Lord Charles, 43, 46, 49

Desaix, General Louis: background and early service, 52–3; captures Malta, 54; at Battle of Pyramids, 56; in Upper Egypt, 56; re-joins Bonaparte in Italy, 57; returns to Marengo battlefield, 61;

killed, 62; achievement minimised by Bonaparte, 63–4

D'Erlon, Lieutenant General Drouhet, 72–4, 79, 81

Early, Lieutenant General Jubal, 161 164, 165

Gates, General Horatio, 21, 22, 23, 46

Germain, Lord George, 18–19

Grant, General Ulysses S., 136, 148, 154, 155–7, 157–60, 161, 165

Grierson, Major General Benjamin H: early life, 135; brigade ordered to attack Confederate rail communications with Vicksburg, 136; enters enemy territory, 136; decides to continue south across Confederacy, 137; wrecks railway at Newton Station, 140–1; further attacks on railway, 143–4; Confederate pursuit of, 144–5, 147–8; fights way across Tickfaw river, 145–6; attacks enemy camps, 147; re-enters Federal lines, 147; report on and strategic consequences of raid, 148; promoted brevet major general, 149; further actions during Civil War, 149-150; commands black 10th Cavalry on frontier, 151–2

Hamilton, Lieutenant Walter: joins Guides Cavalry, 168–9; is awarded Victoria Cross, 171; appointed commander of Kabul Residency guard, 172; defends Residency to death, 173–4; avenged, 175–6; action commemorated, 176

Hodson, Major William: background and early career, 105–6; joins Corps of Guides, 106; personality, 106; forms Hodson's Horse, 109–10; at Delhi, 110–11, 112; captures King of Delhi, 112–

ML:

2/02